After Socialism

Does socialism have a future in the twenty-first century? If not, what is the future for progressive politics?

After Socialism deals with the collapse of socialism both as an idea and a movement. It scrutinizes the economic and social realities that require a critical but much more intelligent alternative of coping with the enormous, mounting challenges that the world confronts. This is a major contribution to contemporary social and political thought written by one of the world's leading critical historians. Gabriel Kolko asks difficult questions about where the Left can go in a post-Cold War world where neo-liberal policies appear to have triumphed in both the West and the former Soviet bloc. In trying to answer them, he discusses:

- the origins and development of socialist ideas
- the contemporary dynamics of the globalized economy dominated by American military, cultural, and political might
- the failures of contemporary capitalism
- the poverty and economic and financial instability – in the United States and industrial nations as well as developing nations – that make our contemporary world so precarious.

After Socialism is a synthesis of Kolko's past work and a critical assessment of why and how critical social thought can be reconstructed. While avoiding the temptations of either pessimism or utopianism, Kolko manages to offer an original and practical solution about the way forward for liberal politics.

Gabriel Kolko is Distinguished Research Professor Emeritus at York University in Toronto. He is the author of thirteen influential books, including *Anatomy of a War*, *Century of War*, and *Vietnam: Anatomy of a Peace*.

Also by Gabriel Kolko

The Age of War: The United States Confronts the World

Another Century of War?

Vietnam: Anatomy of a Peace

Century of War: Politics, Conflicts, and Society since 1914

Confronting the Third World: United States Foreign Policy, 1945–1980

Anatomy of a War: Vietnam, the United States, and the Modern Historical Experience

Main Currents in Modern American History

The Limits of Power: The World and United States Foreign Policy, 1945–1954
(Joyce Kolko, co-author)

The Roots of American Foreign Policy

The Politics of War: The World and United States Foreign Policy, 1943–1945

Railroads and Regulation, 1877–1916
Awarded the Transportation History prize, Organization of American Historians

The Triumph of Conservatism: A Reinterpretation of American History, 1900–1916

Wealth and Power in America: An Analysis of Social Class and Income Distribution

After Socialism

Reconstructing critical social thought

Gabriel Kolko

LONDON AND NEW YORK

First published 2006
by Routledge
2 Park Square, Milton Park, Abingdon, Oxon OX14 4RN

Simultaneously published in the USA and Canada
by Routledge
270 Madison Avenue, New York, NY 10016

Routledge is an imprint of the Taylor & Francis Group, an informa business

Typeset in Times by
RefineCatch Limited, Bungay, Suffolk
Printed and bound in Great Britain by
The Cromwell Press, Trowbridge, Wiltshire

British Library Cataloguing in Publication Data
A catalogue record for this book is available from the British Library

Library of Congress Cataloging in Publication Data
A catalog record for this book has been requested

ISBN10: 0–415–39591–7 (pbk)
ISBN10: 0–415–39590–9 (hbk)
ISBN10: 0–203–08819–0 (ebk)

ISBN13: 978–0–415–39591–5 (pbk)
ISBN13: 978–0–415–39590–8 (hbk)
ISBN13: 978–0–203–08819–7 (ebk)

To Leah and Fishel,
Always searching, constantly thinking,
Perfect parents.
And to Joyce, again, for countless reasons.

Contents

Acknowledgments

Over 40 years ago I planned eventually to write this very ambitious book and it reflects a great deal of thought, research, and considerable experience. In the time that has elapsed the reasons for my finally doing so have increased immeasurably, if only because socialism in all its forms has collapsed and contemporary capitalism is failing, as never before, to build a civilization that can resolve the growing challenges the world faces. Originally, I began my graduate work in the history of ideas and philosophy, and my Master's thesis was on the idea of progress; like most intellectually curious people, I read widely but found that such writers as Bertrand Russell, Charles Peirce, and Morris R. Cohen were the most congenial. I was diverted from philosophy but I did take a minor field in it at Harvard and I always retained an interest in the topic. I have published thirteen books about subjects as diverse as income distribution and poverty in the United States as well as its economic history, especially the federal government's crucial role in regulating the economy. I have written in detail about American foreign policy and its consequences everywhere, above all in Vietnam – and during that war I saw crucial events unfold there. My interest in war over the past century has caused me to do a great deal of comparative history, and why and how immense tragedies occur is very much a topic that has preoccupied my recent writing. While such diversity may perhaps make me a generalist, I have in the course of time done a great deal of homework. What follows is a reflection and an outline of what I have learned and written in the past half-century as well as my thoughts on the present impasse that we today confront.

I owe a great deal to various people whom I have known, and most of them would disagree strongly with what follows. The usual exonerations apply but my debt to them is still no less. I shall leave most unnamed since my observations and views will horrify some of them, even though my basic viewpoint has not altered significantly in the past half-century. My parents, to whom this book is dedicated, were instrumental in my choice of interests, and their intellectual curiosity and freedom were crucial in the way I was raised. I was immensely fortunate. Barrington Moore Jr. was the most creative and brilliant person I have ever met, and his conceptions of the world and ways of perceiving it set a very high standard, confirming me in my wayward intellectual path. He was a dissident and nonconformist, impossible to label. Without attempting to do so, for I was never his student, he also kept Harvard from socializing me and my ideas, for which I am everlastingly grateful. Joyce, my friend and wife, watched this project evolve and helped me in so many ways that were crucial. Needless to say, I hold everyone I have ever known blameless for what follows. I am solely responsible for *After Socialism*.

Gabriel Kolko

Introduction

At the very point that the world is most in need of basic criticism and changes, there are fewer original or searching ideas about the status quo and less opposition to it than at any time over the past century. Wars and fundamental upheavals have occurred and socialism – whether as a theory or as a political movement – is essentially dead.

The prevailing notions – whether socialist or capitalist – about our societies have not prepared us for any of the vast events, ranging from wars to economic crises, that have so marred the human experience over the past century. We live in an age when exhausted analytic concepts, devoid of the prerequisites for coping with daily realities, still hold sway over our minds. Conventional wisdoms, whether from the ideological and political Right, the Center, or Left, are deductive, academic abstractions that fail to explain the increasingly grave problems we confront both at home and internationally. Inherited ideas still burden us with illusions and have not anticipated the main upheavals of our time, and far greater clarity is a necessary precondition, essential but scarcely sufficient, for controlling our destiny.

Virtually all theories' predictions have been utterly discredited, their assumptions of a reasonably stable future have proven false. The past century has experienced increasingly bloody wars and social and political upheavals in their wake. Crises demand and sometimes produce new ideas but ours is an exception. We need desperately a revolution in our perceptions of reality to comprehend the events we have lived through and that now confront us, but such insight must be far less pretentious in order to be more useful and, above all, durable. We should reflect critically and accurately on the past, but – to the extent possible – much more carefully and as modestly as our unavoidable ignorance necessitates. Although we can know far, far more about the world we live in and the human condition, we need also to consciously leave ample space for our inevitable ignorance and constant learning.

This book is about not only the failure of capitalist and socialist conventional wisdom and analysis, but also their practice. I make no pretense of proposing a complete assessment of the past or a precise blueprint for the future but I do advance some fairly general but basic premises about formulating ideas and what must be done to make our future far less precarious. It is a beginning, and I deal not only with the human and social condition today – about the reality humankind confronts – but also with how we should think rationally about our future.

Western society's misconceptions began well before Karl Marx created a brand of socialism that existed simultaneously with – and sometimes also produced – mass movements. Socialism simply inherited most of the nineteenth century's myopia, adding to the illusions of social thought. These assumptions I sum up in my first chapter, but most social theorists tended to believe that societies and history moved through progressive stages until they reached some kind of emancipatory ideal (which they defined very differently), a sort of utopian stasis. And they shared a common optimism if not a mutual outline of a just society. Their visions were incredibly naive, based largely on desires and the dreams of those who produced them rather than a serious assessment of an infinitely more complex and much less sanguine reality. After Stalin, Mao, and Blair, socialism is today irreversibly dead both in practice and theory; but capitalist theories are no less erroneous and irrelevant, and the failure of all concepts, of all stripes, makes the task of reconstructing social thought even more daunting just as our reality makes it even more essential.

I have spent much time thinking about what was fatally wrong with socialism, which now is in political shambles whether it descends from the Leninist or Social Democratic branches, and it has justly lost its capacity to persuade a significant number of people that it holds out the solution for dealing with the grave domestic and international problems we confront. Socialists have discredited their beliefs less by their theoretical methods and prognostications than by their practice, but practice reflected – at least in part – the fact that socialism's analytic moorings were exceedingly weak from the inception. Socialism has become dysfunctional as an instrument both of analysis and of change, but its goals – and most of these were never specific to it alone – remain as valid as ever. Indeed, the ways in which our civilization has developed make these objectives far more imperative than they were when they were articulated over a century ago. It was Marxism, which lacked the critical, contingent assumptions so crucial to its functioning effectively in politics and society both on a short- as well as long-term basis, that effectively incapacitated socialism analytically. Marxism ended as meaningless pieties, as with the Social Democratic parties, or as a religion in the case of Leninism. The states that enshrined its theses have almost all disappeared, and parties in power that proclaim belief in what is loosely termed socialism are anything but radical. The large majority of them behave like most bourgeois parties.

I contend that a critical assessment of the theory and practice of socialism, whether its Marxist or other forms, does not imply a vindication of capitalism in any way. We today confront more problems – economic, ecological, international, and others – than Marx and his followers ever imagined possible. Given its practice and consequences, opposition to what is loosely termed capitalism – the status quo in all its dimensions – is far more justified today than ever. Precisely because of this, a more durable and effective alternative to capitalism is even more essential. But there can be no effective opposition to it without a searching critique of the methods and assumptions that most socialists still hold, for these are not merely naive but also inaccurate – and therefore paralyzing. This requires revising our comprehension of capitalism's historical origins as well as its actual practice today. To make a radical opposition intellectually credible and effective, we must rethink virtually everything that capitalism's nominal critics have believed until now.

Capitalism, in all its variations, is today essentially hegemonic in the world, but only by default. Those who rule it cannot explain it realistically or describe how or why it functions; worse yet, they are unable to maintain the system on a stable basis, periodically leaving social distress and inequities in its wake. Ideologically and analytically, its rationale as well as persistence is due to its mere existence and the interests in it, which gives it the vitality that all systems of power – whatever their ideological coloration – have. Wars have been integral to capitalism and they have only increased with its growth, and preparations for wars provide a measure of vigor to economies before actual fighting begins. Status quos have space and time to continue because the Left refuses or cannot change them much of the time, but periodic wars have nonetheless produced social crises, and modern capitalism operates in a way that neither its loyal adherents nor radical critics expected. Capitalism, despite socialism's demise, is not a rational or stable basis for a peaceful society, and in Chapters 5 and 6 I describe why this is the case. Crises exist without serious critics and serious alternatives. There is an impasse in social thought and changes occur only because existing systems break down, but all too often for the worse.

I also outline the evolution of the dominant capitalist theories of development and the utter inadequacy of their explanations of economic history, the reasons people became rich and successful, and capitalism's failure to create the equity and stability which is an essential precondition to avoiding internecine wars. This requires a reconsideration of the role of the state in the development of capitalism and how it has actually operated in this crucial domain, not only in the past but also throughout the world today. I contend that all of the dominant ideologies have utterly failed to explain reality. Both capitalists and their critics have produced versions of history because they were utilitarian justifications: leftists used it to excoriate the status quo while its defenders produced useful myths to vindicate it. The Left had its illusions about the working class, which fed its optimism, and a significant portion of it condoned whatever folly and evils Bolshevik nations advocated or practiced. It is far too late to nourish any kind of myth – whether for or against the world as it exists.

In great part, the failure of all social theories to articulate accurate, useful visions of the present or the future is due to the much more serious analytic shambles that has prevailed in the intellectual systems of those who defend as well as those who deplore the world as it has existed over the past several centuries, much less what it is becoming. These ideas have no predictive value whatsoever and they do not generalize on the political and social experiences which are the basis of my reflections. Their descriptions are, overwhelmingly, historically inaccurate. All such concepts possess certainty and absolute self-confidence in their screeds, and they offer a good basis for faiths – very different, to be sure, in their visions of ideal societies but all premised on similar analytic errors. But faith is scarcely knowledge or truth, and we simply do not have the conceptual framework for assessing realistically the times we are living through much less the means essential for reversing a course which is leading to economic crises and, above all, more destructive wars. The optimistic notions concocted in the nineteenth century, if not earlier, with their visions of predictability and progress in the human condition, still hold sway over what passes as theory. In fact, a valid predictive social science has never existed, in part because of the deficiencies I shall outline later in this book and the penchant of theorists to allow their desires to define their ideas. They have attempted to explain far too much, thereby explaining far less than can be done with a degree of accuracy.

Social theory, I will argue, must be based on rational intelligence and reason, not simply in the sense of a formal academic enterprise but by reference to actual social experiences and history which attempts to comprehend realities in all their diversity. It cannot merely serve to reinforce our wishes. It must also concede, I will stress, what we cannot know for certain and the limits of our knowledge – limits that surprising disasters over the past century have revealed so dramatically. We must get used to the idea not only that we have a great deal we can understand and do, but also that we will always have important degrees of ignorance as well as constraints which compel us also to cope with an absence of freedom. Indeed, the health of a new and more appropriate social theory and praxis will be due to the realization that while we can do much more, and that while great changes are possible as well as preferable, we cannot treat history and the future like a blank check on which we can write whatever we like. But I assume there is an overriding commitment to perceiving reality truthfully, and that the cultivation or preservation of myths and false hopes – whether socialist or capitalist – leads both to optimism and to mindless irrelevance. False or premature optimism cannot create a self-fulfilling prophecy or change reality one iota but lead only to comforting delusions. The truth, whatever its limits, reveals the fragility of constituted orders as well as their formidable capacities for survival, but a renovated critical social theory that is more than another sham or anodyne cannot be created without devotion to candor and honesty to the greatest extent possible. That alone is the guarantee of its radicalism. But of this, much more follows.

This book attempts a schematic outline of the past and present, from the origin of modern economies to foreign affairs and poverty in developing nations – and much else. But it also requires staking out the relevance of past programs for reform – especially socialism – and the magnitude of problems, whether issues of war and peace, economic, or environmental, to be resolved in the future and the need for politics and ideas that are really appropriate for these burgeoning challenges. Above all, we must now think as rationally as well as relevantly as we can about these questions, because anything less will simply repeat the misjudgments and errors of the past. I offer comments and suggestions for essential changes, scarcely as final detailed solutions but as reasonable and preliminary proposals and – in some instances – necessities. There are no detailed blueprints for the future but observations, assumptions that seem called for, and warnings about pitfalls to be avoided. No one can or should pretend to offer final or comprehensive answers for needed changes, and anyone who does so is, however sincere, a fraud. But we need basic changes quickly if our civilization is to survive, and we have to begin both with this radical assumption as well as a commitment to the use of reason and intelligence in making them. We cannot do everything but we can and must do far, far more than we have. There is no choice but to begin.

What is most urgent today is the definition of the essential broad premises and goals that any political movement of rational social change must have if and when it emerges in virtually any nation, how it is to maintain its commitment to its original promise, and the minimum conditions of reforms that are effective. We do not need – as in the case of Marxism – another sclerotic creed and faith gravely encumbering radical politics. Clarity as well as candor is the precondition of the revival of critical and truly radical politics, essential if the diverse parties of the Left are to confront the crises of the modern age and find and offer solutions that really will prevent the calamities of wars and revolutions from again preempting social change in our age. This axiomatically requires us to confront what was wrong with the broad spectrum of the Left for more than a century as well as why it ignominiously did not fulfill its original promises on so many crucial issues. Both its ideas and practices demand fundamental, comprehensive rethinking. *After Socialism* is an attempt to do so.

Such a seemingly prepolitical inquiry is a necessary but scarcely a sufficient condition for the emergence of movements of social change anywhere, and is not in the least an abstract intellectual exercise. Indeed, it is the absence of such efforts that has made possible the Left's continuing depressing political behavior and the undisturbed perpetuation of a conservative consensus – whatever its formal labels – that has helped produce our world of wars and mounting ecological and economic crises.

We live in a historically unprecedented period of virtually universal disillusion with the vast pretensions of socialists, whatever their tendency, to remedy the world's economic, social, and political ills. This justifiable disenchantment, and the mood of intellectual confusion and depression accompanying it, is occurring at a time that the diverse challenges confronting humankind have never been greater but also when the conservative alternatives to socialism are less able than ever to cope with humanity's problems. The failure of alternatives is the only reason why the motives underlying the original socialist core assumptions are still relevant today and their rational reconstruction remains essential if the world is to resolve its present political and economic challenges. Social democracy's abandonment of the minimum premises inherent in its original commitment to social justice and equity, or the uncritical conversion of the oppressive Leninist regimes to capitalism's economic dogmas, cannot obscure the fact that fundamental, radical answers to a myriad of international as well as domestic political, economic, and social difficulties are needed more than ever. Our task is both to recognize and avoid socialist myopia and articulate appropriate solutions to these diverse problems. Not to do so is to court disaster.

I am highly critical of conventional wisdom and offer no consolation to any advocate of one or another established or respectable opinions. Those who need an absence of contingency in their ideas had better take up with one or another of the many mechanistic philosophies that the eighteenth and nineteenth centuries produced, or better yet one of the many all-encompassing religions, one as pretentious as possible. It is very late for civilization, and the problems to be analyzed rationally, much less resolved, are awesomely overwhelming and we require great candor and unsparing criticism. We must be not only radical and creative, but also aware of our shortcomings, lest our civilization, the good things as well as bad, continue its drift towards more destructive wars and the disintegration of the rationality and beauty which I still believe mankind is capable of attaining.

1 The power of reason

A world without limits

The nineteenth century produced many thinkers who believed in the idea of inevitable social progress and perfectibility, and their ideas have been the dominant influence on most social thought since then. Social theorists imagined few, if any, limits on reformers' aspirations and pretensions or their ability to recast human institutions to fulfill their desires. Whatever their disagreements, both conservative and radical social concepts were consummately ambitious and shared grandiose, universalistic objectives. As each school articulated its notions of the foundations of the historical and social experiences, they created ideologies that ignored many dimensions of history. Both in substance and method, the dominant assumptions and pretensions of social ideas were, to varying degrees, both comprehensive and optimistic. They always emphasized their understanding rather than their ignorance, and their unifying premise was that increasing insight, even certainty for many schools of thought, lay within human grasp.

Indeed, most influential social philosophers believed that progress toward greater well-being, and for some the end of history in a utopian idyll, was occurring irresistibly. The future was immanent in the present, progress virtually guaranteed. This cheerful credo was virtually hegemonic among generations of thinkers until World War One gravely challenged it. Socialism, although the most important, was only one of many expressions of this euphoria. We still live today with significant residues of the nineteenth century's optimistic legacies and visions, and a great many conservative political ideologies still hold to its premises.

Science and mathematics' stunning progress after the seventeenth century, very often correlated to the functional needs of mine owners or manufacturers who had challenges to be solved, led many thinkers to believe that absolute and inexorable laws would ultimately be discovered, giving a decisive impetus to the conviction that profound improvements in society would inevitably follow. One could then apply the knowledge and reasoning that unlocked the secrets of the physical world to the comprehension and control of social institutions. Much more than science was involved in such thinking, however. Hegelian dialectics and pseudo-science masking as a legitimate form of the scientific undertaking also played a key role but negated the limits of science in return for certitude. Such euphoric confidence had great influence internationally. But it ignored entirely that many of the standards of proof and logic that applied to geometry or physics were not relevant to people and human institutions. Worse yet, it was oblivious entirely to the role of politics.

Some exponents of this euphoria, such as Condorcet and the English utilitarians, minimized the tough-minded rhetoric and positivism of an August Comte or Marx stressing the mechanics of society and slighting the causal significance of individuals, but their differences, despite the generosity and permissiveness of their ideas, were more of style than substance. All of them shared a profound belief in humankind's positive power and potential, as well as the benign roles of those who ruled, and to the extent their notions were based on promises and hopes rather than reality, they were all romantic and naive. But the pervasiveness of both currents of thought made for a universal dogmatic vision of the future – and an obliviousness to other, far less rational or sanguine fates that humanity might confront, or even choose.

What unified the most influential systems of social and philosophical thought after 1800 was the unquestioned assumption that historical patterns and events were not only predictable but also devoid of great trauma – war, avarice, or stupidity – and that rationality guided mankind's affairs. The task before thinkers was simply to discover the workings and inner logic of history, to reveal its transcendent reality. Why the future should be so benevolent was based on a leap of faith and an unquestioned belief in progress.

French Revolutionary and British utilitarian thinkers during the eighteenth and early nineteenth centuries provided the optimistic intellectual architecture, and it was the advance of science and its tangible material proofs that most reinforced their optimistic prognostications and the promise of a world much more rational than the one that had preceded it. Science was the guarantor of progress, and no one of intellectual influence considered the possibility that science also contained a latent potential for destruction. The industrial revolution greatly reinforced the consummate sense of power. Such beliefs in essentially one analytic, scientific logic (defined in ways science rarely functions in reality) to guide both the material and intellectual aspects of human civilization, encouraged social theorists' imagination and dreams.[1] Those who sought to possess certitude about civilization's destiny, to comprehend the march of history, were absolutely confident they could succeed in unlocking this precious insight. These social theorists assumed that human goodwill and scientific rationality would always prevail, that their desires and reality were one and the same. Conventional wisdom simply ignored the complex political history of the preceding millennia or the institutions and human mentality that had been created over centuries.

Necessary futures: social laws and the science of society

Eighteenth- and nineteenth-century intellectual and philosophical systems, however important the differences in their methods and assumptions, converged to reinforce the belief that the world's past, present, and future destiny could be not only described and predicted but even, for those like Comte, prescribed. While sociology was scarcely the first to claim societies operated according to some sort of increasingly rational, cohesive, and predictable design, it became, even more than economics, the theoretically most ambitious discipline to do so. It was both complex and intellectually elegant, dealing with universal social behavior and interactions whose organic nature was allegedly reflected in institutional structures and societies that functioned in a unified, predictable manner. Sociology created laws and equations, and it proved them with its own criterion of sufficient evidence. These grand theories emphasized normal relations and order even when they subsumed a cacophony of information, and their methodological assumptions required non-discordant, undramatic regularity. Their logic was inherently conservative and missed a very large part of the often chaotic, irrational human experience over the past several centuries. Sociologists minimized specific times and situations and built static models that fit most, even all comparable societies. Economics was doing the same in its own, essentially similar way – one size fits all, to use a criticism that is now made of the International Monetary Fund (IMF). Social thought was not only misleading but also, where it counted most, dangerous.

Charles Darwin's theory of organic evolution in 1859 inspired thinkers as initially diverse as Herbert Spencer and Karl Marx to articulate "integration," "coherence," and "definiteness" as central to their conceptions of society and grand designs.[2] In a general way, Darwin's account of the irresistible growth of physically superior humans and animals reinforced the Enlightenment belief in inevitable progress in society. By the latter half of the nineteenth century, optimism suffused all social theory whether conservative defenders of conventional wisdom or self-proclaimed reformers produced it. They utterly failed to predict the experience of subsequent generations, and flourished only because of ephemeral intellectual fashions and moods. This crucial context produced not only socialism but also the premises that are today employed to defend capitalism's hegemony. It was, with the minor exceptions I note below, an age of grand illusions.

The search for laws that described sequences of events, the patterns of human behavior, and integrated the main institutional factors shaping society generated diverse methods and explanations for reaching the goal of comprehension, but, with some exceptions I note below, few during the nineteenth century doubted that such explanations could be formulated. Whether an Auguste Comte in France, a Georg Simmel in Germany, or a Herbert Spencer in England produced it, a unified concept of verified, presumably scientific, knowledge of society and human destiny – "laws" – was both attainable and in the process of being articulated. Indeed, the very act of enunciating these organic structural forces would itself greatly reduce the potential idiosyncrasies human beings might create in the social process. The principles governing society and history – what Marx termed as "laws of motion" – were both irreversible and irresistible; all that remained was to discover them. Absolute truth was attainable and it was but a matter of time before science and natural law shaped man's social institutions.

Notwithstanding the overwhelming optimism and belief in inevitable progress and meliorism that defined the century's most influential ideas, deeply pessimistic and anti-rational alternatives always lurked in the background. There were also aristocratic, elitist, anti-industrial and romantic trends, including cults of the individual that were idiosyncratic and dangerous, and some were quite irrational. Neo-medievalism, the idealization of heroes and action, militarism, individualist anarchism and nihilism, mysticism, theories of evil and pessimism, and egoism all had followers; relative to the mainstream of optimists, there were not many of them but they created a substantial literature expounding such theses. Thomas Carlyle, Georges Sorel, Friedrich Nietzsche, Arthur Schopenhauer, and Henri Bergson were their best known advocates. Out of their writings came a cult of deepening subjectivism that Freudians and others later built upon. Different versions of what is essentially pessimism were concocted by Vilfredo Pareto and Pitirim Sorokin, who regarded humans as deceptive and evil. The latter saw Western society as sick and gravely troubled to the core, and Pareto believed inequality was practically a biological law, but they were initially a very marginal, uninfluential minority – even World War One did not alter their isolation, although Sorokin ended at Harvard. But the ascendancy of notions of progress and rationality always coexisted with all its initially far smaller opposites, magnetic to those who preferred such fantasies and exoticism – and who opposed rationalism. Many of these anti-intellectual, elitist notions later became influential and eventually nourished the broad strain of ideas associated with fascism.

But whether theories were naively ameliorative or reactionary, the skeptical criteria that were applied to pre-Enlightenment ideas and received wisdom were suspended when it came to the dominant social and economic concepts that have emerged over the past two centuries. To varying degrees, this myopia and lack of skepticism on essential premises – the need for faith, or call it transcendent confidence – gave all dominant notions and their assumptions of inevitability an influence they would never have enjoyed had thoroughgoing critical criteria been used to formulate them. Classical economists, Marxists, and sociological and psychoanalytic theorists all benefited from it.

This commitment to system-building as the objective of social analysis, treating history as a unified process, inevitably led analysts to formulate various laws or axioms to make the historical experience coherent. This meant a virtually exclusive focus on why and how systems work successfully or well, on functions rather than dysfunctions. Classical economics ultimately proved the most enduring product of this train of thought, and it was predicated on notions of a natural order that defined human behavior and that drew eclectically from putative theological designs as well as Hobbesian pessimistic notions about the inevitability of selfish human conduct. These converged in Adam Smith's economic theory and were elaborated by Thomas Malthus, David Ricardo, and others. Economics was reduced to propositions – not simply laws that replicated those discovered by Newton and others, but even "iron laws" – that were mechanistic assertions of those putative natural laws grounded in the eighteenth century's very diverse legal, theological, and mathematical rhetoric. Theoretical economists liberally tailored these premises to rationalize the economic privileges of those who possessed them. Economics, most theorists argued, functioned in equilibrium, and – if left alone – operated as a functional, essentially static natural order. Theoretical economics, reflecting this nineteenth-century bias which invaded all realms of ideas, ignored the crucial ways politics and social factors affected an infinitely messier and more complex reality. But their absolutely essential premises about individual behavior and the purportedly natural evolution of economic institutions in practice still guides the assumptions and policies of crucial institutions and innumerable governments.[3]

Formalism and theories of society that assumed the existence of reasonably organized and predictable futures have, with some notable but relatively uninfluential exceptions, suffused sociology and social thought in general since the nineteenth century. The very assumption that a society is capable of being both explained and that its future evolution is, in essence if not detail, predictable assumes the existence of coherence and a substantial degree of rationality. Implicitly, whether it comes from autonomous imperatives or logic, institutional or class intelligence, or any combination of factors, the general trend in society was assumed to be integrative, at least relatively successful, and progressive – a part of a rational social logic that moved to a better future. Social breakdowns, much less calamities, had no place whatsoever in such thinking. As for mass behavior, rationality was assumed where it was not explicitly postulated. Stupidity, the failure of intelligence, ambitious rulers immune to the larger public interest, these and other sources of crises were not predicted. The few pessimists who existed were still quite marginal. Crucial historical experiences, past as well as future, were ignored entirely.

A common world of ideas and a largely unified intellectual current existed throughout Europe. Similar discussions regarding the state, liberty, political methods and assumptions, and the like occurred in most nations. Moods and themes were comparable, and intellectuals were in touch with each other – often directly – and they read each other's major books. Literacy created a European community of ideas. It was no wonder that socialism began as a German movement but almost instantly spread throughout Europe. Immigrants – particularly urbanized Germans, Italians, and Jews – also took many ideas with them. Socialism in the United States was largely – though not exclusively – an immigrant phenomenon. Even American universities absorbed some of Europe's intellectual effervescence.

Images of the future and predictions still assumed history would become even more benign or, as with positivism and Marxism, move ineluctably to create far better, even ideal societies. Theories remained large scale, pretentious, and expressed with a complexity that invariably challenged people's comprehension. Such elegant but opaque analyses – which were unintelligible save to a few of the initiated – were their best defense against inconvenient, disturbing exceptions and conflicting evidence. Once such grand theories were formulated they remained largely static, and the more ambitious they were, the more likely their adherents were to defend them precisely in the form they were originally defined. The world's thinkers were therefore utterly unprepared for World War One or its long atavistic aftermath in the forms of Bolshevism and fascism. Within a few years, their intellectual universe had changed entirely, but precious few were ready to acknowledge this reality, much less discard their earlier optimistic assumptions. Essentially, this nineteenth-century ethos and sclerosis has existed down to the present. The result is that most, if not all, social thought is neither valid nor relevant.

Hegel and the quest for the absolute

Georg Hegel's profound influence on philosophy and social thought by the mid-nineteenth century, not only in Germany but also in much of Europe and even in some American academic circles, reflected the search by individuals on all the shades of the political spectrum for a comprehensive explanation of history that argued that the past, present, and future was a coherent whole. This desire for a universality and certainty that resolved all the important issues that might otherwise require both the admission of less-than-absolute knowledge as well as the need for continuous reasoning about human existence and destiny is merely an aspect of the need for absolutes that has caused people for thousands of years to adhere to religious faiths in their many diverse forms – secular included. Hegel influenced many – above all, but scarcely exclusively, Marxists – who otherwise denounced his earlier obscure or reactionary theses but who integrated him into more or less secular ideologies.

Hegel's authority was enormous, and far more significant than his specific ideas, which – as with many grand thinkers – are virtually incapable of being deciphered. Why so many were ready to embrace him and his unintelligibility poses some fundamental questions about the nature of human beliefs, but these can also be raised regarding other, less pretentious ideas. Even if one discards Hegel's notions of a Christian God and the Prussian state as the consummate expression of an Absolute and the Divine Idea that suffused everything he wrote, to accept his presumably secular working methodology, or his arguments in favor of an intellectual system, demands a huge leap of faith. Laws were transcendent and eternal, and ideas had timeless, universal validity. Marx accepted without reservation Hegel's ostensible philosophical methodology and logic, dialectics, but not his application of it, and thereby made Marxism into another form of obscuritanism. Hegel believed in metaphysics and was also an ardent German nationalist, and from this porridge of impulses he articulated a doctrine that rationalized Prussian power and ideology. His chain of reasoning and logic defies a coherent analysis: it is circular, assumes forces and relationships, and appearances versus realities, which only befuddled true believers; those who accept Hegel's system ignore that its meanings and assertions are constantly changing and defy logic, and his philosophy is the height of mysticism masking as a rational process. Hegel was in reality a cynical, ambitious man; innumerable critics have proved convincingly that he had no hesitation about spinning out whatever fantasies that might enable him to become Prussia's official philosopher.[4]

What is by far the most interesting about Hegel, and much more difficult to explain, is why and how so many non-religious people, otherwise enlightened men and women principally on the Left of the political spectrum, found it essential to borrow so heavily from his texts. Their inability to live with those innumerable tensions and doubts that demanded constant reflection on the efficacy of their ideas, and their readiness to comfort themselves with absolute illusions and fantasies, not only were to lead to intellectual and moral disasters, but also reflected the general nineteenth-century assumption that philosophy both should and could be comprehensive in its methods, claims, and goals. Hegel offered a complete "system" whose universal pretensions, extending as far as a Christian Prussia absolutism as an aspect of the natural order, could not be attained save by faith, if at all. People's abhorrence of uncertainty, and the willingness of so many to adhere to fictions, was undoubtedly crucial to his influence. And this raises the question: had Hegel never existed, would a comparably totalistic and ambitious integration of philosophy and history been necessary? And would it have emerged from another source? The answer is probably affirmative. For Hegel must also be regarded as much a reflection of the desire of men and women for absolute certainty and the assurance of total prescience as the cause of their convictions. He confirmed that there exists a large and receptive audience for opaque but superficial, even irrational philosophical systems.

There was absolutely no place in this benign panoply for barbarism – for a Hitler or Stalin – and very few believed that the future would get far worse rather than better. This integrated conception and vision, which pretended to offer transcendent truths, was usually expressed as laws that were comprehensive and unvarying, even absolute. Although theorists could not agree what these laws were, most claimed their methodologies were essentially identical – scientific and value neutral – and many overlapped in important ways, so that Marx could draw upon classical English economists and Hegel to synthesize his own grand system. Even Marx's notion of a so-called crisis was a highly organized one, based on calculable, systematic events preceding it, and its outcome was no less predictable. Ideas came in large sizes. Intellectual ambition was rife, and no analytic constraints inhibited the creation of vast theoretical constructs. Social theories were intentionally very ambitious, and a premium was placed on their being all inclusive.

The nineteenth century for most intellectuals was an age of promise, self-confidence, and illusions. It was astonishingly naive, given the history that had preceded it much less all that was to follow. An essentially optimistic complacency was its hallmark. And its intellectual shadow remains very great today, even after a century of the most terrible experience has shown that such conceptions were a profoundly misleading chimera.

It was not merely that rationality and predictability remain the operative notion of these ambitious theories. They assumed not only an underlying order but also a substantial degree of class intelligence. Even critics accept it, as everything that occurs is intended and logical and interrelated, if only for evil reasons, implying a higher reason. To concede the possibility that major unforeseen events – much less deplorable individuals capable of mobilizing vast followings – might occur could only undermine the dominant optimistic theories' accuracy and value. Grand systems cannot be generalized without predicating an all-defining basic order, and a theory that takes uncertainties and contingencies seriously is not likely to be as appealing or comprehensible to many people as one that simplifies humankind's condition. War, ethnic nationalism and religious fanaticism, racism, personal ambition and opportunism, massive population migration, and a great deal more have no place in the corpus of nineteenth-century theories – even in the many forms in which they still flourish today.

The optimism-meliorism syndrome

The imagination of countless intellectuals reflected this pervasive mood of naive optimism and supreme self-confidence, and the century before World War One was a creative hothouse of notions about society, morals, and destiny. The scope and range of concepts they dealt with encompassed most aspects of the human experience.

The leitmotif of these years was ideas – concepts in abundance, being discussed passionately. Throughout Europe, men and women considered the present and future with the confidence that proposals to make the world a better place would be irresistible and decisive because their very logic and beauty would be persuasive and cause them to prevail. The age, proponents of such changes assumed, was supremely rational and analytic, revealing themselves as both intensely romantic and naive.

Ideas counted, if only because they were said to grasp essential, if not final, meanings and explain the direction of history, and there was a consensus about their power to shape destiny that united sometimes very disparate thinkers – whether they believed in the operation of immutable laws, the efficacy of human intervention, or both. Innumerable theorists of all political persuasions, Left, Right, and Center, merged a scrupulous regard for the logical exposition of ideas with an innocence and utopianism that reflected only their traditional insularity from power and political reality. Contained within their own orbit and subject only to canons of proof that they defined for themselves, they thrived, wrote, and dreamed. Every nation produced them, but some theories were truly international in scope and much more enduring in their impact: Wandervogel, Zionism, Marxism, psychoanalysis, and the like. Many people switched beliefs very quickly; and as dominant ideas changed, so did intellectual fashions. The only thing that was truly constant was a fascination with the power of abstractions, a consummate conviction that reason and ideas really mattered and the human condition, along with the institutions that defined it, would improve greatly once someone revealed the solutions for its troubles. Given the generous motives of most of those who crafted them, it is somewhat unkind to dismiss this renaissance of the imagination as pathetically illusory, but it must be finally judged – as with all concepts – on the assumptions and logic of its theories and prognostications. Their sheer optimism and will to succeed caused men and women to minimize or even ignore those complex problems of society, politics, and reality that required them to temper their enthusiasms. Their eagerness and good intentions encouraged careless reasoning, and slipshod politics was the inevitable result.

Few explicit boundaries between philosophy, religion, socialism, economics, and all the other formal disciplines existed in the nineteenth century. Typically, George Eliot, among the most interesting European intellectuals of the age, was over time fascinated by Hegel and religious theory, utopian socialism, phrenology, positivism, and a host of changing, fashionable notions. Jules Michelet's intellectual odyssey included liberal nationalism, anti-industrialism, and mysticism, and a confused set of propositions which drew upon assorted utopian socialist concepts that were then in vogue among French intellectuals. Fabianism in England attracted spiritualists, Christians, feminists, socialists, dress reform advocates, and many more who were intensely obsessed by ideas they believed certain – once they were understood widely and therefore accepted – to transform the nation and world. Romanticism and a faith in pseudo-science explain dimensions of this mood, and the theories of evolution and positivism added to its credibility. The symbiosis between bohemianism and assorted notions of socialism began in the nineteenth century and was to persist thereafter. What all these doctrines most shared in common, whatever their specific differences, was generosity and faith – thinkers wished to be good and they believed that most people would follow them. Fashions destroy creativity and individuality in all domains, from ideas about society to science, and to overcome them is a prerequisite of innovation, whatever the topic. The nineteenth century was an era of optimism and conformity in ideas.

The large majority of European intellectuals retained a belief in the irresistible power of abstractions to shape humanity's institutions, especially when they regarded science and positivism as the basis of their theories – as so many were ready to do, although some retained a deep respect for assorted theological assumptions. Only part of the cause for their sloppy thinking and indifference to critical reasoning was their belief that their generous impulses and goals justified their holding firm to their assorted doctrines; but there was always a penury of those rigorously critical standards essential for clear thought about society and history.

Mainstream reform notions throughout the nineteenth century were eclectic, and they have continued that way. Incongruous modes of assessing problems and confronting them were common and all too few wanted to disturb the opposition community with probing or disturbing questions that surely would have split them into pieces, creating a high price and alienating often good souls who only wished to change the nefarious ways the world worked. Some, however, for theological or existential reasons always placed a higher premium on personal salvation than intellectual rigor. Better to tolerate nonsense and illusion, many calculated, and theological or utopian baggage therefore persisted throughout much of the next century.

The academic professionalization of theory

At its inception, sociology pretended to be the science of society, capable of discovering the laws of social sequences and even defining society's moral norms. Notwithstanding the reservations that Alfred Weber and a few of the earlier sociological theorists had raised, the dominant trend in sociology was to define general categories that were more or less comprehensive and assumed predictability in society and history. From this belief in systems emerged functionalism and a concept of the world as a fairly rational, orderly place, and while some theorists – Marx is the best known – foresaw crises, they too were to occur in predictable and basically orderly fashion. Crises were also the essential precursors of progress. There was no place in such theories for atavism and irrationality, nationalism and religious bigotry – or for any of the many often chaotic and surrealist realities in daily life about them, the sources of tragedy or wars. In brief, they ignored experience – and history.

To the extent that social theory during the twentieth century was professionalized and became very largely the domain of academics, its deficiencies only increased in many essential ways, not the least of which was that there were bureaucratized intellectuals capable of keeping failed or erroneous conceptions alive. The crucial factors influencing their efforts soon transcended a concern for ideas that are judged solely on the basis of proof and arguments for them. Instead, ideas and theories were articulated and played their functions in contexts where the professional interests of the nominal theorists were involved. Communities of ideas, in the social sciences as well as science, produced conformity to established wisdom and fixed the parameters of intellectual discourse in ways that caused them to cease being critical and innovative. Stated another way, anyone in an academic context must weigh the benefits and personal risks of creative, independent thought and nonconformity insofar as mainstream ideas are concerned. The desire to get tenure makes all too many academics silent or opportunists during the formative years of their careers, after which most no longer have the will or capacity to engage in independent thought. Such constraints, despite their existence, were generally less decisive during the nineteenth century, although Hegel certainly perceived his ideas through the prism of his power and ambition, ruthlessly employing them to advance himself.

The style of discourse that the large majority of professors favor greatly affects the substance of their concepts and most professors confuse the ideas that are crucial in the university with reality. The very few that come to power, as the foreign policies of the United States showed in Vietnam in the 1960s and Iraq today, are no less dangerous than anyone else with authority – and perhaps more. Despite exceptions, academic social theories have attempted to be as inclusive as possible, and comprehensive large-scale, if not universal paradigms and essentially static models are preferable to more modest and contingent ideas. While these assume, as with nineteenth-century theories, predictability and therefore a degree of rationality in institutional and human behavior, the standards of proof are much more constricted than before by the very nature of debates among academics. There is, first of all, a far greater stress on precocious complexity, which tends to increase theories' ambitions and the volume of comparative information they seek to utilize. Such data is often taken as a measure of proof and validity, and quantity and intricacy are frequently substituted for both quality and clarity. Equally ambitious covering laws, arrived at deductively or inductively, are legitimate and common even though many are contradictory and incapable of being reconciled. Elegant and convoluted methodologies thrive even when proof for them is difficult, even impossible, to establish. In such a framework, every idea – the bad as well as the good, or, most often, simply mediocre and banal – thrives. Fashionable myths and pure nonsense in the social sciences flourish and are protected in the name of academic freedom, including propositions that frequently are discredited and forgotten within a few years. A great deal of it is painfully arcane and obscure.

The academic environment is generally pluralistic and absorptive, capable of generating innumerable social ideas, but it also makes possible the perpetuation of erroneous theories. Almost none is ever tested in reality or applied, save those supremely dangerous international relations concepts – very often the product of ambitious people – that are employed by men of power who are attracted to their utility as rationalizations of aggressive foreign policies.

It is, of course, desirable for universities to tolerate every sort of doctrine, whatever their nature and consequences, but such freedom is scarcely a guarantee that theories that are valid will prevail over those that are false; indeed, so far such toleration has been mainly a source of the cacophony of ideas that are isolated from the world of reality as opposed to the one professors imagine exists. It may provide an environment conducive to the propagation of controversy but by themselves universities are no assurance that a resolution of them will occur. For this to happen, mutual toleration and politeness, the hallmark of scholarly people, must be entirely secondary to the desire to resolve controversies by sifting ideas that are likely to be more valid from those that are simply false. Whenever ideas involve bureaucracies, tenure, and jobs, the consequences will always be threatening to truly creative freedom of thought. But for whatever the reason, whether peer pressures, opportunism, or habit, the creativity and genuine nonconformity which is a precondition for formulating alternative social thought on a scale appropriate to the crises civilization now confronts has not existed in the world's universities – or elsewhere.

Whether it is science, social ideas, or any other domain of human activity, socialization plus professional considerations not only perpetuate erroneous ideas but they inhibit new ones also. Such material factors are certainly far from being a total explanation of the inability of social theories to evolve since the nineteenth century, but they are very important to any effort to understand why, especially after the second half of the twentieth century, there has been far less intellectual and analytic progress than conditions throughout the world warrant. Comfortable prosperity has greatly inhibited the task of radically explaining and conceptualizing reality.

Academics assumed an increasingly greater role in formulating social thought as the twentieth century progressed, and independent thinkers were marginalized as never before, isolating theory from the century's traumatic political and social crises. World War One was a terrible, protracted bloodletting, producing intensely alienated men and women who turned to Bolshevism, fascism, and ideas whose influence few had ever imagined possible before 1914. Overwhelmingly, academics failed to anticipate, much less explain them. But an astonishing number of people in universities remained – and still remain – impervious to those great events that have made their ideas irrelevant, trivial, and often completely disconnected from social realities. By the end of the twentieth century, although no alternatives to inherited conventional wisdom filled their place, those formulated before 1914 ceased to have real influence – superficial rhetoric notwithstanding – among countless ordinary men and women who had once believed in them. Economics is a partial exception. Indeed, the fascist and Leninist doctrines that successfully challenged and replaced older notions during the half-century after 1914 are now also rejected. To an extent without precedent in history, disbelief in theories is now characteristic of peoples' perceptions everywhere, above all in those European and Asian nations that have experienced the twentieth century's principal tragedies.

Whenever social and political conditions reach an acute point, reality compels many more people to search for explanations and much greater comprehension. The "normal" theories that evolved from nineteenth-century optimistic ideas failed utterly to predict the very possibility of such crises, especially wars. The closer people are to traumatic events, the more likely it is that some will reassess reality profoundly because the risks of myopia are far more costly than the continued acceptance of conventional wisdom. The dominant grand theories cannot explain the wars, revolutions, and innumerable social upheavals and disorders that have seared much of the world during the twentieth century – and still do so. Traditional ideas, of course, will retain adherents even during the worst of times; alternatives to them have often been unconvincing or flawed in some simplistic manner, and the inertia that sentimental commitments to old ideas produce always exists among those who fear looking at the efficacy and foundations of their own beliefs. Social and personal links keep all sorts of notions alive, for people will not lose friends for doctrinal reasons that appear, ultimately, abstract. But the critical attitude necessary to arrive at a more accurate concept of the truth will persist.

The enormous upheavals that the world has endured throughout the twentieth century have not by themselves led to conceptions of the world that are superior. Bolshevism and fascism proved that it is not sufficient merely to reject moribund inherited notions and that some alternatives to them possessed immense dangers. But a readiness to break with tradition is a precondition for advancing our understanding both of the world and our relationship to it. In fact, the destruction of traditional legacies has far more often than not either produced new illusions or simply created a vacuum of ideas and a perceived loss of comprehension and orientation among many men and women. This void has led to disbelief and cynicism among countless people, and while all this is deplorable, it is far less perilous than a mindless acceptance of those numerous mechanistic fallacies – ranging from laissez-faire economic propositions to Marxist determinism and much else – that the nineteenth century created.

2 The legacies of socialism

Theory

Socialism was the most influential emancipatory ideal to emerge throughout the world after the mid-nineteenth century. Even though Communism disintegrated without wars and revolution during the 1980s, both the idea and the remnants of what was once a great international political movement still continue today – in part because of nostalgia but also because there is as yet no alternative to socialism's former inspiration. Socialism's global importance persisted long after 1914, when its fatal errors began, largely because Lenin's triumph in Russia made socialism as a world system crucial for about a half-century. Marxism was its principal but certainly not its exclusive expression, for socialism descends from a utopian-millenarian tradition which began long before Marx, who merely systematized it in a typical nineteenth-century positivist fashion.

Candidly assessing socialism's ambitious ideology, both as an explanation and as a goad to action, is a prerequisite if critical social theory is to be reconstructed to become a guide to social reality and behavior. We must analyze both its principal ideas and its concrete institutional and organizational expressions – and how and why they failed.

There is no reason why an ambitious social theory should be less complex than historical realities warrant. The desire to attain clarity is a grave liability only if it obscures vital issues – however convoluted they might be – that must be clearly understood. But highly elegant doctrines, whether religious or secular, which pretend to explain human destiny become extremely misleading if their very obscurity requires an act of faith to justify them. Residues of ignorance are inherent in the very limits of knowledge, and such blindness will always risk creating profound errors unless we struggle constantly to overcome it. This means that a lack of comprehension must never be accepted passively, and it must never be necessary to regard a theory as a sacred and mysterious truth. A better way than simplifications and faith must, and can, be found.

Marx's theory evolved at a time when Hegel's philosophy dominated much of German thought, and while it was scarcely the only influence on him, Marx began and ended a Hegelian. Despite Marx and Engels' fundamental opposition to Hegel's candidly reactionary applications of his philosophy to social ideas and politics, they always believed that the basic dialectical methodology was the key to a total understanding of the human experience and history. Many nineteenth-century theorists besides Hegel and Marx formulated axiomatic, optimistic notions, of course. But dialectical and historical materialism was Marx's essential explanatory tool to describe the development of laws of economics, and he believed that it provided a vindication of his predictions on the outcome of history.

Marx also borrowed crucial assumptions from English classical economists, who argued that economics was axiomatic and that "objective" laws guided it. Humankind had to resign itself to their working, and to attempt to alter them was futile, making these writers, with some minor caveats, both determinists and simple apologists for capitalism. Marxism is intellectually a synthesis of Hegel's obtuse dialectical methodology with laissez-faire economics, and both were very much nineteenth-century ideologies.

Engels, for his part, cited Hegel as having been "the first to state correctly the relation between freedom and necessity" in dialectical terms. With feigned modesty, he thought that his and Marx's application of the "most consummate form of philosophy" produced not "absolute truth" but only "the very essence of this absolute truth" – a sort of relative absolute based on "the fundamental law of dialectic reasoning." Dialectical methodology itself was a transcendent doctrine, however great the changes in the world it assessed. From its very inception, Marxism was plagued by obscurity. Hegel's mysticism always suffused Marxism's schema and its attempts to add force to its economics. Marx, but especially Engels, could not divorce Marxism from its original inspiration in German philosophy, which added countless layers of analytic obscurity to an already overloaded theoretical formulation. People were free only to acknowledge the limits that necessity imposed upon them. Belief in the existence of other choices was "founded on ignorance," which Marx thought he had eliminated. Freedom was the capacity only to conform to historical necessity. "The whole process" of history and social development "can be explained by purely economic causes; at no point whatever are robbery, force, the state or political interference of any kind necessary."[1] Historical and dialectical materialism, in the form that Marx and Engels defined it, claimed to be a transcendent and sufficient explanation of the past, present, and future, and it guaranteed certainty. This absolute certitude became the intellectual foundation of socialism in virtually all the forms – Social Democratic as well as Bolshevik – that it took during its crucial formative years.

What is distinctive in Marx were his desires and goals, which were commendable but could have been defended in far more plausible and convincing ways; but he – like so many others – also wanted his system to include inevitability, and this Hegel and the classic economists provided. Engels claimed that he and Marx turned the "German dialectical method" upside down to grasp the fundamentals of economics.[2] But there is simply no Marxism without Ricardo *and* Hegel. Even Ferdinand Lassalle, Marx's only rival in the

German Social Democratic Party (SPD), was influenced by Hegel and Ricardo. As an ostensible scientist seeking to explain the *laws* of motion in terms of determinist natural forces that operated with the inner logic of an inexorable and impersonal dialectical process, Marx did not need to cite his own outrage as a justification for claiming to have a scientific total knowledge of society which allowed him to predict the eventual collapse of capitalism and triumph of socialism. One cannot assign a precise weight to Marx's dialectical methodology as opposed to his economic concepts, and he himself made no distinction between them. But the two were integral, and at crucial points economics could be explained only with dialectical methods, especially to justify alleged transformations in economics that defied purely material explanations. The result of trying to employ Hegel was utter confusion and mystery wrapped around a cause and sense of injustice that was really quite simple and, had it remained that way, would have appealed to more people and retained their commitment far longer. Analytically, it would be far less determinist and far more useful in a world full of unpredictable surprises and changes. Faith, in large part to confront its obscurity and inconsistencies, thereby became integral to Marx's entire system.

Marx merely shared the dominant nineteenth-century certainty in irresistible progress and its belief that an erstwhile science of society was attainable. It was this utter confidence that further assured that twentieth century realities would leave Marxism wholly superfluous as an analytic – as opposed to political – tool. Marx's enthusiasm for Hegel gave him what his disciple, Franz Mehring, called "a magnificent conception of history."[3] Marx's respect for Hegel's methodology never wavered; his earliest and most philosophical writings explored and applied Hegelian categories in depth, effusively approving some of the philosopher's most far-fetched mystical premises. The first volume of *Capital* declared Hegel to be the first to utilize dialectical reasoning "in a comprehensive and conscious manner"; Marx claimed only to demystify it.[4] Engels stated that he and Marx were "the only people to rescue conscious dialectics from German idealist philosophy."[5] However reluctant many of Marx's later followers were to acknowledge Hegel's crucial role in the creation of "scientific socialism," and the assertion that "Essences" which explained the true nature of capitalism exist simultaneously with "Appearances," this was only because they realized that Hegel undermined Marxism's scientific pretensions and replaced it with a metaphysics which demands absolute faith as opposed to confidence that is ultimately contingent on proof.

Marx's economic system cannot even begin to be deciphered on its own terms without this distinction between appearances and reality or essences, although in practice it is incomprehensible however one interprets it. Marx's distinction between appearances and reality – properties and things, including commodity fetishism, as opposed to processes and relations – is central to Marx's law of value and reflects his profound debt to Hegel. Hegel's belief that a unified system underlay what superficially appeared like unrelated or disunited phenomena, and that an integrated and organic whole existed beneath discrete appearances and that there was an overriding superstructure to them, justified Marx's effort to create a unified and total system explaining everything crucial to not just economics but to society as a whole.

György Lukács wrote in 1923 that the Hegelian method, as he interpreted it, was integral to the entire Marxist intellectual project. Roman Rosdolsky, one of the ablest orthodox Marxist scholars of the past half-century, argued convincingly that Hegel's methods are central to many of Marx's most crucial assumptions. It was a major contradiction in Marx's grand economic theory, one which he never resolved; but it was proper Hegelian theory, dialectically correct! It has given many generations of orthodox Marxists a great deal of explaining to do, but in fact the theory remains confused and contradictory – and inordinately complex.[6]

The goals that socialists advocated and the reasons for them could have been far simpler and more easily expressed and defended, but socialism from its inception was hobbled with an incomprehensible Marxist method and mysticism. The strongest argument for socialism is that capitalism has shown itself again and again as an irrational and dangerous basis for building a stable civilization, but this is more an argument against capitalism rather than for socialism. People adhered to Marxism because they were essentially anti-capitalist and believed the theory would somehow make capitalism's abolition and socialism's attainment more likely, but vast organizational movements and even states underwrote both the Social Democratic and Leninist versions of Marxism, and that was crucial. Such a defense of ideas was political and pragmatic, essential to socialism's existence as a mass movement, but it perpetuated its huge and growing analytic incapacity for the sake of myths that proved illusory.

Dialectics condemned Marxism to both obscurantism and determinism, and these complemented each other and introduced an opaque intellectual wall whose very existence allowed its followers to remain comfortably ignorant and impervious to a complex world that requires continuous critical analysis at all times. Dialectics, ultimately, demanded absolute faith, and unquestioning faith of any sort is the enemy of reason. Marxism was offered as a total vision of the world, and neither Marx nor Engels believed that their comprehensive system could be picked over selectively. It had an inseparable overriding logic, requiring one to accept it entirely or not at all. Like all natural law theorists, Marx projected a total organic historical process; not for a moment did he ever consider the possibility of exceptional events, whether political, demographic, economic or whatever, upsetting his presumably natural evolutionary pattern. The future was not a matter of debate, and mankind had only to resign itself to inevitable certainties. Marxism was a whole, integrated creed, a faith, but – exegesis notwithstanding – it was never capable of serving as a continuous and useful analytic tool that changed when circumstances warranted it.

History without surprises

It was inevitable that the nineteenth century's prevailing mechanistic ideas and intellectual fashions also suffuse Marxism. To varying degrees, belief in reason, humanitarianism, and internationalism permeated most, if not all, Enlightenment thought and all of the subsequent variants of socialism – including the so-called utopians and anarchists. English thinkers, especially but surely not exclusively the utilitarians, concocted yet other notions which were a part of the discourse of the times, and the labor theory of value was a product of this tradition. Marx was very much one – but only one – figure of these currents of thought. Most ideas, especially those of associationists and anarchists like Robert Owen, Charles Fourier, Louis Blanc, and others, employed the term "socialism" and suffered from varying degrees of eccentricity and extreme naivety, and Marx originally labeled himself as a "Communist" as well as "scientific" in order to distance himself from their voluntarist excesses and cranky notions.[7] Marx utilized what is now called classical laissez-faire economics – David Ricardo particularly – to portray socialism as "scientific," making it not only systematic but also dogmatic, thereby setting socialism off on the wrong track, from which it was never to recover. Socialism was to be the outcome of impersonal economic laws, not human interventions, much less desires (such voluntarism he deemed "utopian") – inevitable. But Marx, a creature of his times, solved no substantive or philosophical problems. His discussions of the importance of class structures were hardly original; the American Founding Fathers crafted a constitution intended to control the potential role of the masses, and by Marx's time the question of class and power was very much a part of the debates over politics and society. But if the arguments for Marx's formal theory can and should be made because of its intellectual merits, it must also be held responsible for the countless illusions and failures it encouraged – and the striking inability of socialists to change the course of humanity when it most needed it.

Marx and Engels, of course, wrote so much that exegetics can easily create a personal Marx to suit anyone. But at their irreducible core, Marx and Engels certainly argued in their most systematic writings that they explained "the natural laws of capitalist production" and that "it is a question of these laws themselves, of these tendencies working with iron necessity toward inevitable results." Marx claimed "to lay bare the economic law of motion of modern society," and he viewed economics, as did so many contemporaries with their own pretensions to attain certitude, "as a process of natural history." This process of capitalist production operated "with the inexorability of a law of Nature."[8]

But despite their important differences, Marx and most utopians shared much more in common, not the least is that both thought that future history was predictable and contained no surprising terrible tragedies to undermine the universal belief that humankind would inevitably experience greater, if not ultimate perfection. The logic of dominant contemporary thought precluded voluntarism of any variety. Marx was scarcely alone in believing that history had no place for ethical choices. Like many utopians and nineteenth-century writers, especially the anarchists, Marx believed the state would gradually wither away and become unnecessary, both to the masses and to the dispossessed class. If ever there was a utopian notion, based on pure wish-fulfillment, this was it. It ignored not just power but all history and reality, past, present, and future. Marx's intellectual cocktail mixed all sorts of ideas together, leaving future generations who followed in the Marxist tradition to decipher this hodgepodge or simply ignore it and use his imprimatur in the vaguest and most general fashion as a honorific label that implicitly gave them absolution – as in any church.

The utopians' intellectual weaknesses and murkiness had many serious liabilities but they never became as hegemonic and intolerant of dissenting notions as did Marxists. Relatively speaking, the utopians were naive and innocent; most of them had fantastic notions of the power of ideas and social engineering – of voluntarism that believed history was all too malleable. But Marx was utopian too in believing in stasis and waiting for inexorable changes in the economy to alter the class structure – in the primacy of "social relations" – and making his ill-defined socialism inevitable. In its extreme form, as George Plekhanov defined it, Marxism became a caricature of the Calvinist attack on free will and dialectically made necessity and freedom synonymous. Both the utopians and Marx were, in their own ways, deeply flawed, and they refused to consider how the classes they hoped to dispossess might use the state, from police to regulation, to retain power.

Great conceptions regarding history, politics, art, and much else can never be divorced from the intellectual environment that spawns them. Marxism, all of the other notions that called themselves socialist as well as those that did not, can be understood only in the context of the many other contemporary hopes, illusions, and myopic visions of history, science, and society. It accepted the fundamental and universal premise of dominant social theories that humanity's future was subject to controlling forces, and even laws, that could be predicted in advance – and therefore were scientific. That all events in history are in crucial ways mediated by people – rulers, politicians, heroes, and the masses – was essentially ignored in the optimistic theories that the Enlightenment, Marxism included, generated. To have reasoned otherwise would have added an unpredictable dimension to the historical experience, challenging the intense self-confidence which was the hallmark of the age.

Marx, as did many laissez-faire economists, utilized purported materialist analyses as an antidote to the emphasis on volunteerist abstractions in contemporary social theories, particularly among "utopian socialists." His efforts could have had enduring value as a crucial aspect of a more subtle analytic framework that took into account essential but often very variable political and social aspects of humankind's history – including how politics might shape the societies that succeeded capitalism. But he linked a materialist interpretation of history and the importance of class analysis for comprehending societies to a whole series of nominally related assumptions on the nature of economic institutions and its ostensibly predictable direction, thereby submerging valuable ideas with those that were naively determinist.

Marx and Engels believed that they had, in a wholly scientific manner, revealed the inevitable crucial forces that would determine the future. Neither Marx nor Engels can be exonerated for the ideas and follies of their followers; they merely pursued the founders' intellectual methods and uncritically accepted their pretensions. By ostensibly objectively describing the laws of production and the role of workers in the economic process, Marx could dismiss the utopians who depended on ethical and normative notions. For most utopians, socialism was an ideal and human will was essential in attaining it, implying ethical norms for human conduct rather than merely a necessity. Some utopians, of course, also believed there were laws making socialism inevitable, but most saw voluntarism as crucial. Marx claimed socialism was not a question of desire but of impersonally revealing and describing the outcome of an autonomous economic process that possessed its own dynamics. Marx never articulated a notion of the individual's role and responsibility in determining future events. He and Engels believed human behavior would conform to those larger institutional forces that shaped history. There are countless traps built into Marx's vision of history, not the least the extent to which it encourages individual passivity in shaping the future – with all the personal and ethical implications this engenders. To him, socialism was never dependent on the political action or will of its adherents. That was his fatal error.

Marx's entire theoretical framework, principally *Capital*, is poorly arranged and overloaded with long discursive, simplistic expositions of quite minor points that often have little or no relevance to his grand theory. Marx's difficulties were only partly due to the economic theorems he took from the classical economists, and which he predicted would create economic crises. Many of his economic observations were acute even where incomplete, but he failed to anticipate factors that might cause different outcomes than those he forecast. Rival capitalist interests, how political intervention might affect prices and competition, and much else that was decisive in the history of modern capitalism, escaped him. That capitalists would obligingly obey Marx's economic laws and accept being abolished, along with their privileges and perquisites, without acting in concert with each other or vis-à-vis the state, is the height of naivety – on a par with the workers making revolution according to Marx's schema. The fact is that Marx actually based his entire system on his wishes and ethical judgments rather than a "scientific" assessment of options, both to capitalists and workers. Marx was oblivious to much that was crucial, but he ignored, above all, the problem of wars and their immense implications to all political and economic aspects of traditional orders – including their very existence. The immediacy and decisive roles that wars played demanded a far deeper and richer analytic framework, one less dependent on the glacial economic processes described in *Capital.*

One simply cannot calculate history in terms of the development of productive forces, its "law of motion," from which class struggles evolved. This vision of the progressive development of capitalism to socialism as a consequence of fairly predictable economic processes is a comforting myth but exceedingly poor history and prognosis. Marx posed the wrong criteria, and the worst peacetime economic crises – and there were many in various nations – were far less galvanizing on people than the effects of wars, which Marx ignored entirely in his cosmology. Socialist politicians of all stripes tamed and exploited the working class when there were no wars and, for better or worse, capitalism in one way or another co-opted the working class during peacetime. Marx did not count on the way its leaders mediated the proletariat's anger and thereby mitigated capitalism's severe social dysfunctions. He ignored migration – even then a mass phenomenon – as an answer to increasing poverty and the industrial reserve army, a vast event which alone would have ruined his essentially mystical as well as idealist Hegelian assumption that there is a collective consciousness among workers which at the critical moment would eventually cause them to act in unison to overthrow capitalism and create a classless society.

It is a fact that the working class finally became radicalized and a force for fundamental change, but almost wholly in connection with wars, when its leaders could no longer deceive many of them. While workers should, and indeed do, have a proclivity for certain assumptions and modes of action, Marx turned highly contingent possibilities into inevitable necessities and sacrificed the nuances which would have made his system of thought more relevant and durable. What workers have in fact done in the historical process, and their crucial significance as historical actors, played no part in Marx's theory – he was purely wrong. But the readiness of the working class to act under certain circumstances is a fact, one difficult to predict in advance but nonetheless of decisive importance. The working class's role in history is scarcely irrelevant because Marx got it all wrong, but there is no innate proletarian impulse to revolt at the time and place of a radicalized bourgeoisie's – which includes Marx and most theorists who lionized him – choosing. Its potential is often aborted and distorted, but that it will act – given the appropriate circumstances – is a reality of which we cannot make too much, or too little. Why it behaves as it does, with social stasis being the outcome most of the time, and the parameters of its possible behavior, is a crucial and complex question that Marx simplified inordinately.

Marx imposed a Procrustean logic that destroyed the far greater utility that a socialist theory might have played with an open methodology capable of dealing with complex and unpredictable events. But Marxism cannot be faulted for its unique myopia. All determinist philosophies produce the same problems involving fatalism, human passivity, and optimism – and to this extent they are all unscientific and their pretensions are truly utopian.

Marxism's special significance emerged from the fact that it alone, among all the ideas articulated after 1850, provided the world's radical causes and oppressed peoples with a socialist ideology that was a bitter critique of capitalism as well as an exceedingly vague inspiration of a future moral society. But along with it, and never of interest to more than a tiny minority of socialists, came an astonishingly opaque ideology in the form of historical materialism. Socialism flourished because it provided a unifying organizing belief around which mass movements could be built but it always lacked an intellectually adequate analytic and intellectual base. Marxism, in brief, created a very weak foundation for the most important emancipatory ideal of the modern era.

Marx as a classical economist

For Marx, predictable laws of economics governed past and future history, determining political events and social dynamics and subsuming the main currents of the historical experience. Marx did not confine his explanation to any specific nation, though it was based largely on British evidence, thereby leaving it open to universal application – at the very least to the more industrialized countries. Notwithstanding his hatred for their ideological applications of the laws of economics, Marx's theory of production and exchange drew entirely on the axioms of British classical liberal economics. He especially utilized David Ricardo's labor theory of value, and although he disputed some of his applications of it, he believed Ricardo possessed "scientific impartiality and love of truth."[9] But he continuously cited classical economists, some dating from the seventeenth century, to confirm his analyses. Just as there is no Marxism without Hegelian mysticism, there is also none without the bourgeois economic theory that rationalized British capitalism's worst deeds.

Like all nineteenth-century economists, Marx was oblivious to those dimensions of politics and society that were crucial to the way economies really function. Marx was not wholly impervious to the social and political consequences of economics, but by contrast to his pure economics he was extremely casual in his utterances; he had opinions and desires but very little information. His basic premises are deductive, which meant that new facts had little, if any impact and his theory could not evolve – which socialism desperately needed to do. Like most of his contemporaries, he was a romantic, predicting in his case a classless, free society devoid of exploitation. "Inevitability" was simply defined to confirm his preferences, and Marx's socialism was a leap of faith rather than a careful weighing of historical possibilities. But the economy until then was governed by immutable laws, an assumption that all economists then and, most since, have also believed. Reality has eluded them all. Marx failed to prepare his followers for the political and social options the ruling classes might resort to, and he gave no inkling whatsoever of the self-serving, arbitrary and authoritarian behavior of the leaders of the proletariat. Economics in this constrained sense is simply not the way to comprehend much more complex social processes and human behavior, and it is of no value in articulating a program for social redemption. By itself, it is grossly misleading.

It is not necessary here to summarize Marx's laws of the rate and mass of surplus value, the impact of machinery on industrial economics, the whole process of capitalist contradictions, and the increasingly intricate layers of assertions he utilized to build his total system. Marx believed that the very future of capitalism depended on the forces of production and exchange, involving among many things the composition of capital and rate of profit, and he shared the classic economists' fascination with the explanatory power of numbers. He argued that existing economic systems – and therefore the social orders that were mere reflections of them – were both functional and necessary for the duration required for their economic contradictions to produce fundamental radical change. Before that process occurred, nothing else could prove decisive. There was a logic and progressive rationality to every aspect and phase of capitalism in the short and medium run, guided by the imperative and immutable laws of economics based on what Thorstein Veblen called "the hedonistic calculus," and there was no place in Marx for decisive exceptions: stupidity or dysfunctions, but also no capitalist cunning to overcome purely market forces.[10] Capital in modern industrialized nations could be accumulated only by those clinical mechanisms Marx outlined – mechanisms he took mainly from Ricardo.

Marx had very little awareness of history, which would only have made him much more sensitive to the complexities that actually influence human destiny. Marx has been accused falsely of historicism – discovering the future by studying the past – but in fact he did little more than focus on abstract, largely ahistorical economic theorems. From these he projected an inexorable future at least as utopian and ill informed as any concocted during the nineteenth century. But an assessment of Marx's ideas on their face value cannot explain the specific critical events which link his stages of capitalism together, dialectically transforming quantity into quality. As one reads through the first volume of *Capital*, the layers of Marx's analyses and assertions accumulate on top of each other, each crucially interdependent and linked. The next two volumes of *Capital*, which Engels completed, made the components and assumptions of his intellectual edifice more awesome. The outcome was superhuman: purely economic factors relate to each other and become a sufficient explanation of the future of world history. Marx worked through the stages of economics to reach the general law of capitalist accumulation, which embodies a host of propositions regarding the composition of capital – constant and variable – the tendency of profit, the concentration of capital, and much else.

This extraordinary architecture of concepts, and the relationship between them, was frequently so tenuous and abstract that Marx and Engels often cited the existence of "mysteries" and "secrets," especially surplus value and rates of profits that are altered in ways that "the secret of its existence are obscured and extinguished." At such crucial points, as with transubstantiation in the Catholic Eucharist, Hegel's dialectics were often both utilized and cited as confirmation that such qualitative changes occur. Before *Capital* was written, the rate of profit remained "a mystery." Indeed, with "The trinity formula" of capital in the social production process, Marx and Engels often explained it as comprised of "secrets" with a "mystifying character" that they alone resolved. Dialectics justified these theses on the historical stages by which capitalism evolved.[11] Marx unlocked the "secret of capitalistic production," Engels claimed, to make socialism "a science."[12]

Given the sheer intricacy of Marx's system and Marx and Engels' inability to weave it into a logical whole with convincing evidence, Hegelian dialectics remains the core for making essential connections between major economic events, and given the consistency with which they advocated it, not merely before 1848 but thereafter, that it should be so was inevitable. Roman Rosdolsky, who endorsed Marx's "deepest meaning" as perfectly valid and insightful, convincingly illustrated the degree to which Hegel and dialectics are crucial to Marxism's doctrines. Marx's frequent resort to the reality of "essences" as opposed to "appearances" in explaining the "real inner movement" of capitalist production, was comparable, in Marx's words, to "the apparent motions of the heavenly bodies [that] are intelligible only to someone who is acquainted with the real motions, which are not perceptible to the senses." For Marx, capital at various points involved "incarnating itself in fleeting commodities and taking on their form," and he frequently resorted to Hegelian method to resolve such enigmatic economic transformations.[13] Dialectics, however, demanded faith; and without faith, one cannot believe in Marxism. Marx did not conceive of his ideas as simply a basis for further analysis of a complex, changing world but as a final, total explanation. If one did not accept the entire body as it was offered, it could not bear close scrutiny. It suffered the same faults as all religious and philosophical doctrines that pretend to cosmic wisdom.

An elegant theory is useful only insofar as its complexity provides meaning and insight; ideas should be neither more nor less complicated than required for clarity. Neither simplicity nor intricacy, in itself, is an asset. Both can be liabilities if they perform no analytic function. The problem of grand theory is that it can more easily hide errors by claiming that exegesis can fathom its layers of doctrine to clarify its meaning. It never has done so. If a theory demands such efforts then it suffers from serious defects. In Chapter 4 I consider such issues in greater detail. But one of Marxism's leading defenses was in fact its incomprehensibility, which always gave hope that it could somehow be clarified with Marx's own words to answer objections. Socialism would have been far better served if it had been on an analytically stronger base, less pretentious but also more convincing as well as comprehensible. In a word, both simpler and far more useful.

The real question is not so much the limits of their doctrines but why and how Marx's and Engels' theories held so many people, not just intellectuals, in their grip for so long, and this can only be answered by considering how Marxism had powerful political, organizational, and social consequences and was instrumental in creating large organizations with an identity. Theory, in any case, by itself rationalized the ideas and myths that justified vast movements. Concepts, whatever their nature, can exist because of their inherent validity and utility, but they are much more likely to prevail for a long time if they serve as a useful mobilizing myth for organizations and social forces. A convenient myth, from this viewpoint, can in the short run prove far more valuable than an idea which has an inherent value in comprehending reality. Marxism was a convoluted corpus that from its very inception argued for doctrines that proved analytically useless for those who adhered to it. What they received in return, however, was an article of faith – a confidence in inevitable redemption – and, perhaps above all for most of its adherents, membership in a vast cause. Socialism therefore emerged in the world's political vacuum as an important force but it lacked a comprehensible, relevant analytic foundation. That it was to persevere as long as it did was due not to its wisdom or insights but to the innumerable tragic follies of capitalists – wars above all.

Countless people in the late nineteenth and early twentieth centuries were attracted to socialism for reasons having little to do with Marx's formal theory. Socialism became a surrogate religion for many Jews in Eastern Europe who had grown out of a faith in the conventional orthodox theology but still retained a national identity of which socialism became, for many, a crucial expression. Wherever they migrated they took their brand of socialism, in the forms of the Bund and Labor Zionism, with them. It surely gave Zionism, both in Palestine and elsewhere, much of its impetus in creating what was initially a syncretic system combining a glorification of the peasantry, labor, and what today would be called ecological values with an anticapitalism of which Marxism was the penultimate expression. But many Protestants were also attracted to socialism's notions of human as well as institutional perfectibility on earth and its vision of an inevitable march of history toward equity and justice. For men and women such as these, socialism, which was tantamount to Marxism for the large majority, was a secular religion, one that was quite consistent with the larger notions of inevitable progress inherent in the basic romanticism of the Enlightenment and the articles of faith of the Age of Reason. As inheritor of this tradition, Marxism had a charismatic power that far transcended the boring prose and mysteriously convoluted logic of *Capital*. Marxism's strength and durability was to a large extent a reflection of people's such as these desire for a secular faith that promised, at the same time, an essentially Messianic deliverance from the present and an ideal future. But to realize this promise, the masses were crucial.

The masses

Many of the dominant nineteenth-century theories of society were based on the presumed existence of universal, even scientific laws, which were predictable and essentially immune to alteration by capricious factors, ranging from people, peculiarities in the social structure, or to unpredictable events such as wars. Marx too treated the behavior of the masses, political leaders, and even capitalists as effects of, or responses to, putative laws of motion, not the cause of change. But essentially Marxism argued that the masses, after undergoing the rigors and trials that capitalism was predestined to impose upon them, would inevitably replace – whether by force or ballots is not crucial – the old order of capitalism with a socialist system based on justice and equity.

Marx and his followers were wrong in having an idealized, ahistorical view of the masses, endowing them with both an automatic and mystical role in creating a new world. The people are far more complex in terms of both their composition and possible responses to oppression; they generally react, if at all, when wars occur. They also migrate, and migration's role was a crucial, obvious phenomenon toward which Marx as well as most of his contemporaries were oblivious. The nineteenth century's idealization of the masses was no more accurate than to state that they will not act under any circumstances. Marx, like his contemporaries, did not deal with real people, who had emotions, tragedies, pleasures, loves, and hatreds, but with abstract humans who did not exist in reality. After the Paris Commune of 1871 he should have known better. Specific historical circumstances often have a complex logic of their own, frequently unique in every instance, and may push perilous forces to crucial roles and create dangers no one imagined existed. There was no place for chance and surprises in his reasoning, as if everything decisive could be predicted. But as events showed, surprises were commonplace and of the essence, virtually the rule over the past century.

For Marx, workers possessed a collective general consciousness, but Marx was concerned only with economic processes, defined impersonally and not in the least linked to politics and a social mentality which the relentless, invariable process of capitalist accumulation forged. In Hegelian logic, the universal defined the particular. Dialectical logic therefore defined what subjects were crucial to the study of societies; the working class acted in response to much larger and impersonal forces; Marx treated them as an object and was scarcely interested in their moods, possibilities, and personality. Like most socialist theoreticians, he gave the proletariat short shrift.

Marx's core ideas were first articulated systematically in *Capital* and he never modified them, leaving generations of his disciples the formidable task of explaining and rationalizing them in the light of subsequent events in the advanced capitalist nations. Marx's "absolute general law of capitalist accumulation" showed how the emergence of the growing industrial reserve-army and the falling rate of profit created the decisive forces of change within capitalism. Again "with the inexorability of a law of Nature," "the immanent laws of capitalistic production" produced "the revolt of the working class, a class always increasing in numbers, and disciplined, united, organized by the very mechanism of the process of capitalist production itself." The contradiction between the mode of production and the socialization of labor would reach "a point where they become incompatible" and "This integument is burst asunder." "The expropriators are expropriated."[14] Marx and Engels never attempted to describe what would then follow.

Marx's system prejudged the nature of the working class's responses and actions, which in accordance with his abstract scientific pretensions were predictable and invariable. Marx's workers are not so much homogeneous – though they are that also – but abstract. In no way were they allowed to interfere with the inherently neat logic of his theoretical formula; they were not real human beings. He was unconscious of nationalism's hold on the mind of the working class, and the way it was a far more enduring and influential opiate of the masses than religion ever was. He ignored migration entirely. That workers and the masses would be indifferent to radical politics or preoccupied with purely personal interests and matters the great bulk of the time was something toward which Marx was oblivious, and of course he did not consider the specific circumstances when its action was indeed possible or occurred. To have done so would have conceded that the historical experience and the world is far more complicated than his theory allowed. He never doubted that when economic laws reached their culmination, the class structure would be profoundly affected and change; the masses would respond accordingly, in the extraordinarily vague but presumably disciplined and united way he refers to in *Capital*. Marx claimed to replace the voluntarist utopian socialists' ethics and desires with impersonal science but he merely clothed his own dreams with scientific pretensions and denied the constraints of reality, which would have demanded a much more open analytic system of thought if it were to have future value. Marx misjudged both the nature of science and the problems of social change.

Marx and Engels' concepts of the state and road to power did indeed evolve somewhat as their ideas began to gain adherents, especially in Germany, or as events, as in Bonapartist France, stimulated their thoughts. They commented on a great deal that occurred during their lifetimes. These changes were not so much opportunist as a reflection on the underdevelopment of their earlier notions, as well as new conditions which allowed them to establish growing influence over German Social Democracy. But for practical purposes, neither Marx nor Engels developed a coherent theory of state, and in common with all laissez-faire economists, they explicitly excluded the role of politics and the state in affecting the accumulation of capital and its distribution, much less the way political power could be used to enhance, protect, or regulate economic power. Politics, even with their modifications over time, never caused them to alter their systematic economic theory of change in any way, which remained timeless and impregnable.

Marx and Engels' euphoric proclamation in 1848 that the workers could attain the ends "only by the forcible overthrow of all existing social conditions" does not explain their subsequent ideas. The first volume of *Capital* does not specify precisely how the "expropriators are expropriated" but only the economic forces that make it inevitable.[15] As the German Social Democratic Party grew, eventually to become larger than all the other European socialist parties combined, Marx and Engels both sharply criticized and modified many of the positions it was considering, and while Marx especially deplored its reformist compromises, they assiduously related both personally and politically to what was to become the dominant faction within the party, establishing a deep and reciprocal rapport with it. They were attracted to the potential for real success in Germany and they abandoned altogether their earlier apocalyptic visions of the sudden proletarian seizure of power; in 1891 Engels endorsed the SPD's thoroughly parliamentarian strategy. European socialism, to a considerable degree, was thereby to become synonymous with Germany's experiences, and the SPD assumed the role of the Vatican over the continental movement. Marxism became the intellectual property of the country of its founders, stultifying the mentality and concerns of the national movements.

The problem, in essence, is that neither Marx nor Engels had a coherent notion of the political process leading to socialism, much less what socialism embodied in practice. Engels in 1877 outlined an economic "law of nature working blindly, forcibly, destructively" that would "socialize" the forces of production, at which point "The proletariat seizes political power" and takes possession of property in the name of society. The state then "withers away" in a manner that is left entirely vague.[16] But the Paris Commune in 1871 led Marx to make yet other observations, which both he and his critics interpreted to define the meaning of the proletarian dictatorship. But no amount of exegesis can overcome the fact that Marx and Engels had no consistent theory of the state or politics; they also believed the state was unimportant in defining the direction and outcome of economic processes, which were independent of them. They never even considered how state power might influence and abort economic processes and the proletariat's ability to fulfill *Capital*'s prognostications – the occasional letters and articles his disciples cite notwithstanding. What Marxism was to mean politically was to be defined by those who followed Marx and Engels. It was not merely that they adhered to their original apocalyptic theory. The events in the real world were both too demanding and exhausting for more than the impressionistic commentaries both made.

The argument against Marxism is not just the validity of its philosophical cosmology of dialectics, or its application to social reality as Marx and Engels defined it. It was simply false to imagine that economic processes of production and accumulation alone could provide an adequate basis for predicting the future of a considerable part of the world, and one can only measure Marxism by its fundamental predictive failures and total inability to define socialism in a manner that prevented its systematic perversion as a historical force in the hands of those proclaiming themselves as both social democrats and Bolsheviks. Marxism never provided an analytic or programmatic political or ideological foundation adequate to cope with the awesome tasks that rational and democratic reform required in so many nations for dealing with the multiple economic, political, and social challenges they confronted. Its failure was in fact no more nor less than that of all social thought that emerged in the nineteenth century, and this very absence of rational alternative theories to Marxism made its perseverance more plausible.

By default, Marxism filled a huge vacuum in social thought and, above all, it provided idealism, and it was the unwillingness of so many well-intentioned men and women to accept a void in either domain that caused Marxism to remain credible. But however much its defects were shared widely, Marxism (and hence socialism) created false illusions and hopes, as well as insufficient moral and political guidance and clarity when it was urgently needed before World War One. At that crucial time history bypassed it entirely, and socialism's failure as a political movement from this point onward was linked to its unwillingness to oppose the war consistently as well as its inability to articulate a far stronger and viable intellectual basis for the objectives of equality and social justice. Marxism became another expression of utopianism as nationalism and war traumatized politics and societies for the remainder of the century. Socialism's legacies were betrayed in countless ways, and today there is an immense void in ideas and inspiration in our disillusioned, cynical world.

That capitalism is an irrational and humanly and physically destructive basis for organizing societies, much less international affairs, in no way validated Marxism's analytic premises but it made it seem far more relevant than it was in fact. Its adherents ignored and tolerated its fatal errors when they should not have done so. Sharing many of the specific criticisms or even some of the same objectives as other opponents of capitalism, it still had the burden of proof to confirm the tenets of its analyses. It did not, and could not, do so. Anti-capitalism and Marxism are in the last analysis two very distinct issues, and one can and should be critical of capitalism's nefarious impact on the human condition without being a Marxist. Our problem is not defining worthy objectives but our understanding of where – and how – history is going and why socialism as an alternative to capitalism failed.

3 The legacies of socialism

Organizational successes, and failures

The decades immediately after Marx's death in 1883 were years of great socialist organizational and political successes in various European countries, seemingly vindicating his ideas and the movement devoted to them. Power became the fascination for all socialist parties, whether Leninist or Social Democratic, just as it was for the bourgeois parties, and their common practice reflected this obsession. There were many reasons for socialism's failure which cannot be attributed wholly to its lack of intellectual signposts, but the absence of a relevant theory was crucial; its exploitation by ambitious people was another critical factor, one about which Marxist litany was utterly silent when realistic guidance would have been helpful – even if not decisive. Socialists were theoretically underdeveloped when they confronted the great events of the past century, but they were also badly led.

Socialism and authority: the organizational imperative

Socialism's great prosperity had a rationale and momentum that made ideas superfluous in the short run, not the least because Marxism prophesied that history was on their side inexorably and its believers had little need for further inquiry. Doctrine remained virtually the same as when Marx and Engels died. Growth, above all in Germany, made the formidable problems of ideology and analysis seem not only superfluous but even dangerous insofar as successful conventional wisdom was concerned. There was always an inherent tension between socialism's organizational and intellectual tasks but its explanation and responses to contemporary crises were to prove fatal when World War One broke out in 1914.

The difficulty was that European politics could not be understood on the basis of *Capital*. Marx's causal assumptions were clear, and his claim to omniscience meant that any further clarity that was required would have to be found within Marx and Engels' abundant but very dense and diverse writings – ranging from unfinished manuscripts, short essays on everything from current affairs to Balzac, letters, and the like. Marx and Engels had no one but themselves to blame for the eventual analytic and moral debacle of the vast world movement that looked upon them as infallible mentors, for they believed that their ideas were the complete and sufficient authority for future generations. Those heretics who were tempted to build a more defensible and rational set of theories had to be ready to confront political and intellectual ostracism, a price that greatly discouraged creative modifications of inherited Marxian ideas. Socialist thinkers might have expanded their theoretical and analytic boundaries, but organizational hegemony required their conformity to the founding Marxist creed, and so socialism existed until 1914 under the constraints of the organizational imperatives of successful parties and movements. This inhibition proved fatal to an emancipatory ideal whose potential importance and role grew as European capitalism became utterly and irrationally destructive.

From its very inception, Marxism produced innumerable exegetics who dredged all of the masters' words for possible courses of action. The more reality had to be explained in terms of what they wrote, the more esoteric and opaque Marxism became. Socialism reached a level of obscurity that made it intellectually elitist and incomprehensible to any but a very small number of its cognoscente, mainly professors, thereby reinforcing those hierarchical organizational tendencies inherent in any movement, whatever its doctrine. The masses who believed in socialism were motivated by far simpler and understandable motives than its ideology: anger with the way the world worked and its injustices. To repeat a crucial point, socialism in both its main forms succeeded not because of its ideas but because it was an organizational reality – and critical.

The German party

Marx and Engels deemed themselves the ideological and political leaders of the German Social Democratic Party, "our party," and the SPD to be the leader of the First International founded in 1864 – an assumption that most socialists shared. Both strongly criticized the charismatic Ferdinand Lassalle's initial influence over the SPD. Lassalle died in 1864, but his articulate and dramatic indignation and romanticism continued to appeal to the German masses and his influence over the party's program persisted. Many of Marx and Engels' differences with Lassalle were contrived, and they all relied heavily on Ricardo's labor theory of value and even Hegel. Their allies – August Bebel and Karl Kautsky above all – in 1891 managed to extirpate Lassalle's ideas from the SPD'S official program. The large majority shared only the party's protest against capitalism's injustices; its systematic Marxist theory remained incomprehensible to the vast bulk of its supporters. Formulae on the relationship of constant to variable capital are not the stuff from which mass movements are built. Marxism was always compelled to coexist with what they denigrated as utopianism. Not only did Lassalle's ideas remain widely read, but even the American utopian, Edward Bellamy, was popular in Germany. But the details of SPD's platform at this time and its political strategy embodied assumptions that went far beyond anything

Marx and Engels ever wrote about after the mid-1850s, by which time both had largely discarded the apocalyptic romanticism that had inspired their youthful 1848 *Communist Manifesto*. The SPD was a growing Marxist party, highly successful at politics.[1]

It is a much greater error to overemphasize the role of ideas within the SPD than to dismiss them entirely, and the animated discussions of issues within the SPD before 1914 were far less significant than the social and political environment from which they emerged and in which they functioned, a context that often determined which doctrines were selected, and why.

Everywhere it occurs, excessive adoration and respect for leaders is a reflection of political underdevelopment among the masses, and those in authority will always suffocate whatever political literacy and creativity that challenges them. Authoritarian movements come in various sizes, some obviously worse, but German Social Democracy was from its inception addicted to canonizing men and their ideas. After 1891 Marx's followers sustained this tradition of hero-worship, treating his doctrines as an orthodox creed.

In 1915 the German sociologist Robert Michels described Social Democracy, and the much larger trade unions that controlled it after 1906, as a huge bureaucratic structure, nominally committed to socialist ideas but functionally a system of social mobility for men eager to make their way in its vast, powerful world of unions, newspapers, and associations of every type. All political movements have attracted opportunists much more interested in acquiring power than in their principles, and socialism was no exception. Ambition was far more of a spur to action than ideology and mediated every aspect of the party's life. The leaders of the SPD acknowledged before the war that they were a state within a state, and later historians have elaborated variations of Michels' basic thesis to describe Social Democracy and the labor movement as a subculture and social-cultural milieu. It reached into the lives of millions of workers in their neighborhoods: their pubs, social existence and countless voluntary associations, a huge youth movement, and much else. It was a haven within a hostile world of exploitation and deprivation. Its raison d'être was far less the creation of a future socialist world, whose form was rarely described, but an aid for coping with capitalism's immediate challenges. Socialism became a social network not only in Germany but also in countless other countries, and all factions on the Left – from mass parties to the most sectarian cults – organized this way. To be a member of this universe, one acceded to the very general ideas that united it, a small gesture that gave much in return. As such, Social Democracy's community was successful, essentially isolated from the life and institutions of the ruling and bourgeois world, and this success strengthened its existing leaders and its doctrines. Marx's obtuse ideas were scarcely the adhesive that bound this world together. In every nation it has developed a substantial following, socialism has been based on its fraternal roles and organization – its human structures – immeasurably more than ideologies. Useless ideas thereby endured; what mattered for its adherents was the personal society a party created.[2]

Social Democratic leaders were too preoccupied with managing their own expanding orbit to allocate much time to doctrine, which remained orthodox Marxist. Their rule was never imposed with an explicitly authoritarian organizational concept, as with Lenin, but by a large consensus within the party. Finesse and determination overcame whatever internal opposition emerged from time to time. Until about 1911 there was nominally both free discussion and a free party press. In fact, the small number of men who ran the party and unions could count on most of the large party bureaucracy supporting them because they were neutral, a kind of civil service. German Social Democracy established the supremacy of authority and discipline over critical reason, creating the crucial precedent in the development of socialist ideas, one that condemned it to intellectual sclerosis. Lenin's organizational premises were very different but his belief in the necessity of ideological hegemony had the same practical consequences, and whatever its very diverse justifications, socialism in both its historical forms developed in an intellectual vacuum; the organization was everything, ideas essentially expedients in the struggle for power. Most successful parties, whatever their ideology, operate in a similar fashion. Marx's doctrines survived intact not because of their intellectual coherence or cogency, but because the states and parties that endorsed them had power – with rewards for the obedient.

Marxism's first critical test as a theory – the debate within the SPD after 1898 over Eduard Bernstein's Revisionist doctrines – was constrained decisively by the organization to which it had seemingly given a raison d'être. The substance of this sustained, profound controversy is infinitely less important than the very fact it occurred and, above all, the manner in which it was resolved and the ulterior motives of Bernstein's critics: Karl Kautsky, Rosa Luxemburg, and the men who ruled the SPD. The party was politically increasingly successful, its full-time bureaucracy was burgeoning, and it had scant reason to subject its Marxist creed to a critical dissection. Discipline was more important to the party's leaders than clarity, and Bernstein – his commendable goals notwithstanding – was scarcely the thinker to illuminate the exceedingly complex reality facing it. From the viewpoint of substantive descriptions of social reality and dynamics, time and events were to prove that everybody involved in these debates was tragically wrong in all crucial regards – World War One and the emergence of Nazism confounded virtually everything all of them asserted about the future.

It was not merely that the optimism intrinsic in the legacy of all nineteenth-century social theories precluded the realism that might also have led to a much more accurate sense of the complexity of history and its dangers. When staying on the right side of power or loyalty to inherited political wisdom becomes crucial in defining important analytical issues, it is impossible for vital questions to be resolved objectively, denying socialism the capacity to comprehend decisive questions that might have enabled it better to respond to the grave challenges it was to confront. Bernstein, from this vantage, was simply a troublemaker.

Bernstein argued that German society was far more complicated than the simplistic SPD notion of the working class as a growing proportion of the population, and it would not by itself become, as Marx had predicted, the decisive force in society. He implied that the party's exclusive focus on the proletariat and its alleged isolation from the rest of the nation ignored crucial realities. He offered a set of theses on the nature of the German social structure, critical comments on dialectics and Hegel, and more, asserting that he was still a Marxist, which was certainly not the case and scarcely more than a specious justification for his determination to remain within a powerful party that also shared the associational attributes of a church as well as a fraternal order.

All of the participants in this debate possessed a considerable degree of opportunism and cynicism, which throws a pallor over the way it proceeded. The SPD, in any case, wished to preserve its Marxist theoretical legacies intact, essentially for organizational reasons. Again, the controversy's real significance was its indication of the party's refusal to permit free discussion that could cause it to modify its basic doctrines even on matters of detail.

The SPD's leaders felt quite comfortable calling themselves revolutionary in the sense that socialism would inevitably replace capitalism when it collapsed from its own contradictions in conformity to Marx's dramatic predictions; the party was not intended to make a revolution, but to inherit one beyond anyone's ability to initiate or to hinder. Acceptance of parliamentarianism, even with the severe constitutional restraints that the Prussian-dominated authoritarian system imposed, was perfectly consistent with such a stance; Marx and Engels had approved of it. These constraints isolated the working class both politically and in terms of their very social roles and opportunities, and the SPD's local activities were in large measure a natural response to these hindrances. The party's emphasis until about 1910 on insulating itself from the rest of the nation, with only a minimal reliance on parliamentarianism, was really a reciprocal interaction between its legal and social isolation as well as the party leaders' own vision of moral and historical superiority – which produced great success within these boundaries. Before 1907, it focused more on building the unions and its own institutions rather than in seeking offices, and it was not until 1912 that it emphasized elections; in that year the SPD became the largest party in the Reichstag. The party leaders wanted free discussion but they restricted it to local and marginal issues – they regarded Bernstein's heresies principally as a matter of discipline in questioning official doctrine, which was inadmissible, but they also objected to the fundamental criticisms of Marxism contained in his notions. Initially, some SPD leaders wanted to ignore him in the hope that interest in his ideas would vanish, but most of the party's hierarchy regarded him as a threat to a doctrinal status quo they believed congenial with their hegemony over the working class and its vast institutions.

It was in this context of attacking Bernstein that the traditional leaders of the SPD catapulted Rosa Luxemburg, a hitherto obscure Polish Jew, to fame as a major party theoretician. She entered the scene in 1898 at the instigation of an ambitious, doctrinaire local party newspaper editor and millionaire adventurer, Alexander Israel Helphand (whose pseudonym was "Parvus" and in 1917 worked with the German government to spirit Lenin from Switzerland to Russia), and then August Bebel, the SPD's Marxist leader. Consummately ambitious herself, she played with radical abstractions – a type of intellectual that has been the bane of the socialist movement since its inception. Her essays, later published as *Reform or Revolution*, were a defense of orthodox Marxist doctrine. Semantically she favored revolution, but only in the highly constrained, passive fashion the party's leaders deemed acceptable. But Luxemburg's sponsors were not interested primarily in either reform or revolution, and at Bebel's initiative she emerged again prominently in 1901 to defend what Bebel and his peers referred to as "the good old principles."[3] Luxemburg's first appearance was in defense of traditional wisdom – in effect, she was an enforcer of the SPD's ideological conservatism.

Bernstein failed to create a dialogue within the SPD; the principle of the central party leaders' authority over crucial ideological matters was reiterated. In reality, the SPD as a successful party had no vested interest in critical, innovative thought of any kind; more important, this sclerosis was not an immediate political liability. Lenin merely articulated publicly the principle of central discipline and the priority of the organization over ideology; he by no means originated it.

The question of reform versus revolution is entirely abstract, for most, if not all options for action are defined by ruling classes. In fact, nominal revolutionaries and Bolsheviks often behaved like parliamentarians when that was the only kind of activism open to them. Far more important than preconceived notions has been the desire to act whatever form it took. The masses joined movements not because of ideological preferences but because of outrage, and the wish to respond to conditions about them caused them to support a specific party. Events were to prove much more causal than ideologies. Those who advocated either "spontanist" or orderly change were all to be sorely disappointed. Organizations far more often were to bend their principles to accommodate to events – taking them in directions they never imagined possible.

Socialism was dedicated to changing the world and could scarcely afford the sclerosis that mars so many intellectual systems. This immobility reflected the power of party leaders to impose an acceptable ideology. Their ideas were often tailored to meet their organizational needs; their logic or validity in the face of reality was secondary. A great many party leaders believed that the discipline and cohesion of the organization itself was more important than clarifying what seemed to be abstract issues, and obedience seemed a small price to pay for the right to belong to a party that created an intensely comforting social existence. But Marx, Engels, and their followers always asserted they had articulated a complete and sufficient system of thought, the obscurity of dialectics notwithstanding, and there is nothing in Marxism to imply that further clarity was needed.

The dilemma of intellectual stasis in a complex world is that radical adaptations in ideas cannot be postponed indefinitely. Socialism from its inception was analytically paralyzed, pretending to resolve all that was crucial about the world in the future as well as the past; Marx and Engels prevented an intellectually more rational – and ultimately formidable – challenge to capitalism from emerging, as indeed it may have. Marxism's followers created parties to propagate socialism that to varying degrees, ranging from the relatively mild SPD to Communists, were authoritarian and refused to tolerate serious discussion.

If the world had not been so continuously traumatized after 1914, social democracy would have represented a major improvement over the alternatives to its Right, and Leninist challengers to it would never have emerged. The problem is that when major political crises arise, whether involving wars, economics, or both, a party that wishes to lead must be able to rise to the occasion and make far-reaching and essentially radical innovative decisions that enable them to articulate appropriate solutions that will convince the masses to continue to follow them. It must also be intellectually capable of freeing itself from those routines that were appropriate for very different contexts while at the same time guarding the essence of its principled rationale for existence. As a general rule, the SPD and Social Democratic parties lacked both the mental state and mode of operation essential for playing this role, enabling extreme parties on both the Left and Right that had no principled constraints on their ideas and actions to acquire power and to fill the immense vacuum that wars created. As a theoretical system based on the relatively benign and pacific conditions of the nineteenth century, Marxism disarmed all those who took its prognostications seriously. The Social Democratic parties made a virtue of relative moderation and muddling through, and the people who led them were constitutionally unfitted for any other role. Marxism's most important political expression – the German SPD – failed to meet the twentieth century's first great crisis.

Rosa Luxemburg's ideas during 1914–19 illustrate the confusion that marred all socialist theory during this crucial period. Her fame was due to her collaboration at the turn of the century with the SPD's doctrinal police, who later supported the war and became her bitter enemies; Bernstein, on the other hand, shared her opposition to the war at a time when such a stance demanded immense courage.

Luxemburg's basic problem, along with the vast majority of other Marxists, was that she passionately shared uncritically both the mechanistic optimism and prophetic vision built into Marx's cosmology. Marx had predicted the proletariat's inexorable triumphant action in the wake of capitalism's irreversible demise.

Socialism for all orthodox Marxists was therefore in the grip of cosmic forces that determined destiny. As Antonio Labriola, one of the more intelligent contemporary Italian thinkers put it typically in 1896, "this necessity of the *new social revolution* [is] more or less explicit in the instinctive consciousness of the proletariat and its passionate and spontaneous movements."[4] The SPD was firmly convinced that it would inherit the future when capitalism's own contradictions caused it to disintegrate – whether it placed more or less emphasis on parliamentarianism mattered little in the overall context of historical and social dynamics. Many of Luxemburg's crucial premises merely reflected this mechanistic conventional wisdom, and a concept of mass consciousness and the action that would automatically result from it was integral to the large consensus that united all Marxists.

Until her assassination in 1919, she always rejected the image of victory based on "the victorious violence of a minority or through the numerical superiority of a majority," which caused her to criticize Lenin and the Communist Party. Social Democracy "sees socialism come as a result of economic necessity – and the comprehension of that necessity – leading to the suppression of capitalism by the working masses."[5] She always assumed that when the economic crisis of capitalism occurred it would not employ the state to resist the workers. Like everyone else, she never imagined a war of such catastrophic dimensions that it would completely rewrite the rules of politics and power – and capitalism. But at the same time, she was also acutely conscious of the extent to which Marx's laws encouraged passivity in relying on history to accomplish the proletariat's mission; after the 1905–07 mass strikes in Russia that followed its defeat in the war with Japan, she became both a prophet and advocate of mass strikes in Germany as accelerating and guiding the stages to the final victory of socialism. These ostensibly spontaneous events were predictable, if not calculable, and would follow a general model; for someone who deplored Bolshevik elitism as manipulative and anti-democratic, she had her own strict timetable for the working class, and assigned them not only an innate consciousness but also a readiness to express it unfailingly in a manner conforming to her desires. She believed not only in Marxism's predetermined laws and logic but also that voluntarism and human will could accelerate them – a fundamental contradiction she never reconciled. To this extent, she shared with Lenin a conviction that capitalism's defeat through actions that reflected the will of the masses was also important. Given these conflicting propositions, her final position on the Bolshevik revolution and the future of the SPD was contradictory. But in the last analysis hers was the formal logic of yet another romantic intellectual isolated in a framework of totally self-assured and unquestioned premises. History thereby became a blank check, on which one recorded dreams.

There was a pathetic naivety in her quasi-religious conviction. Even in January 1919, days before soldiers assassinated her, she restated her faith that "history leads irresistibly, step by step, to ultimate victory."[6] She also flirted with various organizational initiatives that were to lead to the creation of the German Communist Party – which is why they always claimed they had assumed her mantle.

The war utterly smashed all of the socialists' premises, and their economic fatalism and congenital optimism preordained socialism in all its forms to eventual defeat.

The socialist world

The world of the socialist mass movement was extraordinarily rich, and very diverse ideas coexisted within it. What nominally united these often very disparate notions was a common devotion to the emancipation of society from capitalism and an advocacy of a vague image of a new social system based on equality. But there were many socialist parties, and the most successful created social networks within the working class based on common sympathies and personal affinities which generally made precise ideological issues quite secondary to the average member. Moreover, the kinds of people that responded to socialist appeals, in terms of artisans and skilled workers or the different cultural traditions within specific regions of each nation, were often crucial. In France, Italy, Russia, and Britain marginal and articulate middle-class elements, and intellectuals and bohemians, were drawn to socialism for very diverse motives, ranging from technocratic notions of social efficiency to romantic images of an escape from capitalist industrialization – by choice rather than necessity. An appreciable number of these middle-class adherents remained incorrigible romantics, and romanticism suffuses their definitions of socialism to this day. Via Sorel and a primitive anti-capitalism, a few became fascists, but they were the exception. Before 1917, the German SPD was, by far, the most successful in organizing a mass working-class party; elsewhere, intellectuals were crucial in the formation of all socialist organizations – and most syndicalist and anarchist groups as well. Jews – beginning with Marx and including Bernstein, Kautsky, and Luxemburg – were an important transnational constituency who played decisive roles, especially in Central and Eastern Europe. Zionism and Bundism, which were also nationalist ideas, influenced many Jews.

But as a general rule, nowhere did socialist parties emerge in the fashion and for reasons that Marx outlined, nor were workers radicalized the way he predicted. In every nation the reality was infinitely more nuanced and complicated, and whatever the similarities between many of them, to ignore their differences is to oversimplify historical experience. On the whole, however, while socialism was a variegated, complex social and ideological force, the larger parties organized primarily workers but their leadership came overwhelmingly from the educated, marginalized upper and middle classes – from the intelligentsia in the broader sense of that class. These men and women's ambitions coexisted uncomfortably with their mastery of ideas; in power, many exploited their new roles to enhance their own positions and privileges. In various ways, both social democrats and Bolsheviks were to learn that fame is a spur to leaders, who forgot many of the ideals that they had so ably propagated. The dilemma of leaders, in brief, cannot be explained entirely by their class origins because those who emerged from the working class were scarcely any different. Like the bourgeois parties, neither wing of the socialist movement had thought about the problem of leaders who abuse authority, much less how to control them. Nonconformists and creative people rarely become the chiefs of successful parties of any political coloration, and while socialists were no exception to this rule they desperately needed precisely such individuals.

Social democrats and Bolsheviks alike modified their existing intellectual legacies, usually by ignoring them, in order to enhance their organizational structures' chances of attaining political power. But neither ideology, whatever its nature, nor organizations can by themselves lead to real growth and power; events were far more decisive. Organizations and ideas may help better to relate to these circumstances, but they rarely, if ever, cause them to occur. To this extent, the two main branches of the socialist movement misunderstood profoundly the potential impact of their own doctrines and roles. In practice, success came to socialist parties far more often as the consequences of unpredictable and often uncontrollable upheavals – by the follies of capitalists who have power – than they dared to admit. Then the will to power was decisive, and Leninists had it. But they did not begin to anticipate the complex world that humanity has experienced since 1900.

Ultimately, only one principle united socialists, and that was the vaguely defined ideal of a far better or, for some, even a perfect society based on a measure of economic equality. Initially, Marxism was never a total system encompassing human existence in all its key dimensions, and only the Communists eventually aspired to define it as such. Both wings imposed a taboo on intellectual innovations only in economics and social dynamics. A few subsequently wrote about the whole spectrum of possible future individual and social relations that the two founders ignored or slighted, introducing various libertarian and romantic concepts that most orthodox Marxists found quixotic and utopian. Such dreamers existed everywhere in varying degrees – often as marginal cranks. Whatever their claims to possess unified ideologies, socialist parties and organizations often became ecumenical in practice, although such coexistence did not mean that options were officially sanctioned; the way the various ideas were sorted out depended on the needs and social and intellectual positions of its followers. These included many more artisans and skilled workers than unskilled, and a generous sampling of bohemians in the form of writers and artists. Despite drab Marxist formulae, such creative people found the notion of liberation in various forms most congenial, and their penchant for exhibitionism made them much more prominent in nations, such as the United States, where socialism never developed a durable mass base. Aspiring technocratic planners and reformists, as with the Webbs and Fabians in England, to various syndicalist, guild, anarchist, and nominally anti-bureaucratic currents, had an impact even on Lenin, who read with respect Daniel DeLeon's essays on the structure of industry under socialism. William Morris in England romanticized pre-industrial aesthetic values, while Bernard Shaw and H. G. Wells – in the best tradition of literary exhibitionism – enjoyed the notoriety that their iconoclastic writings on the beastly bourgeois generated. Those powerful egos drawn to the Left, in the broadest definition it, included believers in psychoanalysis and even Wilhelm Reich's orgone theories, *situationiste* artists, astronomers and poets who were council communists, and a generous supply of fascinating and often charismatic characters who could never fit into any organized structure demanding a minimal element of consensus and discipline. Socialism in their hands was never boring, but neither was it political in the sense that it could aspire to transform the real world. More crucial to organized socialism was a highly educated middle class in such nations as France, Italy, and the United Kingdom, elements of the Nonconformist Protestant churches (especially in the United Kingdom, Scandinavia, and the Netherlands), Jews, and other marginal people.

Socialism, especially before 1914, was in practice, as opposed to doctrine, always much more than Marxism. This plethora of noble impulses and good will were, in most cases, not an antidote to the defects inherent in Marxist theory because these well-intended nonconformists lacked analytic aptitudes for dealing with the inevitable problems of coping with a future that is inherently never certain. Oversimplification and complacency – a profound innocence – united all the socialist currents, because an optimistic belief in inevitable progress deeply affected them all before 1914. Some, indeed, confused spirituality and good will with power and further diluted socialism's capacity to reason about the problems of change and to create an alternative society. Such eclecticism, by itself, was not the source of strength it might have been. In none of its forms did socialism as a general proposition have a coherent, unifying rational basis that could transcend the profound complacency that also suffused bourgeois ideologies throughout this chronically optimistic age. Technocrats and social planners who were important to socialist parties in several nations deplored such romantic and subjective thinking, but like positivists of all ideological persuasions, they possessed an uncritical confidence in the efficacy of their own schemes and they shared strong elitist impulses that ignored the way the larger structure of politics and power operates as a constraint on innovative social goals. But Marxism's pretension to be a science of society, and therefore objective and even neutral, reinforced the technocratic strain and cult of expertise that became increasingly influential after about 1900 among bourgeois intelligentsia and middle classes who joined socialist causes. In this sense, socialism alleged it was the logic of progress – or what is now dubbed "modernity." Where men and women drawn from the working class played a greater role in creating and leading socialist parties and trade unions were stronger, as in Germany, Britain, and Belgium, technocrats made no difference to the analytic or tactical resources of the parties they led. In these cases, the social ambitions of their leaders created yet other problems, producing a critical conservative influence.

Moral and political outrage possessed very little of Marxism's formal intellectual structure, but the profoundly radical and inspirational way it educated countless workers won masses to socialism even when they absorbed little or nothing of the Marxist litany. Notwithstanding their serious differences in assumptions and motivations with Marxism, the majority of nonconformists allowed Marxists to lead them, and no intellectual alternatives emerged to prevent the blindness that was to doom the socialist parties to continuous moral and organizational crises – and schism – after 1914. Until then, socialism as a surrogate religion, with all the doctrinal equipment of salvation, redemption, and even Sunday schools, functioned in Germany, Britain, and elsewhere, creating a quite self-contained mass movement that touched all aspects of many workers' lives. Socialism produced a fairly harmless social adaption which made its participants happier people, but it could not confront World War One and its aftermath.

Socialists in general were impatient with many difficult questions, which they dismissed as premature or self-evident – or even unimportant. Romantics will always postulate the ideal as possible, and sometimes even imminent, with scant regard for the fundamental problems of how power is attained and what is to be done with it should that occur. The boundary between romanticism and utopianism has never been clear, and Marx's ideas did nothing to overcome the fact that scientific socialism suffered from the same impatient myopia among its followers as utopianism. In its own way, Marxist simplifications led to a sublime innocence that made it romantic and utopian also.

Lenin and Communism

Lenin built on this theoretical void, but Marxism's crisis began long before 1917. The triumph of Leninism was due wholly to Social Democracy's refusal to oppose World War One effectively, which its analytic failure only exacerbated, and Lenin's victory was only a grave symptom of the basic deficiencies of the original Marxist creed. Lenin's authoritarian concepts, however, were inherent in the practice of parties of all ideological stripes, not simply socialist; he scarcely originated them, and in this regard there was a profound continuity in both theory and practice between the Social Democratic and Bolshevik movements. But while Lenin was never a profound or original thinker, he was the consummate tactician, one of the twentieth century's greatest, the seeker after power and an impatient man who glorified action almost for its own sake – an infinitely more difficult task than formulating ideas. He was also an incorrigible sectarian and schismatic, at best a crank and at worst quite mad, and his victory and the subsequent triumph of the movement he created was wholly inconceivable without the trauma and social and intellectual chaos which World War One and then World War Two produced. He understood full well the intimate linkage between war and revolution.

Lenin created a theory for indignant and angry people who correctly saw the ways of the world as consummate folly, but his ideas had scant analytic value and became the creed for power-in-hand rather than an ongoing basis of relating to the real world. It was this irrelevance that was instrumental in the eventual collapse of Communism, one of the most monumental events of human history, without a war or revolution.

Throughout its history, Communist parties became, by default, the residual beneficiaries of the crises in capitalist societies and politics as well as the conservatism of the existing socialist parties, and they were scarcely the cause of them. But every large system produces its own failures – and the future will be no different than the past – and Lenin was capable of making the very most of the crises of the old order and the existence thereby of countless profoundly alienated, indignant people. At every stage, he remained a single-minded, strong-willed sectarian, coveting power for himself. Lenin was pragmatically ready to grasp the wholly unpredictable opportunities which the collapse of the Old Order and traditional wisdom created, transforming a war between nations into a civil war.

Social democrats never understood how their own failures made Lenin's and Bolshevism's triumph inevitable, and they refused to acknowledge their own culpability in creating the vast vacuum which the Communists filled. After 1917, the main Social Democratic preoccupation was with the Communists rather than capitalism. This obsession made their later recruitment into the Cold War institutions logical and inevitable.

Lenin's theory aside, the very nature of the many struggles which Communist and non-Leninist parties were to find themselves embroiled, from uprisings and underground organizations to full-scale armies, appeared to reinforce the need for a hierarchical organizational structure – authoritarian, with an essentially military command system. During wars, all successful organizations – including those that began as non-Leninist but had their own brand of revolutionary theory – adopted versions of such hierarchies, although the central authority's orders were often interpreted liberally or even ignored entirely at times. The problem is that these parties, and certainly Communist parties that began with Lenin's premises, turned necessity into a virtue and failed to see that an open, flexible structure was far better able to adapt to the peacetime realities they later confronted. There was, therefore, a fatal interaction between the old orders and those who sought to replace them.

Although there were also other causes, depending on each case, this dialectic was to doom most movements of change to frustration, condemning much of the twentieth century to the Left's failures. All successful Communist parties acquired power because they inherited bankrupt regimes that bequeathed them both vast problems as well as immense opportunities. This tragic, essential dialectic between decadent oppressive social orders that produced their own successors almost by chance meant that the latter invariably failed, not the least because revolutionaries in power took as inevitable the predicaments and constraints that the struggle for power imposed upon them and failed to acknowledge and confront them directly. In the end, they created new economic plutocrats and unresponsive class societies, calling it socialism. The freedom of imagination to neutralize these liabilities required open discussion, which the Communists precluded. This absence of free dialogue, above all, was the origin of their ultimate failures.

Never in modern history has a world power disintegrated without wars and revolutions. The enormity and uniqueness of world Communism's collapse, and the profound contradictions and rot that was always inherent within it, demands that we look closely at the roots of its disaster and the continuum between its beginnings as the single most important force on the Left and its total disappearance in Europe and de facto suicide elsewhere. Everything written before the early 1980s about Communism as a general phenomenon, or about specific nations, suffered from gross misconceptions of Communist power – illusions the Communists eagerly reinforced – and failed utterly to predict its enormous transformation. At its worst, the conventional view of Communists was paranoid and attributed to them an almost superhuman ability which they simply never possessed, thereby justifying vast American military expenditures and interventions. It was a mutually useful myth. But even serious analysts gravely underestimated Communism's internal flaws, the element of ambition and cynicism and lack of commitment to socialist ideals that motivated so many of its leaders. To explain Communism's successes because of the repeated tragic failures and follies of the various traditional orders could never be reconciled with the hubris and chauvinism that dominate the political and intellectual milieu of the United States and elsewhere.

The anti-Communists' and Leninists' consensus on Communism's main organizational pretensions prevented both from evaluating the Communist parties realistically, much less anticipating the sources of their eventual demise. Even Lenin's detractors on the Left, from Rosa Luxemburg onward, accepted his claims to command a centralized party, so that the prevailing model of the Communist Party has always been divorced fatally from its functional role. This uncritical definition largely failed to treat Communist leaders as opportunistic seekers after power and lucre and gave Communism's grandiose ideological pretensions the benefit of the doubt.

That anti-Leninist socialists, even after 1917, accepted the Leninists' own model was due to their intense desire not to concede that the Bolsheviks actually succeeded primarily as a result of mass activity and support – and, above all, the evil stupidity of the systems in power – rather than the highly elitist, Blanquist centralism which Lenin consistently advocated after 1900. To acknowledge that an authentic popular movement propelled the Bolsheviks to power despite themselves, and that when the masses are angry and traumatized they support the most conspicuous opposition that exists, however dangerous its ideas, is a proposition that even Lenin himself rejected. To thereby grant Communism a crucial degree of legitimacy is also to concede that the working class and socialism may evolve in perilous and unpredictable ways, a scenario which not merely wholly contradicted Lenin's formal theory but greatly undermined social democracy's and Luxemburg's entirely optimistic, rational model of anticipated mass conduct. Anti-Bolshevik socialists refused to judge accurately the natural history of Communist parties, thereby reinforcing Leninism's fundamental illusions regarding the role of masses on the road to socialism. Leninists deeply mistrusted the people and their capacity for autonomous and effective action, thereby justifying Communist claims to absolute power. In their respective elitist way, each assigned the proletariat its future role; both proved to be fatally wrong, not only about it but also about the way capitalism would evolve and history transformed. Marxism did not prepare its disciples for history's future possibilities.

To comprehend the Communist parties we must first discard entirely Lenin's and his followers' theories and claims. The real challenges they confronted and their behavior almost immediately bore slight relationship to their original doctrines, which were continuously modified to justify action and policies essential to the seizure of power; the Leninists' doctrines never imposed inhibitions upon them. This disparity only grew with time, making Bolshevik theory in nations with radically diverse conditions increasingly irrelevant as a gauge or explanation of the parties' behavior or of those who led them. The many definitions of Communism, or the way that nationalists such as Ho Chi Minh or Fidel Castro came to it by default, are crucial. What this immense diversity of "Communist" parties had in common was their need to find a reason to seize and to hold power, and usually defend it from a foreign-led counterrevolution that provided them with nationalist legitimacy. There was hardly any theory to guide or constrain them but they all had a will to power.

Leninist theory emerged out of a specific political and social context that existed only in Russia at the turn of the century, one which no Communist party ever again encountered. From its inception, there was a fundamental disparity between Lenin's doctrines and his actions. Lenin initially argued in 1902 that the party must be a vanguard of professional revolutionaries drawn principally from highly trained intelligentsia. Such an elite would guide the working class rather than respond to its changing, immediate impulses; it could adapt to future contingencies and the party's very existence would be sufficient to gain ultimate victory. It had to reject internal democracy, and its structure had to be clandestine, rechanneling the narrow trade-union "economism" of "the spontaneous working-class movement" and bringing it under the control of "an army of omniscient people" who came from outside – namely revolutionary intellectuals such as Lenin.[7] Marx had proclaimed the proletariat the agent of future change, but he never articulated the organizational forms that would enable this ineluctable event to occur. Lenin made an elite intelligentsia the personification of the true radical working class. This notion appealed to only a handful of other intellectuals, and it insulted the masses' ability to think and act.

Lenin expected crises to arise in Russia and certain capitalist nations, and they were to be "normal" in the sense that they would be the inexorable result of economic contradictions evolving precisely as Marx had predicted. But all of the great challenges confronting Russia resulted from other factors: the Russo-Japanese War of 1904 and, above all, World War One. In this context, events he never predicted made his initial premises, especially on the function of the party, quite superfluous. The role of the army and of the masses became primordial, and while Lenin never modified the slightest detail of his original concept of the party, wartime conditions made it largely irrelevant; after 1914 Lenin embarked upon a vast series of improvisations adapted to rapidly changing circumstances, so that his principal characteristic was his supreme flexibility, intended solely to win power by whatever means were required. This objective was Communism's only enduring operational principle, and both its theory and organization was wholly subservient to it.

In 1905 he unequivocally criticized the "revolutionary communes" of Paris in 1871, but in 1917 the spontaneous soviets resembled the communes in significant ways and so he cynically evoked aspects of the commune experience to advocate the soviets becoming "representative institutions" to create a "democracy" under the "control and leadership of the armed proletariat."[8] Given intense mass activity and an organizational structure in the form of soviets that the workers and soldiers had spontaneously created without Communists to guide them, a gravely disunited and ideologically confused party leadership, and the lack of a coherent vision of how to organize the future – everything precisely the reverse of Lenin's original expectations – Lenin momentarily waived his profoundly elitist doctrine for a more opportune posture that did not affront directly the peoples' capacity to act or lead.

When Lenin returned to Russia on April 3, 1917, his principal difficulty was with the other, far more cautious Bolshevik leaders. After all, the increasingly revolutionary dynamic was occurring without the intervention of a Bolshevik elite; the interaction between the war, which Prime Minister Alexsandr Kerensky refused to end, the peasants, soldiers, and workers – all the penultimate disproof of Lenin's theses – itself provided sufficient momentum. But in June and July 1917, when he went into hiding, the spontaneous actions of many soldiers and workers, including the many new Bolshevik converts among them, also frightened and profoundly discouraged him as the uncontrollable masses took the initiative. From this time onward, Lenin was in the minority of his party's leadership; he repeatedly circumvented its will. None of the Bolshevik factions could claim the principal responsibility for causing the massive social upheavals that culminated in the October Revolution. For reasons primarily the result of Kerensky's and his generals' monumental follies, the Bolsheviks managed to attain power by using the facade of a soviet government that nominally included other parties, over which Lenin quickly became the preeminent and essentially unchallenged dictator. Lenin's principal message, from this time onward, was the need for "the strictest, truly iron discipline" and "absolute centralization,"[9] thereby creating the essential preconditions for Stalin's personal tyranny. Bolshevism and Lenin succeeded, to repeat a critical point, only because of the traumatic nature of the war. The emergence of the Soviet Union was a reflection of the profound crises in the traditional social and political systems, and had there been no war, or had social democracy really opposed the war in 1914 (it did not even have to succeed but simply make a serious effort), then Lenin would have been ignored as just another crank.

Lenin carried socialism's bureaucratic impulses only to their extreme but logical conclusion. After 1914, despite their leaders' pretensions, in no important nation did truly democratic mass socialist parties exist. Notwithstanding the major differences in degree that remained between the two main branches of socialism, their identical oligarchic practices were far larger than anti-Leninist socialists cared to admit. The large majority in both currents asserted their faith in Marxism. The similarities between Marxism's two major sections are simply far too great to minimize.

In fact, what united both branches of socialism most was the relegation of theory to a marginal status. Theory was a product of organization, not its cause. In the case of Communists, success alone made doctoring theory to justify past actions inevitable, but other socialist parties had their own reasons for not embarking on a fundamental reassessment of what the world had been and might become as a consequence of a traumatic war that had an unprecedented impact on the very core of capitalist civilization. In both cases, no autonomous, critical ideas emerged to either guide or restrain socialism as a historic political movement.

As the Bernstein controversy in Germany proved, an organization that is successful and growing will define theory to justify its conduct – success breeds caution even when further insight becomes imperative. By 1917, the definition of socialism based principally on recitation of the Marxist catechism caused it to lose all of its power of reasoning for adapting to a world in continuous political, social, and economic crisis, and creative thinkers cannot simply rationalize the conduct of a party. This lack of a serious autonomous analytic source of ideas, one not necessarily opposed to either of the two great historical currents but not impervious to its problems or dictated to by them, stunted socialist thought fatally. Socialism became irrelevant to the world crisis as it was emerging; it failed in 1914–18 to become a vital and independent intellectual idea and movement. That failure proved fatal.

Instant parties, accidental triumphs

Communism attained its monumental victories notwithstanding its unwavering devotion to a mechanistic Marxist ideology which predicted the inevitable collapse of capitalism and the triumph of socialism as a consequence of putative scientific economic laws. This failure of analysis was more than compensated for by its resolve to attain power. Communists never questioned the purposes of power, much less the relationship of their actions to their goals, for this would only have imposed inhibitions on what was at the moment most advantageous for success. It was a measure of the intensity of the crisis of traditional capitalist and colonial nations that their astonishing analytic failures did not prevent the Communist parties from burgeoning and, in a number of decisive instances, becoming the victorious beneficiaries of wars and oppression. The twentieth century's major revolutions were the result of spontaneous mass actions, and only the Communists, who rarely predicted them, were willing and able to exploit them. This epic interaction always embodied important accidental qualities.

Communism from Russia to China was from its inception the product of the uneven development between its ideology, which was both irrelevant and opportunistic, and its authority, and it coveted power without any ultimate purpose – or constraints. Although the grave consequences and disasters of its intellectual failures were to show up only later, comprehending them at their inception is crucial for also understanding Communism's eventual peaceful collapse.

Any simplified explanation of the Leninist parties's successes slights the rich diversity and nuances of the modern historical experience. Virtually all Leninist parties have burgeoned and become important in astonishingly brief periods because of crises linked to wars and their immediate aftermath. "Normal" nineteenth-century evolutionary theories, Marx's included, became largely irrelevant when intense, sudden crucial conjunctures profoundly shaped the main events in war-torn nations.

Had the Japanese not traumatized much of East Asia's people during World War Two it would have been impossible for the minute number of Communists, many of whom were privileged former students, to lead many millions of peasants to take power in China and Vietnam. All revolutions, ultimately, are created by old orders destroying themselves and producing vast social and ideological voids that others fill. In one fundamental sense, notwithstanding their sustained ineptness or irrelevance until the crucial moment, leaders are thrust to the fore by accident and circumstances wholly unrelated to their strategies, when sheer luck is transformed into grave responsibilities which then require consummate wisdom and courage. The major tragedies of modern history are to a critical extent a part of an integral continuum, with cause and effect overlapping and merging and creating new forces that reflect, in often crucial ways, the influence of much of what preceded them. This interaction is organizational, as older institutions and people survive in diverse forms, but it is also intellectual. The world Communist and socialist movements did not have the absolutely essential freedom of imagination and analysis necessary to transcend these lingering ideological legacies, and ultimately it destroyed them. They did not merely fail to liberate themselves from the mental heritage of the old order: they never even acknowledged the problem, and in the end Adam Smith and David Ricardo have filled the huge analytic void always inherent in Marxism. We today live in an unimaginably complex and increasingly dangerous world attempting, both on the Left and the Right, to survive with the intellectual ghosts of the nineteenth century. The result is reflected in the massive ideological shambles at all points across the political spectrum.

This context led to emergency conditions which all Marxists, Leninists among them, failed to anticipate sufficiently when they calculated the road to power. These involved the spatial and demographic characteristics of each nation, the nature of wartime leadership and followers, and the relationship of Communist parties to the organizational forms – such as the united front and the Resistance – that were usually crucial in local situations. We must place far greater emphasis on the way Communist parties evolved operationally rather than how their orthodox leaders and their later critics theoretically or deductively explained them. From this perspective, what was decisive was the functional manner by which ideas, values, and consciousness were articulated and organizations created in response to immediate, often unique challenges.

Most, perhaps even all, triumphant Communist parties emerged where there was a great degree of physical decentralization, low ideological and theoretical clarity among both masses and nominal leaders, a high degree of spontaneity, and far less coordination and discipline than orthodox Leninists conceived possible, much less desirable. Where they succeeded, the Communists' centralist, elitist organizational theory was always subordinated to realities all along the revolutionary path, for it was wholly unrelated and counterproductive to their immediate objectives. In a word, at their moments of success, Leninist parties really flourished as mass parties under conditions which they scarcely, if ever, foresaw, for which they were never prepared, and to which they refused to abandon their authoritarian objectives for more federalist, democratic organizational modes and goals that not only were far more appropriate in the short run but also might later have provided Communists in power with a degree of permanent public legitimacy they desperately needed and never attained.[10]

An almost universal precondition for Communist parties taking power, if only in a part of a country, were significant geographic features – distance, mountains, and the like – that the absence of roads, post, and telephones greatly magnified. Wartime conditions accentuated opportunities connected with great space. Such contexts encouraged localism in various forms, often as diverse linguistic, ethnic, and cultural differences that defined relations both between the Communists and their rivals and sometimes within the Leninist parties themselves. While such decentralizing factors were of unequal significance in various nations, they were frequently decisive elements in operational politics. Communist theory failed to even consider such overriding material and cultural disparities or those physical constraints that inevitably eroded the authority that the party expected to have at its command.

Successful Communist parties exploited the advantages that space and decentralization offered to them at the very earliest stages of their struggles, and their local sections often exercised a great deal of pragmatic initiative that ignored or even violated centralist doctrines or orders. This was especially the case in China, and the problem, as Mao Tse-tung understood clearly from the inception, is that such localism not only was a source of short-term strength but also threatened his ultimate centralizing goals. He exploited the immediate reality of rural dissidence out of necessity, but he also feared it. But Mao's doctrines combined Leninist dogma and traditional nationalism to create a rationale for economic growth in a powerful, independent China as the fulfillment of revolutionary goals, creating a basic synthesis that appealed to nationalists as well as nominal Marxists. It was from this combination of ideas and consensus that post-Maoist practice and theory has emerged, and economic growth for its own sake became the basis for a modernized China on which all ideological factions, for their own reasons, could agree. Mao merely exploited the best tactical option of the moment, often based on Chinese lore, folk wisdom, and even novels, rather than Marxist theorems to attain power. Formally, Mao described himself as antisectarian, but that meant stressing the exclusively Chinese character of Communism as the means of reaching the masses. He began moving the party toward Chinese chauvinism and renovated traditionalism, but one relevant to modern technology. What is transpiring in China today flows logically from this background. It was for this reason that Stalin correctly dismissed the Chinese Communists as radical nationalists, but Lenin often did much the same in Russia's context. The overriding goal of both was power, and both were committed to a personality cult as the means of utilizing it – Mao became the great sage and Lenin merely became another absolutist czar. In both cases, the outcome of these eclectic syntheses also depended in large part on the responses of Western nations to them.

Although independent local actions represented a threat to the Communists' elitist aspirations, it was an unavoidable and essential – even decisive in the Vietnamese case – precondition for their eventual successes, because these initiatives exploited promising social opportunities when the national Communist leaders were either unaware of them, too hesitant to act, or, more often, entirely absent from the scene. Successful Communist movements everywhere have made a virtue of such necessities. The tiny band of older Vietnamese Communists who survived in the mountainous northern border with China after 1941, for example, was far too inconsequential to initiate the massive spontaneous peasant-led mass movement to end the famine that began in late 1944 and that culminated in their seizure of power in August 1945. The Communists survived after 1945 only because they could retreat to remote regions, eluding French might.

Variations of these symbioses between space and revolt also occurred repeatedly in Europe during World War Two, especially in northern Italy during the final two years of the war, Greece, parts of France, and Yugoslavia. Cultural and ethnic complexities were also frequently important, and they are synonymous with diffuse, less developed societies – particularly where there are mountains. Ethnic and linguistic diversity was often determinant in the emergence and subsequent cohesion and successes of Communist parties in culturally mixed nations, and any analysis must assign appropriate weight to it. Yugoslavia and Greece especially illustrate its significance for comprehending the Communist parties' internal dynamics, as well as a number of these countries' later descent into virulently atavistic chauvinisms and civil wars. Variations of this pattern also occurred in Indonesia, the Philippines, and even Belgium.

The Communist parties' contradictions and crises

Lenin's organizational theory postulated that revolutionaries with the highest knowledge and political dedication would lead the proletariat. Such a sanctified status justified the Communist leaders' monopoly over decision-making, and party members were supposed to dutifully make sacrifices and perform the often changing, even contradictory tasks that their leaders assigned to them.

All social theories, whatever their political complexion, are astonishingly deficient in their analyses of the nature and role of leaders in modern political and social history. Defining leadership as somehow incidental or neutral to the attainment and realization of all political or social forces' goals, rather than being a principal obstacle and challenge to them, is essential to the myths and pretensions of nearly all the political ideologies, as much on the Right as on the Left. To admit that societies or organizations very often serve principally the egos and ambitions of those who lead them is to upset radically the optimistic fashion in which nearly all those on the Left, at least until this decade, have defined the problems of change. Those sustained traumatic political and military circumstances, with their decentralization and spontaneity, that alone suddenly projected Leninist parties into potentially decisive roles, also often made their prewar leadership systems either wholly irrelevant or challenged them in some fundamental manner. But leaders are not all identical and many emerge in disinterested ways and often despite their desires. This was surely the case during World War Two, when leaders confronted great dangers and they were far less prone to see responsibilities as career opportunities.

The dynamics of leadership formation must be linked to specific events in social processes that make leaders' crucial roles possible, or even inevitable at times, and thrust certain kinds of men and women forward. Obviously, the personal qualities and motives of leaders during crises involving immense risks and sacrifices to themselves are very different than those that emerge during peacetime, when the ambitious people who exist in every society, essentially unconcerned with ideologies but obsessed with what Bertrand Russell has termed "the impulse to power," take command.[11] Indeed, the often daring attributes essential for success during wars usually become counterproductive for administering a state during peacetime.

In a vacuum, some individuals will be projected into decisive positions despite their initial desires or intentions, and the nature of their commitments or motives at such times cannot be prejudged simplistically. While it is mandatory to critically evaluate leaders as a general category, we must also comprehend the specific circumstances in each nation. These conditions often became the origins of grave tensions and purges that many Leninist parties later confronted, including newcomers who challenged the prewar leaders. In practice, rapidly changing political crises in war-torn nations often made it impossible for many Communist parties to be guided in the strictly authoritarian, formal Leninist manner.

The very wartime circumstances that greatly magnified the size and potential of Communist parties generally produced a very high attrition of their prewar heads, either through arrests, death, or exile, and there usually emerged a significant group of new leaders. This first occurred in Russia after 1914, and was even more the case elsewhere during World War Two. Of the 240 key Bolshevik leaders in February 1917, 45 (Lenin included) were in exile, 73 were inactive or in Siberia, and over half of the remainder had been arrested at least once because police agents had infiltrated their ranks. At the moment of greatest crisis, the Bolshevik leadership structure did not and could not function in anything remotely like the manner Lenin had projected, ignoring altogether Lenin's consistent refusal to accept its direction. Lenin's leadership theory was wholly deficient both as a guide and explanation of reality.

Leaders during wartime were often charismatic, ready as well as compelled to take great personal risks; they were capable of heroism, and they possessed those special talents essential to fill the void that the disappearance of senior cadres created. They were frequently independent and strong-willed people who did not defer readily to the dictates of the traditional party heads, and they were often so isolated from them that they were usually obligated to follow their own instincts. It is almost axiomatic that the closer someone is to danger, when the party's discipline is more symbolic than real, the less likely he or she will possess those bureaucratic qualities congenial to an absolute hierarchy attainable only in peacetime.

The European Resistance in World War Two, especially before victory was certain, attracted men and women who possessed enormous conviction and strong characters, and who could hardly expect to personally gain anything material from their risks. A large percentage died heroic deaths in the traditional definition of that term. In Vietnam, the Philippines, and China, those who joined the wartime parties and led its military struggles were far more numerous than the prewar cadres. Ironically, both the very best and worst potentials of humankind emerged throughout the history of the Communist movement, and without the sacrifices and devotion of such individuals its villains could never have later been able to aggrandize themselves.

These often charismatic individuals frequently appealed to the masses, making their parties more indigenous and credible, but many had little or no intensive ideological preparation. It was almost impossible for the prewar party leaders to dismiss them immediately without huge organizational risks, either in the form of a failure to exploit rare opportunities or, above all, the potential emergence of rival organizations.

The pre-1941 European heads of the Communist parties, many of whom spent the war in relative safety in the Soviet Union or elsewhere, considered the new wartime leaders' independence a challenge to their authority. It was simple enough to plan to settle accounts with them after the war, when their great devotion and sacrifices were no longer essential. and they subsequently denounced an unusually high proportion of them as "Titoists" and schismatics. The very process of suppressing this creative newer generation scarred many Communist parties profoundly and opened the way to a succession of paranoia and internecine postwar tragedies. But outside Eastern Europe, it was frequently impossible for the Communist parties' prewar leaders to play crucial roles in those places where parties were most successful.

Since the events after the mid-1990s have confirmed that those who commanded Communist nations were anything but capable or prescient men, much less sincere socialists with profound convictions, we must reassess both when and how their fatal deficiencies originated. Communist ideology never remotely predicted their actual dilemmas and behavior; it was this vast disparity between theory and reality that produced enormous cynicism. Ideology became a functional tool, a deliberate illusion to rationalize and consolidate the absolute authority of individuals – a cynical lust for power that helps to explain why the later astonishing transformation of nominally Marxist into capitalist economies occurred so easily, almost inevitably.

The members: the dilemma of mass parties

Lenin's organizational theory reflected conditions in Russia after 1905 as well as his own elitist preferences. But the rest of the world was always very different politically and incapable of being molded to satisfy his authoritarian model. From its inception, there was always a monumental disparity between Communist organizational theory and reality, for the parties always permitted – often encouraged – men and women to join it en masse but denying them control of policy. Wherever Communists ruled, consummately ambitious careerist technocrats and apparatchiks, most of them ideologically utterly neutral, increasingly turned these parties into personal tools. It was their very immunity from the masses that eventually enabled these leaders to abandon socialism and transform Communist states into private rather than class property. For all its problems, the only defense against treachery – if there is any – is a great deal of democracy within a party, and this the Communists opposed in principle. In their final stages, the most decisive and effective threat to the ruling Communist parties' existence was from leaders, apparatchiks, and technocrats within their own ranks.

All socialist theorists, from Marx to Lenin and Luxemburg, failed utterly to anticipate the range of possible workers' responses to conditions of oppression and social transformation. Whatever the undeniably general class correlations, significant numbers of workers have also supported reactionary movements even while the majority behaved more predictably, but often with much less effect. In the end, groups to whom radical intellectuals have assigned some historic role and class consciousness have – and can

– confounded their expectations and frequently remained passive during times of great opportunities. But however impossible it is to predict the working classes' behavior, some elements of it have marched in the past and, for better or worse, some will march in the future if and when the provocation becomes strong enough. Since its inception, socialism has evolved in the context of this overriding, nuanced enigma.

What men and women are, or can or will become, is not often the reflection of their initial impulses and designs but rather of their interaction with specific social and economic conditions as well as the options that repression forces upon them. The potential range of human conduct can and does cover a vast spectrum. Those who try to endure and survive during wartime crisis and trauma, and remain passive in their conduct when an overwhelming system of repression exists, nonetheless may be deeply committed to ideals. They often think even if they do not or cannot act, and they comprised a very large group during both world wars. Radicalization can be a very dramatic but largely brief passing mood for many during temporary social crises, as in Italy and Germany between 1918 and 1920, leaving only a relatively small political residue in its wake, or a slow but protracted phenomenon that subsequently endures for decades, as in the case of French and Italian workers after 1944. Some new Communists were purely ambitious opportunists, attracted by the imminence of the party's success and the rewards it promised, or indeed even ex-collaborators. China and Vietnam actively recruited many of the latter, as did the Italian party. When the French and Italian parties established a power base, mainly in local governments, party membership was a path to rewards for opportunists, of which there have always been (and will be!) many.

But the large majority of the people who supported the Communists or socialists were angry with the world's injustices, and they believed and hoped that these parties would express both their indignation and desires. Which one they joined at a given time or place depended often entirely on which was most active – generally, it was the Communists. They rarely comprehended the complex doctrinal nuances of Marxist ideology, and they simply endorsed their more basic protest rhetoric and advocacy of an end to injustices. The impulse to activism which oppression generates inevitably finds organizational outlets, and this by default made the Communists its principal beneficiaries – there was often no other active party to turn to. That these parties subsequently betrayed those who believed them in no way mitigates the legitimacy or force of the feelings of those who supported them. At decisive moments in social crises, people choose from the range of options before them – whether reformist or more radical – as well as respond to the constraints that rulers impose. Although it was the Marxists' cardinal error to predict the precise form and the timing of mass action to make it conform to their theories and fondest desires, so long as injustices exist, there will be protests of one kind or other.

Human and social conditions created distinctive combinations at different times and places, producing those complex events that repeatedly have mocked our expectations – and our desires. All that has been certain is the inevitability of change itself, whatever form and outcome it assumed, and the endemic instability of traditional societies. It is the grave failures of established orders that have been the basic cause of our recurrent contemporary crises. The unpredictability of mass behavior in the past produced great challenges for all social movements as well as rulers, and it remains a dilemma we will always confront.

Although Lenin insisted that the Communist parties exercise infinite care in training and accepting members, all the most powerful parties – his own included – grew virtually exponentially during extremely brief periods. The Communists' actual organizational development was virtually the exact reverse of Lenin's desires. The alternative was to accommodate to the reality of a huge people's organization and restructure the party democratically to optimize its assets, which would have not only imposed much greater restraints on its leaders but also provided the party with a much greater legitimacy than they believed it required. This relationship between leaders and a mass membership evolved in an ad-hoc way, in the hands of men who coveted power for all those crass reasons that inspire tyrants everywhere, and without a theoretical justification for their authoritarianism beyond an ambiguous and contradictory notion of "democratic centralism."

The October 1917 Revolution itself set the precedent of exponential growth that virtually all successful Communist parties subsequently duplicated. Bolshevik membership in all of Russia grew from 20,000 in March 1917 to 260,000 the following October, when they seized power. The new recruits were overwhelmingly young class-conscious workers and soldiers; very few were theoretically sophisticated intelligentsia with a knowledge of Marxist theory.

The Chinese party comprised 58,000 members in 1927 and fell to 40,000 in 1937, when it opened the floodgates and reached 800,000 members in 1940. By 1945 membership had reached 1.2 million, nearly doubled over the next two years, and was 4.5 million in 1949 – a rise of 112 times in twelve years.

A Vietnamese party with under 3000 members in 1944 about doubled by August 1945, then quadrupled to 20,000 the following year and reached 180,000 by the end of 1948 – a growth of about 70 times in four years. As in China, the massive increase in the party's administrative responsibilities produced an incentive both for ambitious individuals to join the party and for leaders to welcome them. As the state bureaucracy became largely synonymous with the party, membership in it was a prerequisite of power. Since many of them came from the intelligentsia and middle classes, their superior qualifications brought quick personal success and access to relative privilege, enabling their children to rise into the post-revolutionary technocratic elite. A strategic new class was created. In all nations where the Communists came to power, the absence of a separation between the party and the government meant that a state functioning according to objective norms was impossible, resulting in the debilitation and eventual corruption of both the party and state structure.

But even where membership did not bring the perquisites of power with it, or was very dangerous, many Communist parties expanded dramatically. The Greek party increased from 17,500 in 1935 to at least four times that in 1945 – and perhaps much more – at a time when membership demanded bravery and entailed serious personal risks. There were 9000 in the Belgian party in 1939; despite the complete absence of cadres and the opaque motives of its new adherents, it opened its ranks and numbered 100,000 by the end of 1945. The French party went from 328,000 members in 1937 to three times that number in 1945. The Italian party transformed itself from a sectarian elite with 5000 members in June 1943 to 410,000 in March 1945 and 1.7 million members at the end of 1946 – an astonishing growth of 340 times.

There was, therefore, always a monumental disparity between the Communists' elitist theory and their readiness to grow exponentially. To describe parties simply as "Communist" explains too little as to what they did or might do, and Soviet dictates often failed to determine their behavior. Communist parties pursued radically different courses of action, they were disunited on many key issues, forces that affected their behavior were often beyond their control, and all one can do is to closely examine a specific party, its context and internal tensions, and accept its individuality as a historic fact.

On the whole, the European parties were passive agents, repeatedly – but not always – aborting the mass's potential radicalism; but some, as in Greece, were compelled to respond with arms to situations which left them no choice save destruction, and in Asia the distinctive political and social situations they confronted left them no real option other than to fill huge vacuums others produced. Cults of personality reached surrealistic levels in some nations. The complexity of each party's strategic situation, and especially its many new members' often unpredictable and unstable roles, meant not only that various parties differed enormously but also that their leaders often proved incapable of defining and controlling a mercurial environment in which many forces and factors interacted in unanticipated ways.

Try as he might, Stalin never imposed total hegemony over this immensely precarious international movement, setting the framework for world Communism's subsequent schisms. Like the Western powers, the Soviet Union also had to live uncomfortably with revolutions. It too lost control over the course of history, above all outside Europe.

That a chaotic Europe after 1914 should produce a malignant reaction in the form of Communism is far less a surprise than the fact that the movement itself eventually disappeared on its own volition. That the immeasurable evil that Europe's traditional order unleashed on humanity in 1914 never confronted a decisive response from the Left was a monumental tragedy that perpetuated the legacy of massive violence and destruction, culminating in fascism and World War Two.

When revolutions came in Europe and elsewhere, it was due to causes socialists had never predicted and for which they were utterly unprepared analytically and organizationally. They had no coherent, valid theory embodying an analysis of the world's major social orders, the structure and potential of the social classes that were supposed to make revolutions, an adequate prognosis of the revolutionary party and leadership at various stages of the struggle, or a general but viable conception of the minimum criteria that socialists in practice had to meet. Social democrats were utterly bypassed while the Communists improvised responses, intended to grasp power during the maelstrom of change, often succeeding in the short term but in the end transforming war-imposed necessities into virtues, merging Leninism's instinctive elitism with gravely flawed if necessary war organizations. Leninism, like pure Marxism, was utterly deficient as an explanatory system, and it possessed no inhibiting ethical criteria to constrain its exercise and abuse of power. The Leninist obsession with seizing power, along with Communism's enormous ideological and moral underdevelopment, in its most extreme forms inevitably, logically led from Lenin to Stalin, to Mao Tse-tung and Kim Il Sung, to Enver Hoxha and Pol Pot. Their monopoly of power was initially justified as protection from hostile enemies at home and abroad, and while this was often true, as Leninists they turned necessity into a virtue and they were immune to their own people. Their authoritarian systems later abolished those socialist institutional forms and goals that were ostensibly the very objectives of the entire epic struggle. Their former rulers, managers and nomenklatura, then expropriated their economies, creating capitalism.

Communism's foes failed to understand these inherent tensions and contradictions, and accepted Lenin's pretensions and aspirations largely on their face value so that its successes could be dismissed as essentially the products of conspiracies. What they could not concede was that the Communists triumphed, notwithstanding their theory and organization, due essentially to the fundamental weaknesses of those societies many of Bolshevism's later critics defended and, above all, the decisive role of the masses. Party leaders and their bourgeois enemies both denigrated the common people's primordial impact. The type of omniscient and omnipotent party that both Communist leaders and their enemies alleged existed was to a very great degree the product of their respective desires or fears. All deductive, highly structured models of Communist parties ignore the dynamics of modern history and fail to come to grips with the larger reality.

Both Communism and fascism were syncretic theories, constantly adjusting their tactics to changing political environments, and none possessed principles that could act as obstacles to both profound inconsistency and moral betrayals. The lust for power consumed both movements and guided both their tactics and ideologies; power was an end in itself, used to justify every deed perpetrated to attain it. They concocted utilitarian doctrinal justifications as needed. But to varying degrees, most political movements and parties suffer from what is only a less acute version of opportunism. It is everywhere quintessentially a part of the political mentality and process, and it generates degrees of corruption and cynicism everywhere.

Ideas perform many roles in history both before and after social movements reach their goals, including providing an integrative charismatic faith to justify the sacrifices and devotion of their adherents. When a party comes to power its doctrine also possesses the irresistible argument of success, with its many assets for those who accept it and then exploit it for their own advantage. But sooner or later all political movements must have a functional, relevant basis for comprehending and dealing with the continuous operational problems of managing a society or they inevitably lose their ability both to rule and command the loyalties of their followers. It was precisely this huge disparity between the Communists' analyses, promises, and reality, and their lack of explicit ethical norms to constrain as well as guide them – an ethical bottom line, so to speak, beneath which the party dared not go – that plagued their parties from the inception, producing a mounting cynicism among their leaders and technocrats that ultimately proved fatal.

In all Communist nations, after the generation that first came to power retired or died, a younger elite of ambitious bureaucrats and technocrats enabled a new ruling stratum to emerge from among members of the privileged party nomenklatura, their children, and senior managers. The members of this constituency thereafter habitually engaged in reciprocal bargaining and empire building, becoming self-aggrandizing careerists. With time, they became increasingly depoliticized both in thought and deed. By the 1980s, nominal socialist values and goals had no influence on the leading bureaucrats and managers of the Soviet bloc and China. Their alternative to socialism was not the result of a coherent economic strategy but rather their greed as well as a series of improvisations intended mainly to deal with political challenges confronting the political elite.

No one ever imagined that Communism would culminate in this tawdry manner, abdicating peacefully to the ideological assumptions of its historic enemies to produce a caricature of both capitalism and socialism. In hindsight, however, it should not have been surprising – the seeds were always inherent in the Communists' opportunism and lack of guidelines and ideas. Communists suffered from the acute intellectual underdevelopment that characterized socialism from its inception. Communism was the single most important political expression of the Marxist tradition since its very inception. With its collapse, the nineteenth-century idea of socialism ceased to exist.

Recent concepts of socialism

There were other currents in socialist thought after 1945. All were pure theory, quite unrelated to the practice and politics of the two major socialist movements – which paid virtually no attention to them. The most durable, even if its total lack of drama made it far less publicized, was largely the output of academics, and while many of these writers paid obeisance to Marxism they tended – with a few exceptions – to be less literal in their use of Marx's analytic categories. Not a few were Hegelians but they faced the same conundrums applying it to reality; some were adepts of various psychoanalytic theories. The best known were such eclectic writers as Herbert Marcuse, Jean-Paul Sartre, Antonio Negri, Louis Althusser, and Paul Sweezy. There were countless thinkers of this sort, hundreds and probably thousands, and to sum them up briefly would scarcely be possible save in one regard: they had no influence of any consequence on the real world of Communist or Social Democratic politics. But their talents – which were very uneven – failed to compensate for earlier analytic voids; the new generation possessed verbosity and opaque complexity but they added very little to the work of earlier generations.

Their main theses assumed capitalism to be integrative, relatively successful, and an increasingly comprehensive global system. Prewar Marxists, to a point, treated capitalist nations in much the same way insofar as they assumed they possessed positivist powers of understanding and a certain predictable rationality existed within the capitalist system. A minority gave more emphasis to the limits of integration and they believed in eventual crises, although they remained largely ignorant of how and when they would come.

For the post-1945 generation, accidents, stupidity, failure of intelligence due to bureaucratic, ambitious players, and the like had scant role in shaping institutions and history, and for some none at all. Most assumed that the rulers of the economy and political structures were far abler than they were in fact, and also that critical theorists on the Left can know and explain everything crucial about contemporary capitalism. They left little space for ignorance or error – their own or that of the ruling class. Everything is linked: the system is evil but it possesses a certain logic and works as a part of a grand design – about which there were important disagreements. Globalization, linkages, trilateral and multilateral commissions that ran the world, world-systems, and increasingly comprehensive notions were in fashion for a time but most fell into relative obscurity. Since so many writers were sociologists, such grand theorizing was as much inherited from the general positivist tradition as from Marxism. Everything fits and can be elucidated, and if not then conspiracies were thrown in to explain what is not obvious. Conspiracy theories flourished. Many of these explanations tended to impute intelligence and rationality where there is none, assuming both the will and the ability to attain rational control.

For most people in this tradition, Marxism has essentially been a pure idea, which they accepted on faith, and they fetishized Marx's crucial premises – to use a Marxist term – into a very comfortable profession. The academics assumed Marxist ideas could be separated from the political actions of Marxists and their consequences, and that the pure idea had an autonomous and transcendent value that the conduct of the parties also purporting to share them in no way diminished – which is comparable to divorcing Christianity from its churches. Marxism in the hands of professors finding clinching arguments in the texts made it far more opaque and it was inevitable that their confusion of Marxist discourse in an isolated academic environment with the real world would only further delegitimize socialism. What is today called theoretical insight is really a symptom of Marxism's grave weakness and the final confirmation that it is both incomprehensible and analytically and politically useless. From the viewpoint of reasserting those goals of equity and rationality that were the core of the original socialist mission, these writers' opaque efforts are meaningless if not seriously counterproductive.

What socialist intellectuals lacked in originality or creativity they made up for in institutional solvency, and in the end its members' bureaucratic successes gave their ideas impressive durability – in West Europe but even in the United States. This was certainly not because Marxists are especially favored, but many universities are autonomous and, to varying degrees, give jobs to believers in all sorts of ideas. The few high priests of dialectics – paid mainly by the bourgeois state – live and prosper and seek to preserve Marxism. Most can anticipate being awarded tenured lifetime sinecures for justifying historical and dialectical materialism, many obtain foundation grants and sabbaticals to carry on the task of confirming the original creed, their books are printed and journals subsidized both by academic organizations and commercial publishers, they constantly meet with each other both at home and internationally – often with the expenses for travel and comfortable hotels provided – and they are in general almost as prosperous in academia as their colleagues who advocate capitalism. But this security has failed to make radical professors creative; on the contrary, like their peers they went to too many meetings, and many became quite faceless academic administrators who behaved as their roles dictated. Some of them even taught at universities deeply involved in Pentagon military research, the generosity of which makes it possible for universities to hire them.

A segment of the professorate, not the proletariat, now plays the role of Marxism's social base and audience. For them, ideas define reality almost wholly and Marxist theory lives on as an abstraction, totally divorced from the real world. The working classes and oppressed of humanity who ostensibly have most to gain from social transformation have no interest whatsoever in this Marxist litany, and any attempt to comprehend such a huge difference in perceptions must also include a materialist interpretation of the Marxist professorate.

In science such reinforcing isolation is far less a danger – though here too it is formidable – because ultimately an objective assessment of reality is possible. This is infinitely more difficult when dealing with the human condition in its many aspects. Marxist professors come principally from comfortable economic backgrounds and their concept of the conditions of workers and peasants is almost entirely abstract. Their collective myopia guarantees that intellectual and personal pressures will greatly inhibit creative, innovative thinking. This is not solely a characteristic of Marxism, but of all ideas in general. The social penalties of nonconformity cannot be minimized, but whatever the reason, the many Marxist printed organs and personal contact have – whatever the slight modifications I mention below – served to reify further the original doctrines. Marxism is today inspired much more by the mood of a social club than of a cause.

Ultimately, every theory must be capable of reasonable proof or else it is sufficiently false to be discarded. If its objective is political and it fails to prosper, or even disintegrates, then there can be no doubt whatever of its uselessness. Its final value can be measured not only in terms of its inherent validity, but also by the fact that the socialist movements that Marxism inspired failed to attain their minimal objectives, thereby sidetracking gravely the effort to attain the emancipatory goals so essential for modern civilization.

The effort after 1945 to expand Marx and Engels' ideas focused especially on Antonio Gramsci's seminal and fertile writings between 1914 and 1937; he appealed to Marxist intellectuals everywhere, particularly those close to the Communists. Marx's theories simply were not sufficient to provide the analytic framework for an increasingly complex world, and the heavy dependence of so many on Gramsci was an implicit acknowledgment of Marx's inadequacies. The Italian Communist Party began the Gramsci cult principally as an attempt to broadcast its independence from Soviet political and ideological hegemony. Gramsci's fascinating but often very intricate and ambiguous reflections, ranging from a few paragraphs in a personal letter or an article to longer essays, was the work of a newspaper editor and often written for specific events of the day – and after 1926 in prison. He claimed to utilize Marxism to expand it beyond the parameters of its original doctrine and methodology. Yet just as no one dared to admit Marx was outdated or irrelevant, Gramsci's ideas were also treated as infallible. Authority was indispensable to the disciples of both men, who refused to accept the tensions inherent in a critical perspective, not the least because the original impetus behind the Gramsci cult had far less to do with the validity of his ideas than the Italian Communist Party's eventual divorce from Soviet Communism.

Gramsci could reflect on the half-century after Engels' death, enabling him to assess the crucial period through the 1920s and update Marxism. He had a broad if superficial grasp of economic and social trends in West Europe and the United States. As with Marx's journalistic impressions, which eschewed theory and dealt with real events, his too were also among his most interesting work. Gramsci was subtle and brilliant but also extremely confused intellectually, and he went through various phases. He attempted to synthesize many of the very disparate idealist, syndicalist, anarchist, and elitist notions that flourished in Italy after 1900, above all those of Benedetto Croce and Georges Sorel, and was influenced by some of Europe's critical bourgeois sociologists, especially Max Weber, many of whose political and social categories he utilized. At the outbreak of World War One he shared Mussolini's position of "active neutrality" in favor of the Allies, which was tantamount to joining them.[12]

The complexity of Gramsci's ideas superficially made them appear astute but they were contradictory and he never reconciled them. At its core, they were often empty. But this also left his subsequent disciples – as with Marx – free to define an ideology that most appealed to them, leaving his theories rich picking for exegetics. He was in transition intellectually his entire brief life, juggling ideas with verbal panache, and although he had been secretary of the Italian Communist Party and defended Leninist theory, Stalin became intensely suspicious of him. His last eleven years consisted of writing an enormous number of letters from prison, where he lacked information and was unable to develop his thoughts in a coherent manner. His principal focus on culture and philosophy was only partially a response to his isolation; the ideas he produced in prison had been inherent in all of his thought – and the larger intellectual milieu in which he was formed – before then. Intellectually and politically he was both brilliant and unstable, but his continuous fascination with new ideas and his personal style makes him both very sympathetic and interesting.

Gramsci was a romantic, who evoked a vague spiritualized and voluntarist definition of socialism – "idealist Marxism" it has been dubbed – that was much more attractive to many than the more rigid categories of analyses Marxist theoreticians usually employ. His seminal discussions of culture and hegemony, or the importance of the human will and voluntarism, derived from an idealistic tradition and provided Marxism with a more human face. It was scarcely what Lenin or his successors had in mind, and it was a confused congeries of ideas, including the need for a command party of which he had been the head. However subtle or convoluted his choicest ideas, Gramsci only added another layer of obscurity to Marx's basic analysis.

The New Left

Another major current was the so-called New Left, which flourished mainly in the late 1960s and early 1970s, and it stressed imagination and spontaneity. Its flamboyant actions and statements made it highly visible, giving the media something to focus on. It was perfect for rebellious youth in many nations, and most of these ultras – Weathermen, Maoists, or Trotskyites among assorted cults of action – were eventually to become respectable occupationally, dropping out of politics altogether. A high proportion of its figureheads and members in France, the United States and elsewhere were Jewish, and a few later became prominent neoconservatives.[13] The New Left ranged from anarchist to ultra-Leninist, giving all sorts of leftist cults and even remnants of the Communist parties temporary infusions of desperately needed members. Rebellious and exuberant youth cultures have existed in various nations since at least the nineteenth century, and most stress spontaneity and are ideologically amorphous. The New Left was a product of the world rage that America's Vietnam War was to trigger but it left scant record of its existence and was essentially a symptom of socialism's terminal condition.

The New Left's ideology within every country was astonishingly diverse, very often only impressionistic, but everywhere it attracted many of the same kinds of people: earnest idealists, optimists to the point of incredulity, and while some were psychologically unstable most were generally truly well-intentioned, good folk. Very few were working class in origin. Elements of it were simply fantastic; some were also disciplined (in their own way) arch-Leninists who sustained themselves on a gruel of imaginary imminent events and forces. But most were simply dreamers. Indeed, there was a strong continuity between the New Left that emerged after the 1960s and the romantics and bohemians who have always played important roles in diverse socialist and radical movements in many nations since their very inception. In the United States it was literary and stressed the importance of imagination, more in debt to Joe Hill and the Wobblies than to the dry academic prose of Marxism, and incorrigibly romantic and apocalyptic – especially when it came to black militants who postured for this audience. Intellectually, the New Left was the least reflective of any radical group, especially – but hardly exclusively – in the United States. Ironically, what described itself as "New" was in critical ways really the very oldest Left resurrected, devoid of Marxist strictures but totally lacking a critical reassessment of how and why politics or economics – and the world – operate, much less those rational preconditions for improving it significantly. It was exceedingly pleasant for its participants but it confused its desires with reality.[14]

The utopian Left was anti-political insofar as it refused to regard the function and nature of power as central to its own tactics. It idealized its leaders and their words to an inordinate and dangerous extent. Romantic heroes such as Che Guevara, Castro, Mao, or Ho Chi Minh undermined political literacy because belief in demigods, their alleged nobility and wisdom, stymied desperately needed thought on how and why social change occurs. Part of the New Left believed that pandemonium by itself had virtue and led in a positive direction. Many simply wished to prove that their commitment was serious; machismo and willingness to take risks was its measure, a criterion that placed a decisive premium on action for its own sake rather than reflection. Demonstrations were de rigueur. Radical utopianism led to pop radicalism and protest, and for many of its adherents was simply a form of entertainment, often dignified with the term anarchy, but it was far more a reflection of confusion than an antidote to it.

In its worst form, symbols were substituted for clear ideas capable of being discussed rationally; peace buttons, portraits of Che, T-shirts, posters, music, and the whole iconography of protest and dissent thrived. Pop Leftist and folk, rock and other singers played an enormous role in both mobilizing young people and preventing them from better comprehending much more significant political issues. Lifestyle youth culture that claimed to be radicalism was so extensive in the United States that it was a mass fashion, based on swarming among young people who ultimately had no measurable impact on American politics or its political literacy. It was escapist and politically incoherent, lacked a social base, and was only a reflection of the historic underdevelopment of the American Left in all of its forms. Similar cult-like organizations exist everywhere, and sentiment and friendship kept many organizations, including very big ones, going, with human ties acting as a surrogate for ideas.

The New Left believed that by the sheer triumph of good intentions, as well as mass support, the will and ability of rulers and the dominant class to survive would not become a potentially decisive obstacle to socialism. Ideas would triumph easily, not merely over ignorance but also over interests and power – which has never been the case anywhere. Utopians believe that choices occur in a vacuum in which no decisive limits are imposed on what one desires. Neither the so-called practical nor the utopian wing of socialism has ever steered successfully through actual challenges, which are frequently cacophonous and nominally unpredictable. Both were equally naive and simplistic.

The Left everywhere since its inception has always attracted fascinating, often flamboyant characters, whose charisma in turn enlisted much larger constituencies who respond to heroes to guide impulses that they themselves could not articulate. The German SPD flourished first under the inspiration of Ferdinand Lassalle, whose social ideas and dramatic legal cases shocked some Marxists in the party's ranks. The British labor movement appealed to romantics of every persuasion – literati, assorted interesting people with often very esoteric, mystical notions, and the same was true in France, the Netherlands, and elsewhere. In the United States, Greenwich Village played a crucial role in the formation of syndicalist and socialist organizations. Similar essentially authoritarian heroes, whether religious or secular, have succeeded since time immemorial because of the intellectual underdevelopment that has affected a significant portion of men and women throughout history. The Right suffers from it at least as much. A great many of socialism's followers have adored prophets and saints, whose ability to retain the masses' admiration cannot be explained as a form of rationality. As undesirable as such collective myopia is, it still remains very much an aspect of the human condition.

Virtually everywhere socialist movements emerged, a portion of the intelligentsia from the educated socially and economically secure middle class or, not infrequently, marginalized members of the aristocracy, were instrumental to their foundation. Had those who descended from the poorer masses been much more important, as was the case in the SPD after 1900, yet other problems did or would have existed. But in the final analysis, socialism's inadequate analytic and theoretical basis was predestined to be a fatal flaw regardless of the social composition of its leaders; it was the decisive source of its being overwhelmed by the century's tragic history.

On the whole, when one adds together the secular adventurist revolutionary notions, the Christian-pacifist cult of innocence, uncritical Third Worldism – the belief that most movements in the developing nations are somehow automatically radical – and synthetic, eclectic varieties of wish-fulfillment that thrived from about 1960 to 1975, little of permanent value emerged from the so-called New Left experience. The hard thought and work that addresses the countless challenges that confront humankind in so many nations was still desperately needed, including the recognition that a great deal more than will-power and good intentions are essential to overcome the enormous evils of capitalism. In Europe alone, Green parties emerged, however unevenly, to expand the scope of political dialogue in a very partial but nonetheless positive manner.

The New Left was in large part originally a rejection of the sclerosis and bureaucratization of the Socialist and Communist parties, but it was also encumbered by its original romanticism and utopianism. And just as many earlier, less flamboyant parties and organizations thrived because they were based on deepening social and personal networks that gave its members a raison d'être far beyond nominal ideological justifications, the same desire for community sustained the New Left. The need and desire to belong bound people in a common cause. When social networks are very intense, and the natural and enviable desire for friendship and human contact becomes more important than clarifying key problems, issues that are contentious or divisive are bypassed and ignored. A great deal of error – sometimes bordering on the irrational – survives by default, thereby causing terrible mistakes again and again. All organizations, Right as well as Left, have suffered from this flaw. Friendship or loyalty to an organization is a very admirable and desirable quality, but when mixed with political goals whose success demands the application of reasoning, it can easily destroy a movement. A movement that stays alive despite its follies or the sheer nonsense of its ideas will compound its errors, and although it will satisfy the needs and interests of its members, it cannot change a society for the better.

The failure of mainstream socialism

The socialist parties in the twentieth century often came to power principally because of the catastrophic behavior of Europe and Asia's rulers. But victory by default was, and is, never a sufficient basis for holding and exercising power wisely. Social change requires an intense commitment to values and core principles, but it must also include a very great deal of serious thought, knowledge, and work to succeed – and an awareness of the ongoing need to reason constantly is an essential precondition. Socialist parties, as well, often allowed themselves to become personal vehicles for charismatic personalities who could win elections and rarely saw their obligations in this broader context, creating frustrations and disappointment that will continue until those in power are ready to make choices consistent with their pledges.

The socialist parties in Europe, on the whole, never synthesized successfully their moral fervor with deep intelligence, and they ended the twentieth century both fatigued and deflowered, surviving only because of inertia and the ambitious people who ruled them as well as their adversaries' lack of alternatives. These parties exist principally by default and nostalgia because no better socially idealistic option to them has yet been articulated.

In the major European nations, Social Democratic leaders were masters at politics and political finessing who knew how to build political coalitions and find the price of most of those rivals within their parties (or the ecological movement). The most cynical and unprincipled rose to the top, and fiscal opportunism became their hallmark so that ultimately one is hard pressed to tell the differences between Social Democratic politicians in the United Kingdom, France, Germany and elsewhere and their more candid and honest conservative rivals. The British Labour government's "modernizing" under Tony Blair emasculated the trade unions, whose membership fell from over 50 percent of all employees in 1979 to under 30 percent in 2000, and as a matter of policy privatized innumerable industries – including such historically public services as health and education. What is certain is that economically, and in terms of their class structure, all of these nations after the advent of socialist governments (in France with Communist participation), often after years of rule, still resembled the traditional social and class systems. Even in developing nations, the socialist movement in the latter part of the twentieth century was marginalized both intellectually and socially, usually becoming indistinguishable from centerist parties whose explicit objective is to manage capitalism efficiently. Nominally committed to institutionalizing far greater social equity and justice, most of them did not conflict with fundamentally conservative economic strictures, which the IMF and similar institutions defined for them.

To confuse the value and desirability of a cause with those who lead it runs the serious risk of rationalizing people whose motives and power must always be subjected to critical assessments. The history of the twentieth century confirms repeatedly that noble causes that confront oppressors from without can also end up with oppressors from within. The hero of one epoch can, and often has, become an obstacle and even a tyrant in another. Good causes are permanent, but those who guide them are mere mortals who must be judged accordingly, and the only safeguard is to oppose uncontrollable power by anyone or any party. But those who supported liberation movements everywhere often feared that to advocate such nuanced and potentially critical standards would undermine the larger cause. A mindless Third Worldism assumed that almost all those who called themselves national liberation movements and engaged in guerrilla war, whether against a foreign power or internal tyrants, somehow also transcended those dilemmas of power and responsibility that existed elsewhere. In the end, a whole gallery of people whose subsequent action was exploitive, dysfunctional, or tyrannical were exempted from the criticism they amply deserved, and the slogans and myths generated before the victory of liberation movements served subsequently to assist their betrayal from within.

Socialism as an idea in all its forms, whether Marxist, Social Democratic, or Bolshevik, has ceased to be a mobilizing ideology throughout the world, and the belief that equalitarianism is a socially desirable goal has largely perished with it. But we cannot ignore the fact that the greatest triumphs of these movements came during and immediately after wars, when socialism succeeded not because of its intellectual merits but due to the huge political and ideological void and the follies of old regimes. Wars will occur again, of course, and even fairly localized wars in Europe are possible; socialism's success by default may reoccur once again, but for the past several decades socialism has ceased to be a credible alternative to the status quo in peacetime.

Nationalism and varieties of secular ideologies have also failed, above all in the Middle East, where religious Islamic fundamentalism and obscuritanism has flourished as an alternative to both socialism and nationalism. The United States supported religious fundamentalism as well as secular tyrants for decades, but there is no gainsaying the reality that secular movements also discredited themselves, largely – but not exclusively – because their leaders were venal and opportunist, and ceased to be credible to more and more people as true advocates of far-reaching changes in society. What is crucial is that fundamentalism and irrationality has marched into an immense political vacuum but often, as in the vast Islamic world, sets its sights on the basic transformation of status quos of every sort, ranging from hedonism and secularism to the unconscionable pursuit of personal interest above all else. As much as we dislike these alternatives, which are ineffective as well as obscuritan, such irrational religious options oppose the status quo in much the way the idea of socialism used to. In their own way, they seek basic changes. Had socialism not failed as an inspirational ideal these currents would never have emerged so powerfully.

In a word, the world comes in complex and often equivocal packages and the way people behave socially varies greatly. And for many of the same reasons that socialist parties were successful we should expect a return to mass discontent and action, although its organizational and intellectual forms cannot be exactly predicted. That socialist and Communist parties betrayed so many people in no way mitigates the legitimacy and authenticity of the masses' anger and alienation, nor will their impulses to protest be suppressed in the future because socialism as a political movement is today discredited.

4 The role and limits of social theories

Countless ideas are perpetuated for reasons that have nothing to do with their intrinsic coherence and validity. Those which legitimize official and conventional wisdom are the most durable, and virtually every state has examples of them – nationalisms of various sorts, many of them being recent fictional inventions useful to those in power, are the most prominent but scarcely the only essentially mindless justifications that reinforce existing authorities. There are innumerable doctrines of cultural superiority in various guises; all religions and most nationalities have variations of them. These illusions, and the abstractions they spawn, are the source of much human folly and misery – of persecution and wars.

Such creeds are generally highly dysfunctional as a basis for confronting reality when leaders take them seriously – as they repeatedly do. During peacetime, politicians make ideologies and rationales pragmatically suited to the moods and political or social needs of the moment, above all to attain and hold power. But while the practical functions ideas play should be appreciated, they must be – the sooner the better – assessed for their inherent logic and validity or else they become another obstacle to clear thinking. In many cases, of course, a doctrine or theory's legitimacy for most people is the authority and power – whether political, religious, or military – of those who assert it and have a vested interest in the sanctity of a dogma. Then ideas simply become a method of control. Ideas do not explain reality but justify the action – or, more often, inaction – of those who rule. While there are countless examples throughout history of such essentially authoritarian processes at work in many nations, and the United States is today the best example of the dangers such intellectual fixations pose, any survey of the past two centuries will produce numerous other illustrations.

The dilemma is that conventional wisdom breaks down quickly during wars, and war – and the climate of opinion and thought that bloodshed produces – is very much a central aspect of human history. Ideas as well as societies then come apart but they do so under crisis environments, producing critical intellectual innovations and responses which established orders dread. But these very often are hasty, irrational reactions that compound the illusions and mistakes of the old orders rather than solving them, leaving a symbiosis between the old and new societies that is often an obstacle to genuine progress. The evolution of Communist societies is the best example of this baneful synthesis but there are all-too-many others.

No grand theory of any sort, religious or secular, has survived the ravages of human experience in an immensely complicated world which has undermined all highly structured propositions regarding the future of societies. Logical analyses of them have been even more devastating. Theories, and the assumptions they embody, rarely accord with social realities and they become in most instances articles of faith in which experience ceases to be a criterion for judging their relevance and truth. But we live in a profoundly troubled era which requires a great deal of intellectual innovation and originality appropriate for our contemporary social and human crises, and this demands that we discard most, perhaps all of the existing paradigms and conventions which are so fixed in the ideas of all ideological persuasions.

Most ideas, ranging from the obscure to those that are better known, are not intended to buttress authority. The perpetuation of ideas and thinkers totally independent of established, dominant power is an altogether different matter; assessing them requires more subtle analyses. But the vast majority of these concepts do not change with events and are equally sclerotic. They also fail to cope with human and social predicaments even though many purport to address, if not to answer them. The social networks that grow around simplified icons, slogans, and ideas produce informal as well as formal organizations, and these usually become obstacles to critical, clear thinking. Friendship is but one reason why questions are not asked about received wisdom during "normal" times; people usually cherish human relations above intellectual clarity, which is often fraught with debates and tension. Respectability, and the desire for it, is debilitating also, and it is a menace to creative thinking not only when friendship is involved but also in universities, the media, and society in general. All such factors bar original nonconformist thought. The desire to discover the truth must entail a willingness to challenge conventional wisdom in whatever field which is the object of one's inquiry – and to accept all of the potential consequences, some of them very substantial, for doing so. Only a tiny minority is ready to pursue such an innovative course.

It is not, ultimately, that there are more variables in social science than pure science, for they are distinctions of degree and not of kind, but their analytic similarities are ultimately more crucial than their differences. Creative work in social and pure science requires very radical qualities of character, and the absence of it hobbles progress in both science and social science. The scientific method assumes a critical mentality that transcends the specific results of any inquiry, and it is inherently subversive of established wisdom in pure science or theses about society. It explicitly rejects absolute certainties, whatever the subject, and it cultivates doubt. Many conventional and even widely accepted but counterproductive and misleading theories or notions linger on for reasons of sentiment and inertia long after they have any resemblance to reality, much less any predictive value. But theories that are incomprehensible and unfathomable are worse than useless, a trap to defeat reason in the name of mysterious profundity.[1]

Social ideas are far too important to be subject to the standards that govern academia, where obscure theories come and go and make slight difference. We desperately need criteria and canons of thought appropriate to a usable social theory and program which abjures cosmologies even as it seeks to confront and, if possible, solve large-scale issues. There can be no final or absolute social program and philosophy in the grand sense and it was a fatal error – inherent in Marxism – for the socialist project to believe it needed one. But although there is no finality there must be analytic progress and all ideas are far from being equal. Outright error or nonsense does not have to be considered legitimate even if tolerated. The standards of proof we now require include both the consequences of theory in practice as well as the resolution of philosophical questions insofar as that is attainable.

The intellectual parameters and mood of the times are crucial to the perpetuation of ideas but crises – of which wars are the most important but scarcely the sole source of intellectual ferment – compel nonconformist thought processes to be greatly accelerated and ideas to change. All societies assume certain intellectual premises, however absurd they may be, and discarding conventional wisdom is the necessary precondition of creativity in any field, whatever it may be. The context and degree of urgency is always crucial to innovation, but innovation itself is no guarantee whatsoever of greater clarity or validity in the ways theories are articulated, much less their intrinsic value. They often are a step, or more, backwards, with greater obscurity and irrationality triumphing over attempts to develop more sensible and relevant social theories.

Social theories in peacetime have performed countless functions, ranging from providing those who rule with convenient myths and rationalizations, or a pragmatic basis for specific policies, to theses, tenure, and various academic exercises. The effort to articulate them is not necessarily invidious, and relatively disinterested seekers after truth have also existed, but the mainstream, well-known theories have overwhelmingly been propounded by those in or near the centers of authority. These centers usually define priorities and fund topics of prime interest, not just in science and technology, which has been obvious since the emergence of mining in the seventeenth century, but also in all of the social sciences, and those who say or write what those in power wish to hear are rewarded in various ways – from professorships to media attention. But the moment that specific ideas become profitable or functional they enter into another category and the arguments for them are often highly suspect. Although true believers of ideas are numerous enough, even for obscure and absurd ones, motives are often most relevant, and while the meretricious does not in every instance explain why some notions thrive, the belief that pure, disinterested inspiration explains the success of a social vision or doctrine is, at best, exceedingly unsophisticated in an age when the media are so powerful in molding public opinion.

Ignoring entirely that he had a consummately naive vision of philosophy as an instrument of progress, John Dewey was correct in arguing that philosophy was a reflection of existing cultures, which judged truth by the functional consequences of certain ideas for society.[2] But he pointed to only part of the problem because the survival and perpetuation of absurd and irrelevant theories of no value to the powers-that-be, long after they are plausible and their very existence is an obstacle to clear thinking, is partially due to the reluctance of most people to oppose prevailing notions and thereby sacrifice respectability and the main chance professionally; but it is also linked to the inability of a minority to live in a void without an idea or inspiration and no credible option to conventional wisdom. In the latter case, holding one idea in a lifetime is all that many individuals can manage. Such pure inertia and intellectual laziness on all sides is crucial, even if other sources of the perpetuation of myths involving power and interests are more decisive.

Ideas are assuredly not valid or false because of their consequences but it is essential to carefully consider what the effects of a certain belief might be in estimating its utility. We cannot be satisfied (as are instrumentalists) with this criterion as a sufficient basis of evaluating propositions involving concepts of reality or the truth or falsity of philosophical propositions, but we very often do not have a definitive basis, despite self-criticism and a lack of complacency, for rejecting or accepting ideas; their practical effects cannot be ignored lest our beliefs or action unintentionally prove negative – if not much worse. Ideas are not valid solely because they are socially or organizationally functional, and a belief that they are leaves the door wide open to every kind of irrationality and opportunism, whether religious, assorted atavisms, nationalism, and the like. It can also justify the repression of thought.

An anti-instrumentalist methodology is anything but a simple key to solving many of the questions of choice and social engineering that routinely confront us in the course of responding to challenges. Many of the critics of John Dewey's instrumentalism were no better able to produce answers to social problems or, at least as crucial, overcome the difficulties that prevent people from doing so.[3] There are limits to any philosophy, and while this certainly does not justify impressionism, subjectivism, or pop styles, these constraints must be acknowledged. Reason has to be central to the way one approaches problems and solutions, because ultimately it is a transcendent method that is relevant to every notion, whether in science, religion, or whatever, and an essential precondition of rational thinking; by itself it is no guarantee of success. But if the traps inherent in any intellectual project are to be avoided then a commitment to rational thinking is a requisite – a necessary one but far from sufficient.

The importance of judging ideas by their effects, despite the fact that the final evaluation of the efficacy of conceptions to reality goes far beyond consequentialism, has increased with time because weapons are far more destructive and the meaning of options is intimately linked to the way proposals confront the issues of war and peace. The entire debate over instrumentalism, more justifiable before 1945 and the atomic age, has become irrelevant. Choices are increasingly a question of their implications to the very existence of humankind. Ethical arguments, whether secular or theological reasons are given for them, are more and more powerful and functional because our survival is scarcely an abstract issue.

The dilemma is that much of human history is disorderly, its inherent complexity often makes it unpredictable, and the logic of science rails against those dominant historical and economic theories that are premised on order and predictability. All explanations of society that assume it are, on the whole, misleading. To formulate a new and more durable social theory one must first define what theories should and can and cannot do and what sort of criteria we should impose upon the very project of generalizing on the past, much less the future, of mankind. Essentially, we must first concede the substantial limits of all theories and knowledge of human beings and societies under various circumstances – and proceed from there. Because we cannot know everything does not mean that we can know nothing, but we must have a far superior theoretical basis for relating to an incredibly complex reality than the vast majority of social philosophers articulated over the past generations. Such a recognition of the limits and constraints of knowledge, indeed, has always been inherent in the scientific enterprise but insufficiently acknowledged by all too many thinkers. By reemphasizing the constraints and limits along with the value of theories based on critical reason, we can create a far more durable social theory that does not minimize the role of freedom or accidents in history. We can know much more than we do but we can never comprehend everything that we would like to.

For practical purposes, final truths and descriptions of an independent reality and truth – an objective reality, whether in nature or societies – are not the goals of rational thinking, and to assume we have attained them can be the source of great illusions and profoundly counterproductive. In a word, not only do we not need to grasp absolute knowledge but also we should never claim we have done so; we do need to think rationally, which requires that we accept an element of contingency in our ideas. It does not mean that we shall be proven wrong but rather incomplete. This does not imply that all ideas are equal or relative, but we have to comprehend their limits and the contexts in which they were created – and then proceed to confront complex realities. What is absolute is the very process of critical thinking, which means that institutions, ideas, and contexts that lead to the destruction of this process are irrational. Suicide is not an option, either for sane people or social organizations, and we can formulate criteria for irrationality at the same time that we dismiss the ideas of absolutes as irrelevant to coping with theories and societies on an ongoing basis.

Historical destinies

Despite important differences between them in methodology, ranging from subjectivist beliefs in a divine purpose to claims of having scientifically justified a doctrine – and a plethora of other assumptions – most pre-1914 theories believed they could predict the general contours of society and humankind's future. These theories were rarely, if ever, pessimistic, and ideas of necessity and putative laws abounded.

The debate over historical method and the very nature of the historical experience has generally occurred at a relatively much higher level of abstraction than notions emerging from economics or sociology. And while it is largely grist for academics, the discussion over historiography also touches many of the important issues that the more pretentious social theories claimed to resolve. A brief review of them is useful.

In economics, to name but one field, many basic premises ultimately can or should be proven or disproved (but are usually not!) from concrete historical experiences, but much of what passes as theories of history ultimately cannot be verified one way or the other. But the logic and scope of historical method as most of its practitioners employ it promise exceedingly ambitious concepts even as its results have been unsuccessful. These impinge on not only how historians write but also how a much broader constituency perceives social dynamics and society in general.

All too many of these so-called historical laws are trivial and vague, achieving a nominal wisdom about methodology at the expense of sufficient clarity to be really useful analytically when confronting realities. That the methods of history can in principle be rational, and comparable to the methods of generalized science, does not mean written history is also functional. Theoretically, at least, absolute laws and truisms based on fixed principles and laws may (or may not!) exist to be discovered but this fact alone does not necessarily produce useful or meaningful results and it leaves far too much unanswered. Until now, historical theories based on erstwhile laws have not borne fruit convincingly. But the pretension that such laws exist has led to dogmatism and illusion in the past and poses the same dangers in the future. Philosophers who argue such laws can be uncovered rarely write histories and have scant knowledge of the problems and array of choices confronting those who do so. These debates have proved meaningless and irrelevant.

There are many methodological obstacles to asserting that final knowledge or the truth has been attained, not to mention that such claims often become justifications for actions whose consequences are destructive. Anyone who says they possess truth has the burden of providing incontrovertible evidence for it. When offered by sociologists, political theorists, or the like, such theories are usually far too imprecise and cannot account for the many examples of unique situations and factors – or events that have many causes. If they offer ideal-types as essences of reality, as Max Weber and others did, the dangers of such heuristic abstractions – which are, at best, really hypotheses – exist in proportion to the way these concepts resist facts and events and function intentionally as defenses against uncomfortable disproof. Ideal-types possess an immunity to refutation precisely because they claim a heuristic, indeterminate status that merely gathers pieces of information until more insight is available. They become a surrogate for genuine knowledge which demands verifiable inputs and constant testing. Science aspires to attain completeness and its hypotheses can eventually be verified as true or false. No one can be opposed to theories that do not allege to be more than finite, heuristic concepts but all too often they refuse to admit their limits and become timeless abstractions that are misleading if not false. Societies and history are far too complex – and important – to encourage facile generalizations.[4]

If given the choice, we are far better off admitting we always have a degree of ignorance in whatever we do and say – which does not prevent us from being rational and choosing alternatives, but it is an antidote to dogmatism. A contingent, less pretentious assumption is much more compatible with real intellectual processes – and generally more valid as well. Not to be rigorously committed to honesty and integrity in searching for concepts and theories, and to interpret facts and knowledge to suit those in positions of power who desire sustaining myths for organizational or political reasons, or to satisfy our own predilections and desires, opens the door to false illusions and further error. But "facts" in the pure sciences are very often quite different than those in the social sciences, although in reality hypotheses in both pure and social sciences very frequently are affected by the same lethargic human processes and conservatism which prevent essential changes in both fields.[5]

Science, both in theory and practice, assumes a great deal of contingency and limits in even physics or chemistry, and an accurate definition of what science really is should encourage social theorists to believe that their efforts are not so precarious – nor as enduring as some claim. This rules out laws that are valid for all times and places – and therefore most of nineteenth-century social theory. These specious laws still have immense influence, above all in economics, and are largely very conservative in consequence. They persist, of course, not because of intellectual merit but because there are crucial vested interests in maintaining theories as rationales of injustices – as with the eighteenth-century notion of market economics – and peer group pressures.

While science may have the irregular characteristics of much of history, its basic subject matter is regularity rather than the far more complex explanations of the reasons or causes for specific historical events. Science has innumerable limits, and many erroneous notions plague its progress for a variety of reasons, ranging from ignorance to the lethargic and often hostile ways innovations and new ideas are, among other things, rejected and suppressed for often long periods. But despite the fact that even scientific truths consist of theories and hypotheses that are often changing, it is far more exact than the social sciences and science formulates propositions, even laws, that ultimately can be verified or disproved and often endure for long periods. Science, in principle, acknowledges that it will always be ignorant of a great deal about the physical world; these limits necessarily exist because its subject matter makes it self-limiting, and this assumption is the basis of further progress and drives researchers to learn more. It is self-corrective and is basically committed to probabilities – although in some subjects and instances they are very high – rather than finalities. In practice it is often haphazard, its fields disconnected for long periods, and uneven in its perceptions. Discoveries often occur when the social context, whether military, economic, or intellectual, is ripe for them.

Still, most scientists are often reluctant to accept new theories. Fashions and conventional wisdom destroy individuality and creativity in all domains, science included, and willingness to ignore them is the prerequisite of creativity and progress in all fields. Progress is sometimes due to accidents, and young scientists and those who have not been socialized into the personal networks and ideas that reinforce existing paradigms are much more likely to be creative than older persons who have. Notwithstanding the personal factor which causes scientists to persist when the evidence supporting new theories is initially often little more than faith in mere hypotheses, science produces laws but their consequences are often unpredictable. Whatever the human and institutional obstacles, science has the capacity to produce fundamental new insights, though it often fails to do so for long periods.

Both in the social sciences and science, the social framework both constrains and redirects progress but often provides the funding which makes research possible. Funding is usually crucial to the research's social function. So much of what is discovered in science has as its objective the manipulation of the world rather than explaining its essential nature. In some vital domains we have far too much of it. There is medicine but there is also nuclear physics, and the latter will overwhelm the achievements of the former unless we have the right social solutions.[6]

Reason – limits and all

The best argument for rationality is not that it answers every question, including very important ones, but that it is far preferable to comfortable illusions as a way of coping with the human situation. And despite their limits, some propositions about society and the world have much greater credibility than others in large part because of the way they were constructed. Theories and explanations of historical events are not "relative" or equal, and many are sheer nonsense to anyone who has respect for evidence. Reason alone will not automatically provide meaning to history but it excludes innumerable mystical interpretations of it and provides a rational basis for confronting immediate human problems. Theories and notions in every field of knowledge have limits, but despite the fact that some have far more than others it still leaves us with the heavy responsibility to think both continuously and intelligently about virtually everything. In practice, however, those who proclaim that they have discovered historical truths and causal theories are usually dogmatists who cannot acknowledge the limits of their ideas. They sometimes become dangerous.

It is still more prudent to stress the potential limits of inquiry and the provisional character of knowledge lest we repeat the past century's proclivity to be over-optimistic when articulating grand theories. At the same time, we thereby avoid some – but only some – of the limits that exist on reflection and ideas. We have a vested interest in a rigorous commitment to reality and truth, and the constraints built into them, but we also wish to move forward in terms of knowledge and theory based on it – and there should be no conflict between the two precisely because we are aware of this tension.

The desire to generalize on historical patterns is not doomed to failure nor is it necessarily a poor way to proceed in social inquiry. It is possible when dealing with societies and their development to achieve a much greater degree of probable validity than we now possess, and there is no reason whatsoever to believe that one idea or contention is equal to another. On the contrary, there is an immense amount that can be done to make social theory and actions based upon it more rational and intelligent, with a much higher measure of validity – above all in economics – than those that now hold sway over people of every political persuasion. To believe otherwise is to open the door to subjectivism and relativism of beliefs, and there is no logical reason to do so.

But theories and programs derived from them can create damage and confusion whenever they claim more than they should. Just as there is grave error intrinsic in revelations and mysticisms of every kind, there is also immense danger from the belief that methodologically we have grasped truths for all time because, in principle as opposed to practice, the scientific method and reasoning can produce truisms. But the potential of theory-making is substantially greater than it has been in practice – and both a sense of our capacities as well as limits are essential if a social analysis is more than a simple exhortation of received wisdom or even the plea to think more clearly. Pure theory that ignores concrete situations and examples may be utilitarian doctrine but it is scarcely more than a screed for true believers – the fate of all too many nineteenth-century ideologies, from laissez faire to Marxism. Facts alone do not explain history, and there is a role for hypotheses, but we have to be most careful that theses are not simply deduced from our preconceptions and that they not be reified as self-evident truths valid for all time. We should never assume that valid facts are those that confirm our preferences and prejudices. There are crucial limits on all social theories, but they are ultimately far greater if they are oblivious to the elementary need for ideas to meet both intellectual standards as well as account for as much of reality and experience as possible. Freedom of inquiry is therefore crucial to the process and conclusions of all theoretical – and historical – undertakings.

At some point, a theory that purports to be a guide to action and not simply a description of the world must be judged for its capacity to steer us through the countless problems that humankind faces in reality. To defend the corpus of eighteenth- and nineteenth-century ideas against their post-modernist critics is really superfluous because Bertrand Russell, Morris R. Cohen, and countless others criticized them long before the term "post-modernism" was concocted. Contingency is an integral part of the scientific method, inherent in all discussions of ideal-types, tendencies, or the like. There is no "higher" way of attaining knowledge – such as revelation – and the one thing certain about all ideas is their finite character, and even if some conceptions are considerably better grounded and justified than others, all have to accept the constraints that reality ultimately warrants from even the best of them. Marxism was scarcely alone in delegitimizing itself with its pretensions of absolute certainty. Philosophy and theory without contingency lead to intellectual laziness and a crisis of knowledge, to the repetition of eternal verities. The Left was guilty of such a mentality but most of the illusions in recent decades are cultivated by right-wing market fundamentalists, and to the extent the Left's remnants have sought new explanations they have adopted the market illusions of the Right – leaving them still locked into the false categories devised in the eighteenth and nineteenth centuries. We do not have to disregard past theory or philosophy entirely, not the least because the critical aspects of scientific philosophy greatly assist our confronting problems, and even though this does not by itself answer many of them it better equips us in our efforts to articulate a much more meaningful and useful social theory than has existed in the past. A concern for older efforts can also help us to comprehend the errors in these ideas and the reasons for them, if only to avoid making such mistakes again.

Even when propositions have large elements of validity they must not claim infallibility, because hubris and an awareness of limits are both sensible and justified by experience over the past centuries. Explanations which purport to answer everything end up resolving the least. Absolute certainty and absolute universality do not exist in science, much less conceptions of society. All theories have to eventually be verified, which means they must be verifiable. Whatever our desires, we cannot worry about the implications doubts have for pessimism or optimism because propositions must be judged ultimately for their intrinsic value rather than the psychological needs of their adherents. This kind of critical thinking is skeptical of all conventional wisdom, and despite its liabilities to advocates of change, it is premised on the reality that doubt is less dangerous in critical social thought than dogmatism that also leads to the betrayal of ideals in practice.

But while knowledge should be as extensive as possible, we usually cannot wait before we act, and when we are obligated to act it is best that we think well and retain as high a degree of honesty and insight as possible. The motives and intentions of an actor are therefore critical. A great deal of insight is attainable and we can generalize upon many things – scarcely everything but far more than enough to behave much more rationally. Basic questions that appear like "ethical" judgments, like nuclear and other weapons wracking havoc on people and civilizations, both can and must be resolved immediately. To oppose social suicide may at first glance appear "ethical" but in fact it is a choice in favor of sanity – and therefore rational.

While patience can be justified in the effort to verify a thesis, all contentions and hypotheses are time-bound and so is their relevance – or else anything can be maintained or believed. All too many outdated, absurd ideas are tolerated this way – not just Marxism but a myriad of others. But we are at a point in the human condition that the risks in our civilization's trajectory, combined with the dangerous state of science and technology, require certain priorities and actions before final proof exists to justify them. They may be fallible but they are also essential because the time we have to resolve grave challenges is very finite – if it has not run out already. Circumstances have created new parameters and priorities of judgment and evaluation, and these demand certain choices rather than others – quickly. We cannot casually try to attain the most difficult goals, but when the risks are so great then the prospect of failure cannot deter us from attempting to achieve the seemingly impossible. The nuclear arms race requires a far greater urgency than factory organization.[7]

The function and limits of rationality

Political positions rarely emerge full blown but they also evolve under the pressure of external forces and people's responses to them – including options and necessities. We should always assume a degree of ignorance, a premise that in itself reduces blindness and gives us a better and more coherent basis for dealing with a future that is never as predictable as most established theories contend. Such a process is invariably sloppier and more contingent than we prefer but what we think or believe will often be time-bound and very much a part of transitional conditions. It is only by nourishing rational and realistic alternatives that we can respond to often unknowable events and crises that we have yet to confront. Often, but not always, there is a range of possible responses we can choose from based on our ethics, objectives, and knowledge of alternatives – and virtually any of them would be a quantum improvement over the haphazard and usually ignorant way earlier generations have met the crises of the past century.

The standards of proof that exist in scientific thinking, including its limits, are crucial. Social theory must not attempt to attain the status of sacrosanct received wisdom and its descriptions and ideas must be pluralistic and capable of being reexamined. Theories that survive such a process are thereby more convincing and those who accept them have reassurance they are not wasting their time with another dogmatic ideology. The function of social theory means that while there are normative priorities in formulating it, and not merely a scientific attitude, there will nonetheless always be a tension between a desirable, if not perfect, social program and knowledge; this means we must live with a measure of contingency and doubt. But doubt is far less dangerous than the illusions inherent in certitude. Here our motives are paramount, assuming that we do not wish to delude ourselves with a belief in some kind of inevitability; all theory must have the capacity to be adaptive. We do not have to know everything before we act and we cannot assume that all the great issues of humanity and society both can and should be resolved before we do. A theory must be capable of a credible degree of verification because we need a realistic basis for confronting new problems lest our misconceptions become a dogmatic liability. There have been far too many tragedies in the past for absolute certainty but a greater degree of confidence in both means and ends is essential – and possible.

Theory is highly desirable so long as it does not produce more obstacles to understanding, which means it must be comprehensible. We have lived with the dominance of opaque theorists for some centuries and we now know far less than we should as a consequence. Their ingenious verbal exercises have been oriented to their peers, other intellectuals, or seekers after some faith; some have merely rationalized existing power. The human experience is not comprised of just discrete events which do not interact and produce new permutations, but neither is it bound by laws of motion of any sort – whether in economics or any other aspect of human behavior. We must find our way again, more modestly but more surely, and where recurrent patterns or problems exist we must carefully note them. We need a descriptive and predictive theory which is neither Panglossian nor too obscure and esoteric to be unlocked by mere mortals. It must be reasonably useful because one that is not is worse than nothing, leaving us completely disarmed with illusions in coping with the future. Social ends must be based on realistic assumptions but these too can be rationally evaluated to an important extent, especially in the light of the past century's experiences. An operational view of alternatives and their consequences is possible, but we need objectivity to assess them – which requires a high degree of honesty as well as a desire not to fool ourselves and others. That basic values and goals are determined in many cases by extra-rational means and interests is not crucial so long as knowledge and science (in the contingent sense I have explained) is used to critically evaluate them. There must be an interaction between knowledge and values, and this alone makes it possible to justify one choice over the other even when absolute, final proof does not exist. It is preferable to keep the results of this process on a general basis so that the specific institutional means for satisfying a goal are not considered sacrosanct. Ethical choices may not be "scientific" in the sense of finality but neither are they arbitrary, because both self-preservation and sanity rule out innumerable alternatives – most of which have been implemented and brought countless disasters to the world. These I begin to spell out later in this book.

A rational theory of knowledge cannot produce a rational description of a social system if the structure itself is capable of immense possibilities and is too variable and inherently unpredictable. Efforts to schematize it cannot exist independently of reality. There are many things we can generalize upon with a reasonably high degree of accuracy but we cannot generalize on everything and there are simply too many contingencies for intellectual complacency. Indeterminism can itself lead to pessimism that encourages cynicism and inaction, but a fatalistic, mechanistic optimism is equally dangerous. Neither approach is warranted or is confirmed by historical experiences; an important element of tension is inherent in any useful, valid social theory, and those that cannot live with it are better off with faith in one or another absolute creed. This leaves us with the need for rationality and a high degree of contingency (or modesty) and the best argument for rationality, as I have repeated so often, is that with all its limits it still remains the most functional approach to a myriad of human and intellectual problems. The inherent dangers of other modes of thinking mean rationality has a negative virtue – it avoids many mistakes but it certainly does not automatically answer every problem that demands explanation. It holds out promises even when it does not always or automatically fulfill them. But we cannot judge a mode of reasoning, system, or theory simply because we dislike its consequences, because then everything is credible and we can believe anything that pleases us because there are no canons of proof. Methods have to be judged on their merits but we must retain the assumption that we do not want to merely solace ourselves with conventionally accepted myths.

But there is a decisive problem: we are very often compelled to react to critical events and to formulate a theory or broad analysis when contemplative, unrushed thought is impossible. Inaction and passivity is simply another way of responding to events, and usually it is the worst choice. We often have scant freedom to order reality in a way we desire, and if we are honest we acknowledge our finite capacities even as we attempt to prevent the very worst from occurring. There is never a sufficiency of knowledge, which means we often act with degrees of ignorance, but when foreign and domestic challenges arise, ranging from those every war creates to a myriad of other possibilities, we must respond to them. They are often upon us when we least expect or we are unprepared to deal with them as we would optimally wish to. Doctrines succeeded in the past far less because they comprehended or described historical reality than because they were often the only options available at critical moments when changes were inevitable, and success was rarely due to their brilliance or appropriateness but by default. The entire history of socialist and Leninist movements is testimony to this symbiosis between crises and conventional wisdom but the same lack of alternatives explains much of the triumph of fascist movements and the reason mindless conservatism and religious obscurity persist at the present moment. This is scarcely a desirable way to meet the monumental challenges – political, military, and ecological – that the human race now faces.

The challenge the world has confronted for a very long time is to understand not only the limits of theory but also its strengths, and to respond to reality much more wisely than people have up until now.

Surprise or not, it is crucial, to the extent possible, that people who want changes know what they are doing, and rational thinking is a prerequisite, not a guarantee, of clarity. There are many problems that arise suddenly and some are fundamental – not the least are those that involve the very existence of our civilization in the light of the diffusion of the means, both low and high tech, of physically destroying it. Levels of "truth" required or the validity of analyses and proposals are linked to the methodology for proving them but also to the urgency of the goals that are implicit in their assumptions – in a word, time. Humankind's survival is a key criterion for evaluating social options, and the way alternatives, premises, and institutions help or hinder achieving it are crucial dimensions of the quest for rebuilding a critical social theory. The arguments may be called utilitarian or consequentialism, but whatever we term it there is far more justification for institutional sanity rather than suicide, and that is crucial. To repeat a vital point, social arrangements and premises that maximize the chances of achieving peace and resolving major political and economic problems are infinitely preferable to those that lead to destruction, and this exceedingly radical assumption rules out most of the options, premises, and thought processes that have guided humankind for the past century. To this crucial extent, we can confront surprises rationally – and radically.

There is no reason to believe that the solution of epistemological issues is the route to the salvation of social institutions or that meeting humanity's most dire needs depends simply on attaining clarity. We can aspire for only so much, more in some areas than in others, and the contingencies inherent in knowledge are greater in certain topics than in others. Knowledge and insight is a necessary condition of action but it is scarcely sufficient; there is a great deal more that must be done to attain that and the choices of action are far less amenable to resolution simply by thinking. Ultimately, reflection and objective clarity cannot be the only way we choose social goals, and class bias and interests will be crucial in their selection, but pure bias must never overcome a rational estimation of the cost and consequences of specific decisions and options.

A valid, predictive social theory has never existed, and most that were offered have been discarded and forgotten – thereby making disproof superfluous. We still must respond to the world we live in and the disastrous direction it is heading, but with the knowledge that there are limits to what we are doing, yet also that we must do much more with fewer pretensions about inevitability and righteousness. Patterns, trends, or tendencies that accept major contingencies cannot be laws in the invariable sense that we define the latter. That there can in principle be a science of society and its components is largely irrelevant. In our time-bound context, the difference between what is theoretically possible as opposed to rational and appropriate ideas and action, between certainty and contingency leavened with finite intelligence, is decisive. In this book I have focused on how theories have been used – and misused – in the past but I also seek to enunciate some of the relevant guidelines in dealing with the future – including avoiding repeating mistakes that all too often have been made over the centuries. We must be aware how intellectual traditions, above all in the universities, encouraged ambitions and ideas that were pretentious and promised a very great deal but ultimately proved grossly misleading for purposes of both analysis and action. Worse yet, they persist in some crucial areas, especially economics, and have been corrosive of the clear thought that is possible. Notwithstanding this, the grave immensity of the myriad international, ecological and other problems we confront demands a new critical social thought that is both relevant and intellectually defensible.

Social theory has not only to explain or describe but also to predict to a reasonable, if not comprehensive, degree. The scientific status of a theory is a false issue and an inaccurate simplification of the nature of science. A theory can be operationally useful and retain a capacity for self-criticism and, ultimately, for change. Concepts which predict a fixed historical trajectory or progressive stages are simply misleading, and such pretentious visions should not be the goal of social theory. The entire twentieth century, its wars, human destruction, and chaos is testimony to the chimera of all the nineteenth-century stage theories, with their benignly optimistic scenarios. There simply is no substitute for constant human intelligence and a commitment to averting disaster for humanity.

Tension in ideas is therefore both inevitable and essential because social theories are not academic propositions, products of self-confident wise men, but they must relate to realities and needed changes. The function of theory is to postulate goals; some will be imperative objectives for the very near future, particularly those relating to war and peace, but others will be less urgent, and despite the fact that they may be unachievable immediately they are both rational and necessary to the health or existence of society. Sooner or later, they must be attained. Institutional prerequisites of meeting important challenges confronting the world, or social groups within it, are the ingredients of which social analyses and programs are made. Changes can occur by stages, with the means advocated examined at all times for their efficacy and appropriateness. We cannot have absolute faith nor absolute doubt, and we must avoid simplifications. Either of these two states of mind is dangerous in the longer run. It is very risky to have unbending confidence in a theory or doctrine just as we cannot spend all our time lacking confidence in our program or actions, but neither is necessary if we are intelligent about the efficacy and limits about what we say and advocate.

Theory must be simple enough to be tested by experience but also sufficient to explain adequately our society and its direction, both in the past and where it should go in the future – neither more nor less. It should never exceed the complexity that is minimally required and it must never be based on faith, for this courts endless dangers. The problem, also, is that the world is institutionally and historically very intricate and theories often fail to capture its nuances – which is why art and poetry flourish and often describe reality more forcefully. We must respect individuality and complexity, which requires richer and more nuanced perceptions and modes of analysis. We can generalize and theorize on whatever is amenable to such forms of thinking – and constantly subject our thoughts to critical analysis. But whether there is a comprehensive theory or not, we must always understand how institutions and societies actually operate. There is no substitute for knowledge.

Thought processes are too often telescoped when there is a lack of social time for reflection, and crucial decisions are made too recklessly, but there must also be an environment in which they can evolve without inhibition. One of the reasons for the fatal schism in the socialist movement at the time of World War One was that social democracy had long been intolerant of basic intellectual innovations – in the name of the true faith, it was sclerotic. The worst option, and all too often the most frequent catalyst of innovation, is when ideas are concocted as justifications for facts already on the ground or actions already taken, as in the case of Leninism. The result is that defective ideas replace yet others and a state and a movement's interests – which mainly justify a new status quo – compound the faults inherent in thinking hastily and pragmatically. In effect, whether the political inclinations of their proponents were conservative or radical, their thought processes did not deliver the insight or analysis which allowed more effective responses to social, political, and economic challenges. There is no substitute for rational reflection under much more ideal circumstances. There may never be such conditions for theoretical contemplation but we must do far better. What is crucial is that our thought processes always retain a rational mode of analysis regardless of its specific applications or the constraints that events impose on them.

We rarely, if ever, need convoluted, complex theories either for analysis or action. It is not only that they are an obstacle to both, making either ultimately far more difficult and contentious, but also that no highly intricate theory has survived the courts of experience or careful examination – either in economics, concepts of change, or what have you – over the past two centuries, and they generally justify the exercise and abuse of power by some dominant, privileged minority. Some matters are very difficult inherently, but there are also crucial issues – war and peace being the most obvious – that are patently simple, and it is quite obvious what is necessary to keep our civilization from destroying itself.

Balancing the tensions of ideals and experiences

There is an element of ambiguity in every philosophical position and also in every political act, but people frequently must make important political decisions lest obvious evils triumph because of human apathy. Patient reasoning is very often not possible, and this is even more the case at the present time because philosophical issues have been deferred and we do not have the insight which more rational thought over the past generations would (and should) have produced. Inaction, whatever the reason for it, is also a crucial decision, and it is usually the wrong one. The question today, more than ever before, is survival. But theory has been formulated largely in a vacuum. Wars and wholesale slaughters are scarcely secondary to the way we must perceive social realities and options, for they have defined the past century's history.

We can never wait for ostensible historical laws to unfold before we take action and make critical judgments. History has been far more complicated and tragic, and human foibles will, notwithstanding critical constraints on our choices, play a far greater role than nineteenth-century scribblers and their followers allowed. There is no substitute for constant critical thought and no alternative to action, and there is absolutely no guarantee that generous amounts of either will succeed (or fail) – and we have no rational option but to attempt to apply both. Even granted that some social outcomes are more likely than others, the human experience is full of risks and we confront a variety of social possibilities, ranging from the noble to the deplorable. There is simply no certainty, but we have far fewer chances of righting wrongs and dealing with society's pressing internal and international problems if we are passive and do nothing.

We cannot apply careful, rational reflection nearly so easily when we are compelled to confront surprising emergencies. We often are forced to make hasty judgments as existential choices. Wars produce revolutions and total social breakdowns, and people must often relate to and accept options that later seem abhorrent. Ideals, even specious ones, are crucial to the success of innumerable causes and motivate people to essential sacrifices which also make success possible. Revolutionary and chiliastic religious morality that evoke individual sacrifices and certainly have been crucial in affecting historical changes, and we can cite countless examples, ranging from China and Vietnam in the 1950s and 1960s to Afghanistan and jihads in the early twenty-first century. Ideas are often very influential and causal because they offer those who believe them scope for idealism and action even when there is neither intellectual nor factual justification for them – which is usually the case. And their political premises, which deal with the efficacy of all they do, is frequently mythical – and false – and their sacrifices are ultimately for naught. This was surely the case with Bolshevism and other socialist currents. Success was often due largely to objective forces interacting with mobilizing illusions and myths. We should not divorce ideas from the practices of their followers, much less exonerate a doctrine that is erroneous simply because it evokes essential actions. We cannot destroy old myths, from religion to economic theory, by creating new ones. A cause that is undermined by a reasonable respect for facts is a false one, utilitarian or not. Social theory should be translated into a basis for praxis, certainly if it is to be of more than academic interest, but it must also try to be truthful and not be simply functional and another variety of false consciousness. Unfortunately, all-too-many social theories, both critical and otherwise, have been articulated in an accidental, sloppy fashion. There is a great deal wasted time to be made up, both in terms of the way ideas are formulated and the way they are implemented and tested.

In the last analysis, the best defense of a good cause is truth, and a cause that cannot bear the weight of serious analyses is not worthwhile and perhaps dangerous also. We have every incentive to avoid deluding ourselves, and to prevent this from occurring we must have intellectual freedom and encourage critical inquiry. The only way to avoid cynicism and depoliticization, which the denial of reality produces, is the truth. By this I mean the unsparing critical assessment of the mainstream's myths as well as those fantasies its critics propound – as they often, with great naivety, do. We must build contingency into our basic approach even when the ends we want to attain reflect our desires. Certain issues – war and peace are the most notable but scarcely the only example – long ago ceased to be subjectively motivated capricious goals. There is a logic to some objectives dictated by the process of reason, and the folly of war is one of them. But any cause that requires illusions and the suspension of critical reasoning, whether they involve the political process or agreeable myths regarding the working class, iron laws of any sort, and the like, is too fragile to deserve our allegiance.

At this juncture of human history we desperately need both a critical method and social ideals appropriate for the multiple crises and challenges we face. For we now stand intellectually and organizationally sorely wanting after attempting to confront modern civilization with the ideas of the eighteenth and nineteenth centuries, and there is an immense amount to do.

5 Capitalist realities

Economic development, the state, and the myths of the market

What kind of world do we live in, and what is the relation of reality to theory and social thought? The purpose of this chapter and the one that follows is to give a broad outline of what we confront in both understanding the world we live in and changing it.

The economic theory that today dominates the conventional wisdom of politicians and establishment economists alike is the product of Adam Smith and British and Germanic writers of the late eighteenth and early nineteenth centuries. It confuses the economists' benign predilections for the way people *should* behave with what they actually *do*, as if men and women's motivations are utterly calculable and immune to greed, group influence, or illusions and ignorance. Even worse, it is wholly oblivious to politics and states, for politicians are often decisive to who wins and loses in the economy. Its appeals are mainly to intellectuals who cherish nineteenth-century zeitgeists, and it is still conventional wisdom in economics despite the fact that most economic historians have shown it to be pure mythology. Marxism incorporated many of its crucial premises.

Liberal economic theory, in the anti-statist free market sense, is used as an argument against anyone advocating social priorities that would hurt those who now benefit most from the status quo, but it in no way describes how economies operate in practice. In the real world, most business people are practical individuals who deplore the market whenever it means price competition. Over the course of time, they have resorted to political means to avoid competition or created alliances with potential rivals to control prices and output, embarked on mergers, and more: when one course failed to attain their goals of stability, they switched to other means. Business people in the United States and other nations who have had the time to read the theory have always regarded it as an academic exuberance, quaint but irrelevant. Pragmatism toward politics on behalf of profits has provided the only consistency of their actions. At best, business people possess a few banal sentiments formulated well over a century ago but they lack doctrinal coherence, and have relied only on an opportunism of ideas – theory has always been unrelated to how the system really operates.

The political context in which all economies function differs from nation to nation but is usually decisive in economic success and development in most of them. The very few efforts by business people to conceptualize the ways in which state's affect how an economy operates are full of inconsistencies; they are utterly pragmatic. Success is due to the facts – making money, ruling societies, objectives and priorities that are accepted – and the ideas underlying them are ill-defined, vague shibboleths that are unable to explain the form or logic of their actions. The function of ideas, such as they are, is to give the status quo a moral patina. In large part because of the analytic deficiencies of the status quo's opponents, these apologias have been successful. The credo evolving around the notion of "market capitalism" is stronger today than ever – but its believers ignore history entirely.

The failure of Marxism was in important part due to its dependence on Ricardo and the laissez-faire analytic tradition, with its impersonal assumptions about economics and human behavior. The crisis of Left thought has been matched by that on the Right, in large part because of their many common intellectual assumptions. Capitalism's institutional success and power has given the Right a great deal of room for maneuver and plenty of adherents but today it too suffers from an immense theoretical void and it has no methods or ideas with which to confront and find solutions for the continuous new problems of reality.

The capitalists' fatal dilemma is that they also have responsibility for managing the existing system and their analytic misconceptions constantly prevent their doing so effectively. One consequence of their myopia is both instability and, at least sometimes, financial loss. Economic practice in virtually all nations has not been the result of coherent ideologies or strategies but rather of incremental actions, many designed for immediate political ends, which are linked together and justified in ideological terms – the "market," "economic freedom," and the like. The real system is the sum of its parts, whose only cohesion is power in one or another form, whether political or economic. Almost nowhere can economies be explained or understood in the systematic ideological terms that most professors formulate. In the twenty-first century we lack a conception of an operational economic system that has no real coherence other than its own priorities, privileges, and power. There is a theoretical impasse on all sides of crucial issues, on economics and much else, and we must not allow it to confuse or mislead our perceptions.

States and economics

Economic historians have reached a broad consensus on how economies actually evolved. States have always played crucial, often decisive roles in economic development, especially where the distinction between public and private property has been blurred, and the purely market forces that laissez-faire theorists enunciate have rarely determined the outcome of economic development. Both the speed and direction of growth and change have been profoundly affected by governments, some places more than others and these differences are important, but it suffices to say that the political process in economic development has always been significant – and very often critical. The roles the state plays are variable, depending on the time, place, and options available to those with political influence and their economic problems at a given moment. But in most, if not all, developed and developing nations the state has been a source of capital, policy guidance, regulations, and innumerable other vital functions. There is simply no economic theory that assigns the political system the importance it deserves. Marxists scarcely intended to become rationalizers of what is eclectic opportunism in economic development, but functionally they performed the same role as laissez-faire theorists by making capitalism out to be a predictable and impersonal system in which the state played no central part.

Wars have greatly accelerated and intensified the state's economic role, and governments in most large nations of Europe, North America, Asia, and elsewhere played crucial economic functions before and after the bloody conflicts that have largely defined the modern historical experience. Everywhere, to a more or lesser extent, politics and economics have been inextricably intertwined and states manage and affect how economies function – and who is rewarded most. Whatever the academic "laws" of economics and politics, the way history evolves in practice is far better understood with instrumental analyses of social options – above all the often changing priorities and identities of those who govern the crucial political and economic institutions in every nation.[1]

The social composition and characteristics of capitalist classes is exceedingly diverse and there is no single pattern which explains the social basis of success in capitalism. The notion of a simple buyer and seller and a market in a vacuum is an utterly misleading ideological myth. In some nations family and social networks are crucial, and there are castes, clientelism, combinations of these, and the like. In all of these situations the state is more or less important – subsidies, policy guidance, regulation are but a few areas in which it plays critical roles – but it is integral to the entire economic system in countless, if not all, nations. The United States is an excellent example of how vital these informal family and elite roles were in economic development. The Boston-area social elite was crucial in innumerable areas of American economic growth, as were socially marginal entrepreneurs also. East and Central Europe, where Jews were important, is yet another case. In both places and many others as well, those who had access to banks and capital which family and friends controlled had a critical head-start. These are often – but not always – decisive. There is simply no adequate theoretical structure which explains capitalism in all its dimensions, social, political, as well as economic, in large part because of the dominance of market theories and the devotion of its critics to Marxist economism derived in large part from capitalist ideologues.[2]

The rationale for the state's vital role in the economy is far more often pragmatic rather than ideological in most of the leading industrial economies. The ideological myths that were subsequently articulated were in part to restrict the state's activity whenever it fell under the influence of those hostile to existing elites. Most business people seek to avoid competition, whether by voluntary or political means – or both. Their task is made much simpler because politicians need money to win elections and cooperating with business is the best, sometimes the only way of getting it. Although many other factors enter the picture, including a milieu which posits that the interests of business are to be cherished by all state institutions, this financial lubricant has been consistently crucial to the way – and for whom – the economy operates in practice as opposed to theory. Even many original classical theorists tailored their doctrines freely to allow innumerable exceptions for the state to play whatever interventionist roles that elements of the wealthier classes needed or desired, and ideological consistency never inhibited them when the interests of the rich were involved. The question is not the state's role in the economy but rather on whose behalf it will act, and even on the relatively infrequent occasions when it stays out of the economy, some interests gain thereby. When powerful constituencies have economic problems, political intervention on their behalf is more than likely. Economics never evolves in a vacuum, and it is the larger social system and its structure, above all the way existing power affects political mechanisms, that determines the way states behave.[3]

It is impossible to recount the sheer diversity of world history in a short book, but the broad outlines of some crucial national examples will accurately convey a sense of reality.

No nation exceeds the United States in rewriting its own history and in its profound misperception of how and why it became an economic colossus. From its colonial inception in 1620, the United States' economic development was always suffused with political intervention and regulation on behalf of the wealthier population. Europe's nations, of course, all present different cases, but on the whole they pursued a protectionist tariff policy between 1830 and 1844 to 1846, were much more liberal over the next three decades, and moved back to tariff protection from 1877 to 1892, when they embarked upon an even stronger protectionist policy until 1913. Growth, especially of industry, was highest during protectionist periods. Even their exports remained substantial throughout these high tariff years, although not as strong as during the period 1844 to 1860.[4]

But although Europe's economies developed without applying the free trade and open market dogmas that the United States, the IMF, and the World Trade Organization (WTO) advocate today, Europe was always considerably less protectionist than the United States. From 1820 to 1913 – with 1846 to 1861 being a period of more restrained protection – the United States usually had far higher tariff protection for its manufacturing industries than European and other developed countries, and even President Woodrow Wilson's classic liberal ideology in 1913 left US duties on manufactured goods considerably higher than other nations. Only after 1933, when it was already the world's leading economic power, did the United States actually lower its tariffs partially and begin to conform to the policies it has since consistently advocated for others.[5]

The overarching policy of state encouragement of industrialization meant that a great deal of the primary capital for economic development, both in the United States, Europe, and Asia, came from the state and public funding. In the United States, state, local, and federal aid to railroad and canal construction, in the form of immense land grants or capital contributions and subsidies, was of critical importance, especially before 1861. In the South, 55 percent of the cost of all railroad construction prior to 1861 came from public sources, and combined state and local government spending before the Civil War was about $425 million on internal improvements, essentially transport. Federal aid to railroads after 1861 was principally in the form of land grants – well over 100 million acres – and Texas alone allocated another 27 million acres to railroads. Local, state, and federal grants after 1860 – most with few, if any conditions attached – came to about $335 million. Mercantilism, not laissez faire, inspired American politicians throughout the nineteenth century.[6]

In Europe, Japan, and elsewhere, governments played crucial roles in the early industrialization process. Their intervention took many forms, ranging from the actual supply of capital to the manipulation of the banking system to assure that adequate credit was available to entrepreneurs. Theories were far less consequential than pragmatic politicians, most of whom nonetheless also adhered to the myths of free markets. But practice had scant formal ideological justifications, and political leaders generally responded to interests rather than ideas, and to those who had political power and gained the most from the state's actions. Politicians were generally sensitive to bankers and industrialists who favored protection of domestic markets, and many wished to see their economies develop, if only for military reasons.

In France the government had earlier been crucial in building canals and roads, and provided nearly half the capital before 1848 to triple the railroad track mileage. Thereafter, essentially private interests took charge of the expansion of railroads. But Napoleon III and his successors selectively manipulated both the tariff (which was still far higher in 1913 than most of the rest of Europe), credit, and the banking systems to provide a vital impulse to railroad construction, public works of every variety, and economic development – thereby modernizing industry. Not only did the French state play an important and often crucial role in the economy before 1914 and during the war, but also after the war both its actions and definition of its function in the economy became even more ambitious.[7]

Russia, essentially for military reasons, from 1880 to 1914 created an internal demand for the steel and machinery essential for government-sponsored railroad construction. Directly and indirectly, the state supplied these industries with investments. In Belgium the government employed credit banks and its own resources to aid economic development, above all during 1830 to 1850, but when private investors refused to take risks it stepped into the vacuum. In Germany, which was not unified until 1871 and therefore different than its European neighbors, the banks initially guided economic growth and especially sought to minimize competition, leading to the early formation of cartels. By and large, periods of war excepted, the relationship of the German state to the economy before 1939, to quote one economic historian, was "always close, but never close enough to speak of an 'interventionist state'."[8] But politicians sought in various ways to advance the interests of industrialists and bankers. Prussia's Silesian province developed a modern iron and coal industry because the state undertook the basic responsibility, beginning as early as the eighteenth century and lasting in many ways throughout the next one too; it also controlled most lead mining and smelting. Military considerations were its foremost justification, and it also invested – as did other German states – in the Saar. The state set the technical standards for private firms, which until 1864 had to accept directors the state nominated.

In Australia, the government's role in capital formation between 1861 and 1900 – above all railroads and public works of every sort – and especially migration, was overwhelming. In Canada, the state – whether provincial or federal – was decisive in all domains, the railroads being only one, and a high tariff policy encouraged the growth of manufacturing.[9]

There is a virtual consensus on the state's role in Japanese economic development and the crucial part it played in the remarkable rise of that country to its present economic power. The government enacted the fiscal and organizational measures to weave together the quasi-feudal regions into an integrated nation, playing the decisive role in making available the capital essential for economic development. It fostered the emergence of an entrepreneurial class able to transcend the localisms and fragmented nature of Japan's initial industrialization and it radically modified the educational system so that its people would excel in science and industry. For principally military reasons, Japan's political elite before 1945 stimulated development rather than playing an independent role in the economy. It often sold off its crucial economic holdings to private capitalists ready to continue its pioneering development role – leading over time to the growing integration of business and politics.

The government provided the initial capital for Japan's railroad construction in the latter part of the nineteenth century until private investors were ready to take it over, and a similar pattern occurred in manufacturing and especially in those industries most in need of modern technology. From 1892 to 1940, the government share of domestic capital formation was never less than 40 percent but usually well over half. The net effect of its efforts was to make possible Japanese imperialism. This meant the emergence of a handful of industrial, financial, and commercial conglomerates – the *zaibatsus* – capable of organizing the once decentralized, backward economy for modern economic life.

After 1945, however, the interaction between the Japanese state and large companies continued and economic power remained concentrated, albeit more subtly as the state took over many of the functions once performed by the *zaibatsus* directly. Six large banks coordinated what had been the *zaibatsus'* commercial and industrial components. Major firms in various industries now had the government regulate output and competition that otherwise might escape their control. The Ministry of Economy, Trade, and Industry (MITI), operating through about 300 consultative committees, planned and prioritized sector goals and cajoled, exhorted, and otherwise brought reticent companies into line. Quotas and restrictions, subsidized loans, bank credits, and much else played a role in rationalizing and sometimes cartelizing whole industries. The high technology sectors were especially encouraged. While education became more important for success in this context, and new firms became part of the concentrated corporate world, clientelism and family ties still mattered. The interaction between the business and political elites existed on many levels, including the election of a significant minority of business people among the Liberal-Democratic Party members of the House of Representatives. Above all, much of the money to lubricate politics came from business, assuring private control over an activist political structure.[10]

In the rest of Asia, above all those nations like South Korea and Taiwan that industrialized rapidly after 1950, in no place and at no time did experiences confirm the economic theories that, then and now, hold sway over most of the professorate and politicians – and comprise the litany of the "Washington consensus" that the IMF, World Bank, and most international economic organizations propagate. State-led economic development, and access to US aid donated to wage the Cold War in the 1950s, was crucial in both these nations. In South Korea there was from the inception an integrated, symbiotic interdependence between the state political elites and big business and key families, although at the same time a great deal of emphasis and financial support was given to education, providing labor skills that were crucial to economic growth. The result was the extreme concentration of assets and exports in the hands of a small number of diversified, heavily indebted business groups – "chaebols." The "market" played only a scant role, and development priorities, high tariffs, and subsidies were decisive in South Korea, Taiwan, as well as Japan. There was much cronyism and corruption but it was highly effective, at least insofar as growth targets of the favored designated high technology industries were concerned. As a result, today Japan and South Korea have the world's most successful automotive industry. South Korea resembled more the Japanese model, with state priorities imposed on private firms (and easy credits for those that cooperated and a state-guaranteed corporate bond market), yet there were also state-owned firms, many of which were subsequently transferred to private interests at bargain prices. Since the mid-1980s this tight relationship loosened in some important regards and diminished business susceptibility to government regulations, partially under pressure from Washington, the IMF, and similar foreign bodies but also because major Korean interests wanted specific changes that allowed them to tap foreign financial resources; business still had much to gain from the state and it remained crucial. But as the crisis of 1997 revealed, the South Korean government failed to anticipate the risks that deregulation might create. In the three years after the regional financial crisis began in late 1997, the government made available more than $130 billion to banks and investment trusts in straits. South Korea, however, was behind China, Japan, and Indonesia in injecting money into troubled banks after 1997, and at least a half-trillion dollars of government funds were used in the region to rescue private interests. In the end, the corporate system in South Korea resembled its pre-crisis structure.[11]

In Taiwan, the state's role was highly clientelist and designed to strengthen the power of the ruling party, the KMT. Later, business interests began to play a more independent and influential role. But the state retained a central role in all aspects of economic life, had a monopoly – or close to one – in many activities normally privately owned in Europe, and it was only in the late 1980s that the assets of the top 500 private companies exceeded that of the state-owned sector; Taiwan's exemplary development was linked directly to the government's role. And in both South Korea and Taiwan, state-owned firms and strong government protection of domestic companies prevented foreign firms from controlling heavy industries.[12]

Elsewhere, states have pursued whatever policies are essential to economic development, principally for the benefit of local elites. Some were led largely by self-confident technocrats who, as in Mexico or Brazil, were relatively honest, but in East Asia – Indonesia and the Philippines are good examples – or much of Africa, the so-called state economic strategists were often political accumulators directly or indirectly (often working through their family members or cronies) who gain rewards in the form of kickbacks and corruption. Clientelism is crucial in the economic process everywhere, Asia especially. They may begin as military officers or civil bureaucrats, but they end in much the same way – corruptionists. They are linked to strategically placed groups, but specific national situations are often too complex to sum up and important nuances are lost because military officers sometimes perform different functions in different nations. But notwithstanding important distinctions, accumulation via political means and decisions exists in many developing nations at various times, if not always, just as it has existed in developed nations for many decades. Some elites are ideologically nationalist, although ideas tend to play an ever-smaller role everywhere, but many become more pragmatic and essentially are corrupted in varying degrees. Who has political power frequently determines who wins or loses in the economic process and gets access to state resources in various forms – and becomes rich.

In Latin America, to quote a sociologist who subsequently became Brazil's president, "[t]he private sector was not excluded from economies where state participation was preponderant, nor was the public sector absent in the initial stage of industrialization, even in countries of liberal tradition."[13]

Import-substitution policies helped both the private sectors and those basic industries, as in Brazil, where the government held 32 percent of all assets in the top 300 corporations in 1974. Indeed, local capitalists in Brazil and elsewhere often welcomed costly and frequently uneconomical state investments in steel, oil refineries, and electrical power, allowing them to produce their own goods more cheaply and thereby to sell to a domestic market. And taxation of the masses, again as in Brazil's case, generated much of the capital for state-funded economic development and the basic infrastructure. But as economies evolved so too did the needs and demands of private interests, which were overwhelmingly pragmatic and non-ideological: their only consistency was their desire to make money, and this they could do better with selective state involvement in their economies. It was precisely when the Latin American nations abandoned autarchy and linked their trade to each other, making crisis in one of the larger countries events that affected all of them, or – in accordance with the IMF's and Washington's desires – geared more of their trade to the United States, Europe, and East Asia, that their economies became most unstable.

Capitalism virtually everywhere has been intimately linked to politics, an overriding reality for which the IMF and classical and Marxist economists ✓ simply have no theoretical explanation. Alexander Gerschenkron's thesis that "The more backward a country's economy, the greater was the part played by special institutional factors designed to increase supply of capital to the nascent industries," describes the great variations that occurred, because all nations are backward at some point and seek to develop.[14] There are many forms and patterns of economic development, and politics and the state have played and continue to play a dominant role in most nations. In countless cases, men and women of affairs – by instinct problem-solvers who disdain all ideologies – favor the state providing answers to problems if necessary, and often they are the first to advocate properly tailored government intervention. The role of governments in the economy since 1929 has become greater in most countries, taxes along with it, and the real gross domestic product (GDP) per capita has grown with it. In Organization for Economic Cooperation and Development (OECD) member nations the ratio of taxes to national income has increased significantly since 1970 and per capita GDP has gone up even more. Exact causes of growth are difficult to estimate and vary by nation, but no one can show that a smaller government role accelerates it, as conservatives argue.[15]

There are many kinds of experiences, and class structures are rarely static; major changes occur even in the most advanced industrial capitalist nations. Technological or economic innovations may have important consequences for the status quo. Who has political power at any time, and who gains advantages from it, remains absolutely crucial – and often decisive in most developing nations. Whether or not political power precedes economic accumulation, and the extent of this symbiosis, differs from country to country over time, but it is a central theme in economic development that only confirms the decisive role of politics and the state historically. There are countless examples of regulation and protectionism emerging because politically well-placed business people sought it – and the principle has governed economic development in most, if not close to all, nations. There is scant theory to describe it.

Wars and economies

Wars occur frequently and define the realities of the human experience. War telescopes social and economic processes in many nations but our conceptual and theoretical equipment ignores them entirely. Rational social analyses should be prepared to deal with all phases in the evolution of societies; wars accelerate and often transform them, requiring fresh analytic notions – which we simply do not have. Everything can be affected and altered, often dramatically: existing class structures and internal social orders involving the masses, elites, or both, and all aspects of economic development.

The way a nation organizes itself during wartime reflects the nature of its entire social system and those forces, ranging from its class structure to its intellectual processes, that define its institutional life. This overriding fact also affects, usually decisively, which businesses gain most from the immense increase in government expenditures inherent in the process of making war. War organizations rarely transcend the influence of dominant elites and factions in the power structure to attain a more efficient, disinterested way of managing hostilities. Power mediates how nations fight wars.

In practice, neither officers nor civilians in charge of war organizations had the ability or the objectivity for waging the intense, protracted conflict as efficiently as the inherently irrational enterprise demanded. Officers in France, Russia, and Germany could help initiate wars but soon revealed their incapacity to deliver the quick victories they usually promised, much less manage the incredible logistical complexities that wars have imposed since the end of the nineteenth century. Krupp in Germany during World War One, for example, exploited its close relationship to the monarchy to restrict the army's choice of artillery to arms it wished to sell, leaving it less modern than what was then possible. The German army's railroad department – crucial to its plan for fighting on fronts both in the east and west – was incapable of mastering all the technical challenges involved, partly because of its intense desire to maintain the elitist social composition of its senior officers. Industrialists and managers drawn from heavy- and capital-intensive industries, those most favoring cartels able to fix prices and output, soon played a decisive role in Germany. In the United States, after July 1917 business people drawn mainly from anti-competitive large corporations, operating both formally and informally through their trade associations, were in charge of the War Industries Board's procurement. France from the inception of the conflict worked through the Comité des Forges, which the major metal firms dominated and which took charge of arms production. The Comité used state funds to import metals and allocate arms contracts; in the decade after the war ended, the capital the state provided was important to the expansion and modernization of French industry – much of it destroyed during the war itself. This precedent set the pattern of economic *dirigisme* that was to guide France after 1945 as well. In the United Kingdom, the inability of the War Office and generals to overcome bottlenecks in arms and munitions production led to business people being assigned increasing responsibility for ending chronic shortages and confusion.

Business people dominated the war organizations of all the major combatants during 1914 to 1918 and they saw no conflict between high profits for their constituencies and patriotism. This crucial precedent became the fundamental way the modern US and many West European economies have been organized for the protracted tension that has characterized modern history since 1914. But business mastery of the material foundations of war was very largely the consequence of its decisive political power, power which the endemic incapacity of officers to manage increasingly complex technology only reinforced. In such a vacuum, it was entirely predictable that wars would become a means of capital accumulation for well-placed interests. World War Two greatly enriched and expanded their power; despite the military's pretensions, only business people had the minimum abilities to confront the war's decisive organizational and economic problems.

In the United States, men recruited from the giant firms dominated all sectors of the war-mobilization structure; when the War Production Board (WPB) was created in January 1942, some 1000 of its key executives were paid by their employers rather than by the government. Two-thirds of the $175 billion in prime contracts the WPB issued over four years went to 100 corporations, and only ten of these received 30 percent of the total. And, of course, half of the $26 billion in new plant – a sum equal to two-thirds of the cost of all manufacturing facilities built before 1939 – were operated by 25 corporations; over three-quarters of this new capacity was usable after the war ended, and 250 corporations acquired over two-thirds of it at bargain "war surplus" rates.

In Japan, with its military's near-absolute power and pretensions, the *zaibatsus* that dominated industry and finance exploited their substantial and quickly growing leverage to employ government sanctions to impose their interests upon recalcitrant firms. Officers defined Japan's imperialist goals but were incapable of managing the economy. By the spring of 1943 the largest businesses were in charge of economic mobilization and increasing their power in the process. It was mainly these firms that reemerged as the economically most important after the war.

Germany was no exception to the virtual rule that wars become an opportunity for specific interests to prosper – in this case, both local Nazi leaders with fiefdoms but especially the very same industrialists who commanded industry before Hitler's accession in 1933. Hitler understood from Germany's soldiers' and workers' revolts of 1917 to 1918 that the political risks of waging total, protracted war were too great, and his war organization was anything but efficient. Civilian production was sustained, but he also cherished the vain hope that the conquered European economy would fill the demand for civilian goods. Hitler's military had less control over arms output than was the case in any of the other major warring nations. German business people pursued their own self-aggrandizing interests and – complaints notwithstanding – they exploited the opportunities that Nazi conquests provided. After 1936, essentially self-regulating cartels made crucial price and accounting decisions which gave big business much more extensive powers over purely economic, non-ideological questions, spreading their control into previously non-cartelized economic activities.

This reliance on business people has not altered the dominant reality that those who have guided and run the world since the end of the nineteenth century have not, in the last analysis, known what they were doing or understood the consequences of their policies and actions. Their avarice and erroneous sense of power have plunged their nations into deeper troubles. For successive wars have proved to be the greatest threat of all to established orders, and brought many down when there was scant chance of purely economic factors, much less organized political opposition, ever doing so.[16]

The United States: government to the fore

This synthesis of private interest and political power has been decisive in the United States. It has expressed itself in countless ways, ranging from military spending to immense subsidies for privileged private interests for everything from oil-rigs to cotton and dairy products; interest rates or central bank purchases of the financial assets of troubled banks and financial institutions have historically – in the United States and increasingly in West Europe – been determined by the needs of banks, investors, and a tiny but very wealthy minority.

Several estimates provide the general parameters for comprehending the state's role in the United States since it supplied much of the total capital essential to economic growth in the nineteenth century. The concept of total capital, which plays no role in classical economic theory and is today rarely acknowledged in conventional wisdom, has been with us for a half-century and is now irrefutably documented as a decisive element of economic development. To cite but one example, Edward F. Denison's detailed explanation of American economic expansion in the period 1929 to 1969 attributes the sources of growth to various overlapping factors, and public capital was crucial – it was responsible for roughly half of the gains during this 40-year period. Advances in technological, managerial, and organizational knowledge accounted for slightly less than one-third of the expansion during 1929 to 1969. Excluding education, the increase in labor productivity accounted for 29 percent of 1929 to 1969 growth and capital investment about 16 percent. Both are affected by public tax rules. Education, which augmented skills greatly, accounted for 14 percent, while improved resource allocation accounted for one-tenth of the advances in national income from 1929 to 1969. Indeed, it is precisely in literacy, which is to say public expenses in education, that the United States' historical lead over Europe is so striking.

Recent estimates based on more complete data corroborate this general pattern. Ignoring military and defense expenditures entirely, from 1925 to 1988 the stock of public capital amounted to 46 percent of the value of private capital, and states and regions that had greater publicly funded infrastructure grew more quickly than those that did not.[17]

When we consider all of the other factors that play a role in the modern economy, including military outlays, it becomes even more obvious that the relationship between political power and the economy is greater than these numbers suggest. Whatever the important national distinctions or the many ways it is expressed, the general rule remains that all economies have a crucial, often decisive political dimension. To deal with one without the other misses vital realities.

In the US case, there were peacetime precedents going back to the beginning of the twentieth century, when the federal government's regulatory mechanisms were both modernized (in the case of railroads) or created (as with banking and industry). Woodrow Wilson's Administration gave foreign trade a much higher priority than its predecessors, producing an integrated business–government relationship that gave the state a dominant role in mobilizing US resources for overseas expansion – a role it has retained since then. Its consistent desire to help protect business interests from the perils of competition, over-expansion, poor profits, and the like, was nearly always the principal motivation of government measures to regulate the economy, even though it nominally cited an amorphous "public interest" as justification for its actions. But its efforts were thwarted by its consistant inability to create mechanisms that actually solved the problems it set out to eliminate. Even under Franklin Roosevelt's "New Deal," which came to power just as there was unusually widespread public awareness of monopolistic and oligopolistic price fixing and the way the very absence of market price competition retarded economic recovery, his National Recovery Administration (NRA) allowed precisely this kind of price rigging – only to abandon it four years later for an ostensible return to competition. The Supreme Court decisions abolishing NRA practices were not the basic cause of his policy change but provided a convenient rationale for it. In the end, both policies failed to produce an economic revival, but only confirmed the confusion that emerges at the highest levels when the system's procompetitive ideological tenets clash with concrete business interests.[18]

Even after the 1960s, when the role of the state's bureaucracies in protecting various industries became too patently evident to be denied, so-called efforts to deregulate several of them fell upon political shoals, only revealing the extent to which regulation had become a tool of the affected firms – as well as a number of unions that shared goals with them – to control competition and maintain profits. Where industries were divided, as with airlines, alterations were made that satisfied only some constituencies, but where they were united and politically able, as with trucking, they defined the direction and substance of change. But whatever these modifications, consumers only infrequently benefited from them. From the beginning of the twentieth century to the present, the government's central role in employing regulation to create a political economy designed to assure stability with profitability for numerous American industries, above all banking and finance, has only altered somewhat in form but not in substance.

There is the far better known role of Congressional pork-barreling, which is expressed in many ways, ranging from the Army Corps of Engineers' extensive construction projects to the Pentagon budget – the latter comprising everything from procurement of ultra-sophisticated weapons (based on the erroneous premise that firepower can win political friends abroad as well as at home) to bases located in the United States. But politicians must be elected, campaigns are expensive, and they have powerful rich constituents with interests whose support is vital. In the case of the Engineers, districts with members of Congress on public works committees receive, by far, a disproportionate share of the Engineers' budgets. Coalitions in Congress, often linked only by single issues such as contracts or bases, become more decisive than nominal party designations and allow Executive bureaucrats far greater scope for getting budget requests approved.

Constant federal efforts could not make capitalism stable and profitable. Economic forecasting – and actions and policies based upon them – both before and after World War Two and down to the very present, proved too inaccurate to be useful, and were often counterproductive. The desire of the state to introduce rational management, which crucial segments of the business community have always advocated and endorsed, cannot be confused with its ability to actually do so in practice, for no sooner than it resolves some problems it encounters yet others. The greatest single error in assessing the contemporary economic and social structure, one nominal Leftists commit more often than others, is to assume that systems with such diverse political, economic, and ideological components are capable of being more or less rationally managed. They cannot. But by any measure one employs, and even granting the extent to which its intentions have been frustrated, the synthesis of political power and private interests has occurred relentlessly and it has been the only way that the immense federal budget, with its monumental deficits, is approved.[19]

Ideologically, Washington favors the "market economy" and is against other nations giving subsidies or owning sectors of their economies. It will go to quixotic lengths to get countries or regions to introduce "free trade" and privatize such vital sectors as oil. It has an essentially religious faith in the alleged virtues of this doctrine, but in practice it excludes the goods of nations that compete with those many American producers who have allies in

Congress and who create barriers against free imports. The federal government will subsidize vast, politically well-placed economic sectors – ranging from military-equipment producers to big agricultural interests and lower taxes on the wealthy – and it will run up huge trade and budget deficits to do so, thereby ignoring its own litany of a balanced-budget and fiscal prudence it demands of other nations. Living with such extreme contradictions, where the rhetoric that passes as ideology is in utter conflict with the practice, is simply integral to the cavalier, inconsistent, and opportunistic manner that the United States has formulated its credo since the middle of the nineteenth century.

The military budget, now approximately $500 billion annually, is the largest and most enduring dimension of the integration of the state and private sectors but it is scarcely the only one. The Pentagon's contracts, or its sales of weapons overseas, are often linked to the electoral cycle – the first Bush Administration's announcement of the massive sale of hitherto-blocked advanced tactical aircraft in September 1992, just before the presidential election, is typical of the way the military budget is used as a spur to economic activity and to obtain votes. Universities, but especially business, depend on the federal government for funding for the technological research and development which has been so crucial to American industry's successes in the world economy since 1945. Firms that do not work for the military have significantly lower profits on their investments because they do not have access to government-funded facilities. Much the same is the case in other nations.

A much-publicized example of this intimate but typical relationship of the state to private business is the construction and sales of long-distance aircraft, involving Boeing in the United States and Airbus in Europe. Boeing, with active assistance and funding from US government, accused the European governments of actively subsidizing the Airbus's development and displacing Boeing from the lucrative market for large long-distance aircraft – all of which is true. But in the process it revealed the extent to which Boeing, which does over half of its business with the US government, like most military producers, also relies on political manipulation and lobbying to obtain contracts, including for weapons and equipment that often do not work in the ways promised or are even utterly dysfunctional. Boeing placed tens of millions of dollars in venture capital and investment funds run by high Pentagon advisers, it hired – among many others – key Pentagon acquisition personnel and their family (occasionally these are publicized, as with its $23.5 billion refueling tanker order during 2001 to 2003) who were supposed to defend the government's interest when dealing with the company, and the like. The tanker deal was "a bailout for Boeing" in the opinion of some Pentagon officials.[20] It has donated heavily, as have all the major defense contractors, to the campaign chests of strategic politicians and engaged in the usual lobbying, from the President downwards. Boeing also received huge subsidies in the form of tax breaks from the state of Washington and enormous tax advantages and direct subsidies from the US government.

Directly and indirectly, most large military contractors in the United States are subsidized. The Pentagon found many decades ago that canceling highly expensive and technically dubious weapons is politically too difficult, and it occurs far less than warranted, producing immense cost overruns and government deficits. The joint strike fighter (JSF) plane has been in the works for two decades and will ultimately cost at least $200 billion, making it the most expensive military project in history. The United States will pay 89 percent of its cost. The problem, apart from numerous technical shortcomings, is that the enemy for whom it was designed, the Soviet Union, no longer exists. Anemic Pentagon efforts to review these and similar costly programs have met powerful and effective resistance from House and Senate members of states that will lose from cut-backs. Lobbyists, hired at large fees and often their former colleagues or related to key members of Congress, make crucial differences in getting contracts. Budget cuts fall on programs – like public housing and medical care – for the poor, who have no political clout.

The Iraq War, like all wars, created an opportunity for immense and lucrative contracts, and the entire process of spending tens of billions in Iraqi and American funds was eventually carefully investigated by official US and other agencies. They all reached identical conclusions: profits were enormous, as was corruption, and the politically well placed – President Bush's younger brother Neil was the most prominent – were at the heart of the entire sordid episode.[21] But wars are hardly predictable events. Systemic advantages for this elite, ultimately, depend largely on huge arms expenditures and regulation more generally.

The market for military equipment is enormous and largely closed to foreign competitors, in part because the Pentagon decided long ago to maintain a huge domestic arms industry. Historically, the mainstay of US foreign trade was farm products, but these are now in deficit, and arms exports are increasingly crucial to US trade balances. Occasionally the United States' closest allies, like the United Kingdom, complain about the complex regulations which exclude their goods, but nothing is changed. On the contrary, Carlyle, a venture capital firm that manages over $18 billion in assets, hires such foreign luminaries as the former British prime minister John Major, the former Philippines president, many retired senior American cabinet officials, and the first President Bush to help Carlyle pry open foreign markets for defense firms in which it has an interest.[22]

The point is not that military technology be effective but that it should be costly, the more expensive the better for arms contractors. To take one example of the Pentagon's profoundly flawed mentality, no one even thought about the fact that the American military would require water in dry areas; in the Iraq War beginning March 2003 much of the water had to be trucked hundreds of kilometers from Kuwait over dangerous roads – comprising 30 percent of the weight of what was transported. Plans to create "Star Wars" systems and defenses against missiles have existed since the 1980s; they have already consumed $130 billion and are projected to cost $53 billion more from fiscal 2005 through 2011. Along with the JSF, it is the highest cost weapons system the Pentagon has ever undertaken and it has failed most of its tests, the latest being an $85 million trial at the end of 2004. The Central Intelligence Agency (CIA), Government Accounting Office, and Rand experts have shown that most potential enemies can easily overcome it even if it operates successfully; it is a spectacular waste of taxpayers' money. Many military planners oppose it; but Lockheed, Boeing, and other aerospace companies – all of whom would go out of business were it not for National Aeronautics and Space Administration (NASA) and Air Force contracts – have managed to keep funds for it flowing. The Pentagon is weaponizing space unilaterally, a process that will only renew the arms race and bring the United States no security. It is very expensive.[23]

The Iraq War, which employed much of the new and futurist technology that Secretary of Defense Donald Rumsfeld believed essential to the Pentagon's "transformation," was a disaster for many of the expensive innovations used there. Sand alone made many weapons impractical if not useless, to mention but one of many surprises. There is far less oversight and competitive bidding for military spending than the vast sums warrant, and this has been true in every war down to the present – the Iraq War, with its widespread overcharges and waste, if not outright theft of significant amounts of cash, being merely typical. But the bonanza for weapons producers that make robotic and similar exotic devices is in fact a subsidy for them, and there is no theory to account for it beyond the incredibly specious assumption that increased firepower and mobility leads to political victories. Numbers vary, but military spending in the United States remained constant throughout the 1990s, after the Soviet Union disappeared, but increased by almost a half since George W. Bush's Administration came to office in 2001.[24]

Subsidizing US capitalism

Subsidies have existed in innumerable forms in the United States for generations, and here I discuss only a few of the countless examples. What they share in common is that the already wealthy gain the most from them. Like most data, there is no consensus on precise figures but there is fundamental agreement on the general impact of the innumerable forms of federal aid to key constituencies. In the case of agriculture, which began receiving various subventions after 1918, by 1963 to 1964 the top one-fifth of the farmers were receiving – at the very least – 51 percent of the total subsidy income, but this is only a very conservative estimate. During 1995 to 2002, 60 percent of the American farmers and ranchers did not collect any of the $114 billion of government subsidies to agriculture, and the top one-tenth of the recipients received 71 percent of all subsidies. Agribusiness has been a major source of donations to the parties – increasingly the Republicans – and in some states it is decisive. The United States exports its wheat, corn, rice, and cotton at far less than the cost of production, causing countries such as China to restrict imports of these commodities – and disputes for the WTO to deal with. The result of American actions was usually to depress the prices for these commodities globally, more than offsetting foreign aid to many nations. In the case of cotton, US production costs are twice the world price but the 25,000 American farmers who received about $4 billion in subsidies in 2004 were far more consequential politically than the 10 million poor African farmers dependent on this crop for their livelihood. The post-2000 Bush Administration initially hoped to halt, if not reverse, this pattern but found that the rich farmers were politically far too powerful in Congress. Cash payments to farmers will increase substantially – one estimate is an additional $123 billion over the six years beginning 2003.[25]

Proportionately, the United States still spends less on farm subsidies than the European Union and others – combined, the OECD nations spent $257 billion in subsidies in 2003 – and export subventions are the rule in many nations. Besides agriculture, the 15 members of the European Union alone gave private companies $73 billion subsidies in 2004, mainly for research, development, and innovations. Nowhere is there a free market in agriculture or industry in the developed nations. Japan, where the farmers have immense political leverage, has protected – in effect, subsidized – domestic agriculture to an extent that pales every other nation save South Korea. Slightly more than one-fifth of gross American farm receipts in 2000 to 2002 came in the form of subsidies, 18 percent in 2003, as opposed to about one-third in the EU and close to 40 percent in 2003. The sums involved are enormous and the examples endless, increasing the price of food in the EU by 44 percent, but farmers are kept on the land when there is no purely economic reason for doing so. And developed nations export subsidized corn, wheat, soybeans, sugar, and other basic crops to low-income countries, often at far below the cost of production, depriving poorer farmers in those lands enormous sums both in domestic and foreign markets; some estimates are anywhere from $100 billion to $180 billion in lost income annually, and even higher – not to mention greater unemployment. Indeed, if the rich nations were to eliminate the barriers to developing nations' agricultural exports, the benefits would be worth about six times their annual assistance to all developing nations. The World Trade Organization, which has become the main arena in which these issues are endlessly debated, has only nibbled at the edges of existing inequities. Given its role in intellectual property transfers and services of importance to the financial interests in developed nations, the WTO is essentially a vehicle for preserving the poorer countries' disadvantages. No theory takes into account how and why the market mechanisms that ideologists describe or, especially, proscribe for others, simply do not exist in the developed nations. Politics plays no role in economic theory, but politics explains reality.

Subsidies to agriculture have increased in the richer nations since the mid-1980s even as developing nations have halved their average tariffs, far more than the developed countries have done, in large part because IMF loan provisos compel them to do so. The United States is a leading violator of free market principles. About half of all its exports by the late 1990s were funneled through offshore foreign sales corporations, which produced about $70 billion in tax breaks annually to giant companies like IBM, General Motors, Boeing, Microsoft, and General Electric in 2002 alone. The WTO at the beginning of 2002 ruled that such rebates were a form of subsidies to exporters but the political vested interests were too great for Washington to abandon the lucrative procedure, replacing it with $145 billion in tax cuts for companies with foreign operations – and in July 2005 the WTO ruled that this too was a subsidy.[26]

But inequitable as it is, agricultural subsidies are only the tip of the iceberg: many others who favor conservative political ideology also have their noses in the trough of government favors. Independent of export subsidies, there are a large variety of other subsidies. The enormous Pentagon budget remains by far the largest source of political favoritism, but the immensely lucrative contracts it gives guarantee easy passage of the military's annual requests. Over 8300 "pork-barrel" projects went into the 13 annual spending bills in 2002, costing one-third more than 2001. President Bush attempted to eliminate some of these subsidies, including reducing the Export-Import Bank's financing authority from $12.6 billion to $8.5 billion in 2002, but he largely failed to overcome what are now entrenched vested interests. Indeed, there were so many American exceptions to WTO rules on free trade and markets, and so much lobbying from politically powerful constituencies, that by the time the Bush Administration came to power in 2001 the United States was moving instead toward bilateral trade accords which sanction its exceptionalism, and hundreds of bilateral trade agreements allowed American business to arrange global trade to suit its own interests – its free trade ideology notwithstanding.

That money shapes tax legislation to the advantage of specific companies or interests is merely standard operating procedure. General Electric (GE) spends more on lobbying both Congress and the executive branch than any firm – $7.5 million in 2003, plus large donations to friendly, strategic congressional candidates. It is widely credited with significantly reducing the taxes on the foreign income of US companies, and from 1994 to 2003 the foreign profits of the six largest pharmaceutical companies, for example, went from 38 to 65 percent of their overall income even though their overseas sales grew a mere 7 percent. The effective tax rate on foreign income was almost halved over that period. Firms like GE have recast the provisions of tax laws, and an armada of lobbyists deals with every issue affecting their clients. Energy companies are among the most generous donors to the campaign funds of senators and House members, and in early 2001 they were given $20 billion in tax breaks and credits over the next decade, plus large amounts for research in nominally pollution-control technologies. A major reason why American firms invest so much abroad is because the US government taxes them at lower rates, thereby making it more profitable. Corporate welfare, made all the easier when government officials later go to work as lobbyists at far higher salaries, has been the rule especially under administrations that avow their faith in free market ideology. The creed is used against other nations, ostensibly to preserve a "transparent" economy and prevent welfarism for the masses, but even if those who rule the American economy believe earnestly in such laissez-faire ideas, they have never practiced it. Successive administrations for well over a century have pursued essentially the same policies.[27]

Public sector spending in the United States, although lower proportionately than most other industrialized nations because social transfers are also far below West European standards, was still in 1998 almost one-third of the GDP. Much of this sum goes to subsidize the rich rather than the poor, and one reason why this proportion is not higher in the United States is that taxes that are routine elsewhere are not levied. Subsidies can take the form of direct payments, remission of charges, guaranteeing low-interest loans, and supplying goods and services to private interests – the post office is a good example – at less than cost or market prices. Indirectly, the manipulation of Federal Reserve interest rates to aid investors during downturns in the market is routine. It is exceedingly difficult to calculate all the ways Washington aids the rich, but some of them are very large; for example, the IMF, under US prodding, raised tens of billions of dollars after 1994 for Mexico, East Asia, Russia, and Brazil to guarantee that foreign investors would be bailed out when all the predictable great risks materialized. Ultimately, it is the taxpayers in countries – of which the United States is by far the most important – whose bankers loan to high-flying nations who guarantee that the financiers will be repaid and that risk-taking is no longer intrinsic to finance. Wherever one turns, there are comparable examples, many of which have become aspects of the continuous synthesis of the economy and American state. Other nations follow the same practices.

The savings and loan frauds of the 1980s, which cost US taxpayers $2.6 billion in the case of the Lincoln Savings and Loan Association alone, confirmed that the Federal Reserve System existed only to protect major investors and banks from their ignorance and greed. In September 1998 it was inevitable that it arrange the bailout of the Long-term Capital Management hedge fund when its highly leveraged and predictable huge losses endangered 16 major banks and the entire international economy. But the Federal Reserve had allowed the hedge funds the freedom to engage in their dangerously wild dealings despite the fact it has its own reputation as an erstwhile supervisor of the banking system to maintain.

Mergers and acquisitions have fallen sharply since 2000, as have other unregulated means of making money, but banks and investment houses continue to earn it. Today, hedge funds are more ubiquitous than ever: there were approximately 9000 in 2005 and their assets grew 20 times between 1990 and 2003 to over $800 billion, reached about a trillion dollars in 2005, and far more is predicted. Institutional investors seeking higher returns are now their main customers and they are also reaching out to small investors. Globally, they doubled in size in the two years ending mid-2005 and had assets of about $1500 billion. Hedge funds thrive on instability in the economy and both find and feed it, they leverage in well over a dozen highly speculative investment areas and thereby expose themselves to huge risks as well as profits. Many of them thrive on insider information, and some are notorious law-breakers. Largely unregulated, they are increasingly dangerous as they take far greater chances in the junk bond market as interest rates on government bonds, especially those of the United States, decline. Although data on their performance varies radically, they make high returns most years but in 1994 and 1998 they lost money and during the first half of 2004 and all of 2005 earned far lower returns. The fees for managing them are much greater than mutual funds. By 2005, when controls on them were again loosening and more of the large banks and pension funds were funneling immense sums into this highly lucrative aspect of finance, 82 percent of distressed debt and nearly one-third of the below-investment grade bonds and credit derivatives (junk bonds and the like), which they purchase at a fraction of their nominal value, belonged to these highly leveraged funds. Hedge funds are speculators and have in many cases become obstacles to rescuing viable companies threatening insolvency unless they make a large, quick profit. Those who win at it make huge incomes, and in 2004 the leading hedge fund manager earned a billion US dollars while the managers of the top 25 funds averaged $251 million each from fees and gains. They are increasingly, and often, decisive in the corporate world and include people who work for investment banks and are privy to information that allows them to place their own money in ways much more likely to profit – and such insiders are estimated to have made $60 billion more between 1980 and 2000 than if they had not had this knowledge, while the banks themselves made about $120 billion.[28]

Other financial instruments have been invented since 2000 to service banks, hedge funds, and others, and these are even more complex and dangerous. Credit derivative contracts allow banks and investors to move risks off their balance sheets and sell them, primarily to hedge funds. By the end of 2005 these contracts had more than doubled in only one year and had already reached over $17 trillion, and their volume is far greater than cash bonds. The financial infrastructure cannot process the opaque transactions they make fast enough and regulators cannot reach these deals, leaving more of the global financial system to those eager to profit from it. There are other types of derivatives and "hybrid" financing as well, creating a market for junk bonds that would not exist were orthodox economic theory valid, but all these innovations are almost impossible to monitor and regulate – and regulatory authorities have expressed anxieties about them. But they fear that any attempt to control them will drive them to offshore banking havens, where they can do as they like without any inhibitions whatsoever.

By mid-2005 the German and British governments publicly acknowledged what was long known to others: the hedge funds were a major threat of instability to the entire financial system, gamblers who accounted for at least half of the daily turnover in the New York and London stock exchanges. One authoritative estimate was that only about 15 percent of hedge fund managers knew what they were doing, and a further 55 percent, based largely in Europe, had a background in investing but lacked experience; 30 percent were essentially incompetent. There were far too many hedge funds and they were a menace. "Never have so many people," Germany's top financial regulator warned in September 2005, "made so much money with so little talent," and he was "scared as hell" because it was only a matter of time before hedge funds created a crisis in the world financial system.[29]

The US banking and financial system is fraught with dangers in a world full of intensifying trade rivalries, corruption and mounting deficits at home, and much else. More than ever, the whole is no stronger than its parts. Ongoing disputes between various nations reveal that each generously subsidizes their own industries, the best known – but by no means the only – is the market for lucrative new long-distance air carriers. The United States took legal action against members of the Airbus consortium, and in response the European Commission showed that by 1991 the American commercial aircraft industry had received at least $41 billion in support over the preceding 15 years. Since then, charges and countercharges regarding air carriers have been routine; so too are disputes over everything ranging from access to Europe's banana market to American restrictions on imports of every sort, from cotton and steel to orange juice. Purely to assuage Republican candidates for Congress and the voters in the steel-producing states of Pennsylvania, West Virginia, and Ohio, in March 2002 the United States imposed a tariff of up to 30 percent on a large variety of imported steel products for three years, raising steel prices in the United States as much as one-tenth and damaging Brazil as well as the developed nations that have all greatly overexpanded this basic industry. US Steel wanted even higher tariffs as well as $12 billion in government assistance. In September 2001 the Congress approved a $5 billion cash infusion to US airlines plus an additional $10 billion in loan guarantees – but only a year later the airlines asked for more aid, threatening a collapse unless it was forthcoming. But the examples are endless and all prove the same point. Tariffs, pork-barrel gifts, and subsidies are still passed out freely in the United States to politically important industries, notwithstanding the fact that US presidents have preached free trade since before World War One. Together, for an ever-growing variety of reasons, both the American and world economy are increasingly fragile.

Explaining reality

Those who run and gain the most from the US economy have virtually no accurate theory to explain, much less justify, their actions or their rewards. The existing order possesses neither ideological nor intellectual coherence. The people who rule are no better off in terms of ideas than their powerless opponents. What is true of the United States applies as well, to varying degrees, elsewhere.

Still, efforts are made to formulate comprehensive justifications of the existing corporate structures, not just of the United States but Western Europe and elsewhere. The most ambitious is Albert D. Chandler's organizational model, which maintains that giant corporations have succeeded because they are the most efficient and have adapted best to technology and markets. Able managers, in this view, are essential to corporate success, and the status quo is both "natural" and inevitable. But such a fashionable thesis simply does not explain the emergence of the modern corporation, both before but especially after World War Two, when financial speculation increasingly became the basis of executive compensation. It is oblivious to the persistence of competition and change in innumerable economic sectors and the inefficiency of many larger corporate units, recessions or depressions throughout this century, or the ways in which financial manipulation, tax laws and extremely wasteful actions if one uses technological efficiency as a criterion, have played a crucial role in corporate reorganizations.

In actual practice, financial and political rather than technological imperatives have been principal factor's in defining the shape of modern American capitalism, with the state generally performing whatever facilitating roles that circumstances – economic trends, competition, and the like – required. Regulation and political intervention in the economy are very largely the result of various corporations using the state to solve problems that resisted various economic solutions – many of which they attempted first. This was the case not just at the end of the nineteenth century; it is the only explanation of the last decades – and vast chicanery – of the twentieth. There is ample evidence that the contemporary US economy is the product mainly of factors which confirm, if anything, its technological inefficiency and also that those in charge of the economy have the political power and capacity for financial manipulations – acquisitions and consolidations of competitive firms or outright accounting frauds – when conditions demanded it or opportunities beckoned. Enron was scarcely an exception, and the largest investment firms have been deeply involved in the increasingly creative financial manipulation that fed the euphoria in stocks since the 1990s – just as they were a century earlier, before "regulation."[30]

Those who guide the political system and economy are very fallible people, often extremely ignorant and myopic about larger patterns and general principles, but masters at tending their domains and catapulting to success either in politics or business. This mentality has characterized American history throughout the past century, and even nominally very able people, like Herbert Hoover, have been incapable of coping with the problems they confronted – and most were far more incompetent. It is simply a grievous analytic error to assume that those who have or want power know what they are doing beyond their own ambitions – they do not. The theoretical literature misses the essence of rudderless, extremely finite political and economic leaders.

They know how to take care of their constituencies but rarely more than that, and more is generally unnecessary until the inevitable problems arise. This intrinsic fault makes for countless troubles, for which the people pay.

When generalizing upon the nature of the real – not the idealized – US economy, and the recent crisis in confidence that began with the Enron scandal, embracing false accounting and the very confidence we can have in all business data, there are crucial historical facts that must be recalled. Fraud of every kind, stock manipulation and deals to benefit merger managers, investment bankers, and the like were the rule from at least the Civil War onward, immortalized by Charles Francis Adams for the railroads in his classic *Chapters of Erie*, published in 1871. The merger wave from 1898 to 1901 is still, by far, the largest in American history. But whenever they have occurred there was no justification for them on the grounds of efficiency, however it is measured, and neither their profitability nor productivity increased – and the British experience has been similar. Bankers and investment specialists saw an opportunity to make money, restrictive laws have declined or disappeared altogether, and so mergers and acquisitions have flourished whenever they are profitable.[31]

During the 1950s antitrust legislation encouraged companies to diversify into different product lines and form conglomerates, and this was often essential for big firms in economically declining industries. The results were often poor, with high debts and low efficiency. By 1979, people who were principally financial experts were the largest single group in the 100 biggest US corporations, and corporate raiders increasingly treated investments as stock portfolios – their interest was in short-term gains, and driving up stock values was paramount. Profit, not efficiency, was their goal.[32]

Fraud is one technique of wealth accumulation and deception in its many forms is a characteristic of modern capitalism. Its scale and location has only increased with the spread of international investment and trade and executives' pursuit of the fast gains that rising stock prices and stock options offer them. The concept of managers as somehow responsible for the shareholders' interests, a notion which has been popular over the past century, is a quaintly naive theory that utterly fails to explain real behavior, which is less and less based on traditional definitions of investment and profitability due to real productive functions but rather on ever-higher stock prices and speculation. Executives are paid increasingly in options rather than salaries and bonuses, which gives them a material incentive primarily to drive up stock prices rather than engage in making profits for their companies. There is no theory adequate to describe the reality of chicanery which is spread throughout the highest levels of capitalism – the way it operates in practice. The value of the US stock market increased by $12 trillion between 1994 and 2000, and the bubble was too enticing for most executives. At the end of 2002 even leading investment strategists admitted that the probity of corporate America's executives was profoundly disillusioning, and in early 2003 ten of Wall Street's biggest investment banks were fined $1.4 billion – a minute fraction of their gains – for giving investors false information and thereby earning huge profits for themselves.

Anyone who follows the financial press is familiar with diverse peculations. In 1989, to cite but one of many examples, Drexel Burnham Lambert admitted to six counts of fraud and agreed to pay $650 million in fines and restitution, while Michael Milken – after Ivan Boesky, a leading speculator, gave state evidence against him to receive a lighter sentence – went to prison for 22 months and paid nearly $1 billion in fines and restitution for his "junk bonds" capers. In July 2005 Bernie Ebbers was sentenced to 25 years in prison for his part in the $11 billion WorldCom fraud, the largest securities swindle in history. The financial system is based to a crucial extent on personal relationships rather than laws and ideology, and insider memoirs show how this culture leads to greed and fraud.[33] American International Group, the insurance giant, in the spring of 2005 was discovered to have overstated its value by at least $1.6 billion going back 14 years. In 2001, individual American taxpayers, overwhelmingly in upper income brackets, underreported their incomes and failed to pay from $312 billion to $353 billion in taxes – an immense sum equal to about one-third of individual income taxes that were actually paid. Foreign exchange frauds, involving the biggest investment houses in the world, were uncovered at the end of 2003 and resulted in prosecution.

Wherever one turns, dishonesty – including the many ways that creative minds have yet to invent – is the hallmark of countless aspects of the system. It always has been. Forecasts, plans, and budgets are increasingly formulated with investment analysts in mind, producing overvalued stocks which are then peddled by Wall Street to gullible investors and pension funds. The results of such exercises in fictional accounting are a plethora of scandals among mutual funds, which alone managed $7 trillion in 2005, as well as investment houses; it also creates immense gains – and losses.[34]

By 2005 everything was going wrong in and for the US economy, ranging from scandal in every aspect of the corporate world to unprecedented deficits in trade balances and government budgets, to a grave weakening of the dollar as a valued world currency, to a growing technological edge for the key nations against which it competes. The United States' integration in world trade may be a source of strength but it may also increase the global economy's vulnerability. The international economy in the 1920s was more and more united and this ultimately proved a crucial source of instability and weakness. Much the same is occurring today with globalization; the plethora of speculative mergers, individual and bank credit excesses, and similar devices is making world capitalism more rather than less vulnerable to a crash. US trade as a proportion of its GDP has increased greatly since 1990 but its liabilities have grown much faster than its assets and it is now a deficit nation with an immense foreign trade shortfall and budget deficits, all exacerbated by the seemingly unlimited costs of the Afghan and Iraq wars (and even hurricanes!) and borrowings that leave it exceedingly vulnerable.

There are innumerable measures of this decline and dependence and they all point in the same direction: the United States is far weaker economically relative to other nations than it has been since at least 1945 even as its overweening political and military ambitions have remained hegemonic. It is now challenged everywhere, and in all domains, in ways that were unimaginable in the early 1980s, especially as it is mired in yet another futile local war – this time Iraq – that is exhausting its human, military, and economic resources and increasingly alienating the American people. In Asia it faces the exponential growth of China and others, and in Latin America and Europe yet other economic and political developments confront it.

The CIA predicts that in 2020 the United States will still have unrivalled military power but is increasingly likely to pay a "heavy price" for using it; but its economic strength will be "more vulnerable," terrorism against it is likely to remain while global public opinion will continue to relentlessly shift against it.[35] The eclipse of US supremacy, which began in the late 1990s, notwithstanding disagreement on the importance of its causes, is real despite the immensely overvalued stock market and comparable assets – itself a potential source of dangers. Where, and when, all these weaknesses and conflicts end still remains an open question, but the threat of a sustained world depression has never been greater – "the future," as Morgan Stanley's chief economist put it in May 2003, was "even more worrisome."[36] The global financial system, the Bank for International Settlements warned in June 2005, was plagued with unprecedented, immense debts, threatening the global economy with disorder – "time might well be running out" for it.[37]*

The case of the United States

For decades the United States held itself as the example of what capitalism abroad should seek to become. But the Enron and all-too-many other promotional scandals revealed that American capitalism was a hypocritical chimera. Business people in the United States wished to become wealthy, in any way

* "Globalization" is a much-overworked description of today's world economy, which is far too complex to be labeled in simple terms, but it quite accurate in its contention that bankers and investors now have far more freedom to move wherever and however they wish, exacting a very high price from the poorer nations that accept such arrangements. The most common usage of term "globalization," arguing there has been a unique increase of world trade and all forms of finance, the diminution of the power of national states over economic matters, or a flight of industry and especially services from high- to low-wage areas such as India and China, is irrelevant to this book, but I reject many of the tenets of this thesis. Apart from its gross simplifications or ignorance of the way states and businesses really operate, this argument ignores long- and medium-range historical data. The growth of multinationals is less and less in the hands of American corporations. Its principal consequence has not been an increasingly common lifestyle, as many of its critics argue, but greater and interrelated economic instability in ever-larger parts of the world. For an excellent critique of this school, see Fligstein 2001: ch. 9.

possible and necessary, fraudulent as well as technically legal, and that has remained the essence of the system since the nineteenth century.

The Enron case, involving a company that was once nominally the United States' seventh largest, revealed that many major accounting firms are pliant collaborators in issuing deceiving numbers, and that the average stockholder is incapable of coping with the fiscal illusions that companies seek to create. Enron had 30,000 creditors and claims against it reached a trillion dollars. It also unchained a wealth of information on how investment banks have obtained a growing share of the credit risk market, partially by acquiring firms but largely by a willingness to take bigger chances. In 2002 American and European banks had exposure to about a half-trillion dollars in loans in the energy sector alone, many of highly dubious character, and a significant number of them could not be repaid. US corporate debt went up exponentially, starting in 1980 but especially after 1990, and compounding these risks were the rise of hedge funds – which add to the gambles corporations are willing to take.

The growth of stock option bonuses to executives gave them every incentive to falsify profitability data, and over-borrow, especially short-term capital essential for mergers and expansion. Options by 2003 far outweighed salaries and bonuses as a way of compensating executives. Chief officers in many of the large firms that went bankrupt after 2000 made huge fortunes before the deluge. Some, such as the merged Time-Warner and AOL, lost over $50 billion in a short time – in this case, the first quarter of 2002. There is simply no relationship between the basic health – and earnings – of more and more corporations and their stock prices, much less what executives are paid.

Pension funds and investors mesmerized by the promises that mergers and buyouts freely issued had no reality checks imposed upon them, and despite huge bonuses and salaries for those who ran them they ended up as victims of a euphoric stock market which – as it does sooner or later – declines as well as rises. Stocks have increased in value an average of over 8 percent annually since 1945. From 1998 to the fall of 2002, after an orgy of what Alan Greenspan, chairman of the Federal Reserve, called "irrational exuberance," American stock assets fell by at least $7 trillion – the biggest deflation since the 1930s. But they are still too high relative to the earnings and assets of many firms, thereby leaving the system vulnerable. Anyone can make money when stocks are rising, and a staggering proportion of those who managed all firms connected with stocks simply were ignorant – save of what was profitable for themselves. But Europe's pension funds lost at least a half-trillion euros in 2002 to 2003, and Europe's individual traders lost at least 250 billion euros. American equivalents lost even more: 40 percent of the 185 largest pension funds, managing $19 trillion in assets, suffered trading losses in 2002 to 2003.

Investment bankers wish to make money, pure and simple, they have become increasingly aggressive and foolhardy with all sorts of new as well as traditional financial services, and they repeatedly prevent their analysts from releasing objective – and critical – assessments. Misinformation and false information have characterized modern capitalism at every level. Many of the largest investment houses picked stocks that lost significant portions of their value; the Goldman Sachs fund fell 37 percent in value in the 12 months ending July 2002, while the Morgan Stanley portfolio dropped 24 percent (Standard & Poor's 500 index fell 25 percent during this period). Banks, individual stockholders and pension funds, journalists – everyone – are fed information that is often inaccurate and manipulated. Pension funds and investors are suing and settling around these money matters; in April 2003 ten of Wall Street's biggest investment banks were fined $1.4 billion for giving investors false advice deliberately – and later several others were fined $305 million yet again for helping Enron defraud investors.

In the end, many of these financial and economic difficulties are also translated into political problems. Obvious ones arise from George W. Bush and Dick Cheney's careers in business and their own formidable gains in stock options, loans, and compensation as oil industry executives, or the way they manage government regulations ranging from taxes to safety and pollution laws. Variations of such conflicts-of-interest are found everywhere and in every period of time. More subtle, and eventually much more important, is the role of the US government as borrower to pay for its mounting deficits. Whatever ideology both parties advocate, and both favor balanced budgets, when in power they add to the federal debt. Pork-barreling in all its forms, military and domestic, is too much a part of the political and economic process, and deficits are merely a logical concomitant of the way the system operates. There was a deficit in every year after 1980, reaching 6 percent of GDP in 1983 and 4 percent in 2004 – save for three years under Bill Clinton and 2001, when Bush inherited Clinton's conservative budget.

All nations compete for funds that would otherwise be available for the private sector, and by 2001 at least some $33 trillion were in the government bond markets – the numbers are constantly becoming higher. The US government, which is staunchly committed to the conservative goal of balancing the budget, is merely the biggest offender in this regard. It had a $480 billion deficit in 2004 alone, with an accumulated federal debt of $8.3 trillion in 2006 and at least another $1.4 trillion deficit forecast for the next decade. Its annual deficits have grown even larger because huge tax breaks for the rich and declining share prices, which have caused consumer demand to fall, have made a mockery of the Bush Administration's ideological pretensions and compelled it to borrow heavily. US dollar reserves in foreign central banks, therefore, rose $870 billion from December 1999 to June 2003, $665 billion of which was in Asia. By November 2003 this sum exceeded $1000 billion – $775 billion in Asian banks. China, ironically, is among the biggest buyers of US Treasury bonds, having increased its dollar reserves to $207 billion in 2004 alone, nearly one-third of the US deficit. These bond sales allow Washington to pursue its reckless foreign and military policies, the principal cause of its deficits, without causing a crisis.

There are innumerable and growing economic variables, both domestic and international, facing the United States, and how they evolve and interact cannot be predicted – nor controlled by those who have a vested interest in making the transition to a new balance-of-forces in the world economy as smooth as possible. But to list them – deficits, strength of the dollar, trade patterns, and the like – is virtually to state the complexity of the problems and the dangers. The US current account deficit is growing quickly and in 2005 reached over $800 billion, or 6.4 percent of the national income. Such losses cannot be sustained much longer without the dollar being significantly depreciated – unless imports can be sharply reduced, which would require American protectionism and the end of international free trading order, and globalization, that Washington has nominally favored for nearly a century. Congress may indeed implement protectionism, especially for Chinese imports, but there is a growing consensus that the United States will create a world economic crisis one way or another.

Many central bank managers, quite aware of these trends, have begun to shift from the dollar into euros; central banks financed 83 percent of American current account deficit in 2003. Foreigners held 14 percent of all US Treasury securities in 1993 but 25 percent in 2004. The Organization of Petroleum-Exporting Countries (OPEC) countries have cut the proportion of deposits held in dollars from 75 to 61.5 percent between 2002 and 2005 and the euro's share of global official reserves rose from 18 percent in 1999 to 25 percent in 2004. The United States' share over the same period fell from 71 to 66 percent – and the direction is clear. One consequence of this trend is that oil prices, traditionally denominated in US dollars, will rise and nations will be better able to compete with the United States to secure supplies of the precious precondition of industrial growth. This will be even more the case as oil supplies diminish relative to demand if not absolutely.

Asian central banks in 2005 had nearly $4 trillion in foreign exchange reserves, over two-thirds in US dollars. Their dilemma was potential massive losses with the dollar's de facto devaluation if they did nothing and triggering a flight from the dollar if they actively diversified their holdings – risking massive losses in another way. From 2002 to the end of 2004 the dollar still fell in value 20 percent against the yen and 30 percent against the euro. In February 2005 the South Korean central bank, which had already been quietly diversifying out of the dollar, further triggered a flight from the US dollar by raising the issue publicly, urging China to allow its currency to be revalued upwards. When the Japanese prime minister in March 2005 even alluded to diversifying Japan's $840 billion in foreign reserves, the dollar tumbled. So long as the United States runs massive deficits and foreigners finance them, there exists a problem whose risks are potentially catastrophic. International finance is fragile in a way it has not been in a very long time. Sooner or later, there will be a reckoning. Even if Germany, China, Japan and others do not wish to end the causes of US deficit spending they may be obligated for purely domestic reasons to keep their surplus savings at home, thereby ending their ability to purchase US Treasury bonds. There are yet other scenarios that could cause a "hard landing" for the US economy, and more and more quite conservative analysts in high places fear that the United States' and world financial systems are increasingly vulnerable to precisely such crises.[38]

Such a crisis is all the more likely because at the beginning of 2005 the Bush Administration reiterated its public stance on China being a "peer competitor" in Asia and a growing danger. In fact, the United States has encircled China with bases and regards its growing military power as a menace, above all to Taiwan. China prefers a stable international environment in which its economy prospers but it rightfully believes the United States is threatening it. It also must obtain raw materials, petroleum being the most crucial, and its mounting rivalry with the United States in Latin America, the Middle East, and Central Asia is a fact, with potentially far-reaching implications. One of China's assets in the great game for global power is the increasingly vulnerable US dollar.

There are myriad sources of instability that simply did not exist a few years ago – confirming once again that capitalism is a system that is inherently prone to crises, some of which we can hardly anticipate. When one adds largely domestic factors, the risks grow even greater. It has taken increasingly long periods in the United States to recover jobs lost since the last business cycle peak, and "jobless recoveries" are now an aspect of the system – and the dangers it confronts. One-fifth of the United States' workers belonged to unions in 1983, 12.5 percent in 2004, and consumption and real incomes have fallen. The military budget has increased substantially but employment in the American military products industries has fallen by almost a half since 1990 and all employment in manufacturing has dropped dramatically – 40 percent – since 1980. The fact is that the United States' trade balance for advanced technology products has declined and has been in a growing deficit since 2000. The United States no longer produces enough of what the world wants, and if one adds all its potential problems and the unknown ways they can interact, its economy and society are in growing trouble. Economists are frequently wrong, especially those who claim the most certainty for their forecasts, but there is a growing consensus among them that all of these unfavorable trends, ranging from monumental deficits of every sort to inadequate employment growth at home, plus much else, cannot be sustained much longer. The United States is now at a precarious junction. And therefore the entire world is also.

Inherited ideology is simply useless in describing economic history or contemporary realities, and it is sorely misleading whether one deals with nations that call themselves "capitalist" or "socialist." Politicians rarely understand, or are even interested in, larger geopolitical patterns and the ultimate implications of their actions. Depending on the nation and the electoral situation that political leaders confront, ranging from dictatorships to genuine democracies, they care much more about retaining power and, if necessary, public support. Their focus – and myopia – is strictly on the here and now – the short run. There are no coherent descriptions or ideas, whether critical or a defense of the status quo, that adequately describe the way capitalism operates. To comprehend reality – and its contradictions and dangers – we must begin with history and the facts of the time we are living in.

Capitalism at any epoch or stage of its development can never be defined as an exclusively economic system. It is a far more complex social and economic order that manifests its strengths and weaknesses not only in economic terms – as its theorists would have us believe – but in political terms as well, involving wars with all their consequences and in the state and its central role affecting the very nature of capital accumulation. It was precisely in the political domain that capitalism has not only been weakened in the twentieth century, but also strengthened from time to time as war gave temporary respites to its internal economic problems. Data on growth is quite extraneous. What still matters most is the way wars lead to upheavals and change, many of which cannot even be remotely predicted. It was that way a century ago, and it remains the same at the present moment.

6 Capitalist realities

The way the world lives

US President Ronald Reagan and British Prime Minister Margaret Thatcher made a much smaller government role in the economy an article of faith, and private takeovers of state-controlled companies was its logic. Starting in the 1980s, privatization outside of the Communist world gathered momentum not merely because the ideology of the "free market" became increasingly hegemonic but also because the IMF and World Bank demanded that its clients implement the so-called "Washington consensus," providing financial credits for them to do so. There were thousands of privatizations, ranging from basic utilities to whole industries, in over a hundred nations. But nowhere did privatization go faster and further than the virtually instantaneous transition of the former Communist nations – including China and Vietnam – to capitalism, revealing at the same time the decisive relationship of economics to politics.

Privatizing Communism

Privatization in Communist nations conformed to the less-than-idyllic realities that afflict all capitalist economies to one degree or another, above all the one that has done the most to assert the virtues of the "free market" – the United States. The bankruptcy of the Enron Corporation in December 2001, with $101 billion in reported revenue in 2000 and the largest failure in its history, revealed that systematic fraud, irresponsible speculation, and dishonesty were widespread and that political chicanery remains, as always, often decisive to success. Enron made its fortune via the privatization of power throughout the world.[1]

The privatization theory that exists is largely irrelevant to the way it is implemented in practice. It has failed in many cases because the new owners have largely been politically well-connected speculators loath to invest in maintaining services, much less improving them, often skewing income distribution even further and promoting inequality and growing poverty. Growth and higher efficiency rarely followed, although in the short run the state made money. Privatization was good orthodox doctrine but corruption marred it in most nations, whether nominally Communist or capitalist.

But nowhere did it reach the scale of the transformation of the former Communist states, where – to quote Barrington Moore Jr – "the worst features of both worlds, capitalist and socialist," were implemented.[2] Insiders, whether managers or well-placed investors, or those with political connections, were the main gainers.

By the mid-1980s, what is euphemistically termed the "spontaneous" transfer of state property to private hands began in part because the leaders of both the Soviet Union and China sought the support of well-placed managers for their radical economic and political innovations. This de facto privatization produced innumerable forms of property transfers to individuals, and asset-stripping was common, a process that was characterized by corruption and nepotism at every stage. Since in every Communist nation the ruling parties have always been magnets for ambitious, essentially apolitical careerists and technocrats who only sought personal advantages (just as every ruling party has elsewhere), especially after the first generation that came to power disappeared, their nominal Leninist creed was scarcely an inhibition to thievery. The cynical, avaricious men who controlled these nations had long ceased to believe in socialism's egalitarian ideology. When the ruling elite decided that its interests would be better served in a "market" framework, they confiscated society's property. There was a crucial continuity, very often including the same people, between the technocratic and political elites of the Soviet system and the oligarchic economy that followed it.

In the nations in the former Soviet bloc, once the Soviet Union formally abandoned Communism in December 1991, an incredibly high level of corruption and graft, and often violence, became integral to every phase of the passage to capitalism. Encouraged by the World Bank, IMF, and American and foreign advisers, Russia implemented the fastest and largest privatization of all time. They believed that the worst alternative was the continuation of the state economy – what was nominally termed "Communism" – and that it was crucial to employ any and all means to put the economy in private hands as quickly as possible. The oil, coal, and chemical industries were especially raided. Immense depredations and corruption notwithstanding, they calculated, at least the property no longer belonged to the state, and they assumed that the predators would later behave as business people are theoretically supposed to – honestly. Regardless of how they got the property, "the secret of successful capitalism is to respect property rights," one important Western adviser later wrote.[3] Key Russians agreed with them – a restoration of Communism was the worst of all evils. It was essentially a political decision, monumentally costly in human consequences; the result was the speedy transfer of an immense amount of wealth to a minute handful of oligarchs – an event without historical precedent. What they did not count on was that the average Russian would correctly perceive the process as theft and that some of the firms involved – the best known being the Yukos gas and oil company – would seek to use their vast wealth to control the political process, compelling the state later to reclaim and resell some of them.

By late 1995 alone Russia had privatized over 122,000 state enterprises, or more than half the total, but it virtually gave them away free – principally via credits to the managers, access to foreign exchange at a fraction of the legal rates, and comparable mechanisms. Managers appointed during the Communist era took possession of medium and small businesses, and by 1995 they had majority control of the bulk of them and continued to run most of the rest – an appreciable number still received state subsidies and credits. But many of the super-rich also came from the Communist elite, including senior officials in ministries or regions, which gave them access to raw materials and energy; a few were strategically placed Party bankers and knew how to exploit opportunities involving foreign exchange.

Some extremely wealthy oligarchs had been criminals, at least under Soviet rules, and were mainly non-Russian ethnics who were ruthless in the pursuit of riches – a sort of mafia ready to cut shady deals and employ violence if necessary. They used their connections with President Boris Yeltsin, whose reelection they funded, to grasp the most lucrative government property, building fabulous fortunes. There are differing measurements of their power but they all point in the same direction: a tiny group took over the economy's commanding heights. Some estimates claim that they have dominant roles in over half of Russia's businesses. In 2004, before its editor was gunned down, the Russian edition of *Forbes* reported that the 100 richest business people had personal fortunes equal to one-quarter of the entire GDP – in the United States, billionaires control only 6 percent – and Moscow had more billionaires than any city in the world. In 2003, 22 groups of private owners accounted for 42 percent of the total employment and 39 percent of the sales, dominating petroleum, coal, steel, autos, aluminum, and timber – those export sectors best able to earn foreign exchange, much of which stays abroad. One estimate by an insider is that 12 groups control 60 percent of the economy – and even if the figure is excessive it gives some idea of the economic power of a very few individuals. In all, about two-thirds – some claim it was 80 percent – of the state's assets were looted: given away or sold at far less than their real value. By 2003 the concentration of wealth in a few hands was more skewed in Russia than in any nation for which there is data.[4]

The oligarchs, who include at least 17 men worth at least a billion dollars, pay a fraction of the taxes that the comparable wealthy do elsewhere; they have bought up the media and a few have moved into national and regional politics. The most avaricious, Mikhail Khodorkovsky, was estimated to be worth $15 billion and gave millions to his favored opposition parties – ending up in prison. Political ambition brought the oligarchs into direct conflict with President Vladimir Putin, who managed to appear like a defender of the state's autonomy and enemy of the new class of economic predators. Whatever the precise extent of their wealth, the role of oligarchs is decisive and they are in a position to dominate future economic developments. For those who gained the most, however, the rewards were astonishing, and instead of a command economy under the control of a party it is now the possession of a tiny oligarchy.

These oligarchs have become a key focus of post-Communist political life, and it has profoundly influenced Russia's political dialogue and may yet produce important changes. But the fortunes of specific oligarchs vary according to their relationship to the political rulers. There is no oligarchy as we think of it in most other contexts, but only a few very rich men who control huge swatches of the economy but who are also vulnerable, above all politically. Massive corruption by most of the rich produced cynicism and alienation among the people. Bribery of all sorts of state officials, ranging from fiscal to police authorities to those who determine who is drafted into the army, is estimated to be $316 billion over the four years ending mid-2005, ten times the amount in the preceding four years. In the December 2003 Duma election the parties that supported privatization and the oligarchs were virtually wiped out, partly because the oligarchs moved to control politics like they did oil and aluminum, and the population voted for candidates endorsed by President Putin – politicians far from being ideal democrats. The end result of this mercurial and precarious process was political instability, which in turn triggered capital flight by the handful of very rich men. From 1994 to the end of 2003 about $200 billion left the country – almost twice the annual exports and two-thirds of the GDP. President Putin in 2004 decided the oligarchs' political influence through their vast funding and control over the media had to end and began prosecution of only one of the most blatant giant firms, which he accused of avoiding taxes, laundering money, and even murdering rivals. But the oligarchs cut their local investments and precipitated an economic crisis, and in early 2005 Putin was compelled to reverse his course, assuring the oligarchs that the existing privatizations would stand and that they could keep their empires. Capitalism in Russia had become irreversible. But for most Russians, the new system has been a disaster. Real incomes in Russia dropped throughout the 1990s, 31 percent during 1991 to 1993 alone. Russia's per capita GDP fell from $12,604 in 1990 (in 1995 purchasing power) to $7140 in 1998, and then began to rise very slowly mainly because prices for oil and other natural resources grew. Russia became comparable to Latin America in terms of living standards, and poorer than the more prosperous Latin countries.[5]

The nations that were part of the Soviet bloc imitated Russia and entered into a steep, protracted decline which was marked by rampant inflation and greatly increased income inequality – which in turn was closely correlated to the extent of corruption. In countries that were once part of the Soviet Union, in 2000 the GDP was 62.7 percent of the 1990 level. Some countries did worse than others, especially the Central Asian states, which declined until 1997. In 2002, output in all of the Soviet bloc economies combined was still at about 80 percent of the 1990 level. Poland was the most notable exception, and the nations in Central Europe, those that joined the European Union, surpassed their 1989 output. The remainder were still below it, in some cases far below it. But Poland, despite many privatizations that made politically well-connected predators wealthy, was the nation that also privatized the least. It privatized only 22 percent of the stock of the 8400 state-operated enterprises in the first six years and the state retained about 4000 large enterprises. It also experienced the second highest overall growth rate of all the former members of the Soviet bloc. At the end of 1999 its GDP was 25 percent above its 1989 level, good even by all-European standards. On the whole, privatization in the Soviet bloc also favored those with friends in high political office – Poland's richest man is an example.[6]

In 1998 1 in 5 people in the entire Soviet bloc lived on less than $2.15 a day, a standard poverty line in regions where people spend more on heating and clothing, compared to fewer than 1 in 25 a decade before. In 2003 one-quarter of Russia's population was still living below the poverty level. In 1998 1 of every 20 people in the transition economies had per capita incomes below US $1 a day compared to fewer than 1 in 60 a decade earlier. In Tajikistan the incidence of poverty was 68 percent in 1998. If one uses income between $2.15 and $4.30, which exposes those at this level to "economic vulnerability," Georgia and Poland saw the proportion at this level rise while Lithuania remained the same. Health standards have dropped throughout much of the region, especially because there is an HIV epidemic, and the poverty incidence for children under 5 has increased. The transition from the Soviet system to capitalism was a disaster for the large majority of people. While overall core poverty declined in the Soviet bloc after reaching its nadir in 1998, jobs have been destroyed far faster than they are being replaced and, in the World Bank's opinion, put a decisive brake on future poverty reduction. The "big bang" reform that orthodox economists advocated was a disaster.[7]

Russia, which experienced an economic decline until 1998, grew rapidly over the following years largely because of the rising price of hydrocarbons, which constituted 55 percent of its exports in 2002, but this new prosperity is limited to a minority in big cities. Russia has also become a major force in the international arms trade – accounting for one-quarter of it in 1999 to 2002 as opposed to 42 percent for the United States. But the Russian economy that was almost bankrupt in 1998, when the ruble went through draconian devaluations, is still structurally exceedingly vulnerable. Most destabilizing of all, the majority of the Russian people do not consider the new oligarchs as legitimate – an issue that has now become highly political and may yet lead to a reversal of the great bonanza of corruption.

No existing theory explains this intimate symbiosis between politics and economics that now controls Russia. American advice and pressure had created the worst of capitalism and communism. But Washington also extended the North Atlantic Treaty Organization (NATO) to Russia's very borders, sought to limit its influence in the Central Asian nations that had once been a part of the Soviet Union, and is building ultra-sophisticated arms in space. Communism had disappeared but the United States still sought to constrain Russian power. Russia was far weaker and internally troubled but the Cold War largely continued.

Bolshevism's emergence throughout the world was wholly a consequence of capitalism's irrationality rather than the strength of Lenin's ideology and tactics, but it proved to be an illusion to believe that "socialist" economies could proceed simply from statism to the market. They are all fatally encumbered by conflicting basic values and institutions, and these produce cynicism and various pressures – political, morale-psychological, and others – which create a variety of unpredictable crises in these societies. Neither socialism nor capitalism, at least as we define them on paper, has emerged in these nations but rather a new synthesis that combines the worst antisocial consequences of each, producing a hybrid system that is not morally or economically effective or legitimate. The failure of Communism has simply led to the failure of its successor – now called capitalism. Corruption and disillusion are rampant, and moderately coherent and operative social systems are being replaced by arbitrary, inefficient, and debilitating ones with profound human implications – the disappearance of social services to begin with. These new systems are producing traumatized masses, anomie and unprecedented human disintegration in diverse forms: crime, psychological disorders, AIDS, and the like.

Asia's Communists adopt capitalism

The Communists who rule China and Vietnam have relegated the equalitarian premises of socialism to some indefinite nirvana in the future. China, with its extremely cheap and efficient labor, is a paradise for foreign investors. China is now among the three highest recipients of foreign direct investment in the world in absolute terms, the first as a percentage of the gross domestic product. But the Chinese Communists have maintained the fiction of socialism, and political constraints there and in Vietnam have made the process of transforming their economies to capitalism much more convoluted and far more gradual than it was in the former Soviet Union.

Deng Xiaoping's coalition took over the party in 1978 and he allowed key managers and regional and local party leaders who supported him all sorts of perquisites, ranging from subsidized raw materials and electrical power to foreign travel permits for relatives, and freedom to turn their provinces into largely autonomous fiefdoms. Deng was principally motivated by a desire to construct a clientelist regime that was stable and he fostered a consensus based on reciprocal favors and benefits to his coalition members. Ideology was merely a highly flexible, convenient vehicle for rationalizing policies adapted for purely opportunistic reasons and scarcely a guide to action. While politics, including family ties, more than any single factor explains who won or lost in China since the mid-1970s, Deng was aided immeasurably by the fact that most of the senior party leaders no longer believed in the party's ostensible ideology. This was due not only to the utter chaos and cynicism that Mao had created for decades, equating discipline with ideas, but also to the fact that many were nationalists who believed that any economic strategy that made China more powerful was legitimate; and many were party members simply because it was a prerequisite for advancement. The Chinese introduced capitalism much more slowly than the Russians but they have always insisted that the Communist Party maintain political hegemony – and it has done so. In 1987, partly to gain political support but also out of genuine conviction, Deng introduced a "contract responsibility system" that allowed the managers of state-operated firms to gain unprecedented autonomy. De facto, this became a form of "spontaneous privatization," giving managers control of assets, mergers, and the like – combining the advantages of both capitalism and socialism. Procedures for transferring state resources to private and foreign investors were greatly expanded at the end of 1993, and the fiction of socialist-ownership was preserved as a pro forma ritual.[8]

In 1996 the ninth Five-Year Plan set the goal of "corporatizing" those large firms that accounted for about two-thirds of state enterprise assets, and managers of these firms often could go to state banks to borrow the funds to purchase these companies at a small fraction of their real value. Many still maintain the fiction of state-ownership even when managers buy out the company, but the rights that the state as opposed to new owners have is often opaque. Stock exchanges were created. By various methods, cronyism and corruption being as important as any, the Communists have abolished most of the state control over the economy, including land. State-operated enterprises (SOEs) and banks – many of which are really quasi-private entities – have coexisted parallel to the burgeoning private sector but have fallen sharply in importance; in 1978 the SOEs accounted for 78 percent of industrial output but only 23 percent in 2000. State firms accounted for 82 percent of the fixed assets in 1980 but 55 percent in 1998.[9]

Estimates vary, but one knowledgeable Chinese economist calculates that nearly $4 trillion worth of state assets were transferred from publicly owned companies to insiders from the early 1990s through the end of the decade. Enamored by the high growth it has attained, in late 2003 China decided to begin to privatize virtually the entire remainder of the state's holdings and not only to allow private investors to take over what they want but also to permit foreign interests to enter hitherto closed sectors of the economy. About 550,000 of the registered private firms in 2005 used to belong to the state, but the legal status of the remainder is, in large part, dubious. Every stage of this vast transformation involved a massive shift in property from nominally public to private hands and – to repeat a crucial point – it has been characterized by nepotism, corruption, and graft. This favoritism extends to party members in every way, and retirees from party and state organs receive pensions almost half higher than former employees of collective enterprises. In 2005 the state was still selling its enormous equity in firms listed on the stock exchange, but its role remains purely nominal, and the legal hangover from having once been socialist is merely a huge administrative headache. And because there are few rules to constrain the new capitalists, China is also an ecological disaster, rapidly losing arable land and water.

But despite such problems, the Chinese managed to obtain a very high growth and a rising standard of living – in the 25 years under Deng, the GDP increased from about $300 billion to over $1 trillion. But progress in eliminating poverty for roughly 250 million people has been geographically very uneven and inequality of income has risen dramatically – I shall return to this complex topic. And since this inequality has increased most rapidly during periods of lower per capita household income growth, in due course this trend will become an obstacle to development and poverty reduction.[10]

High growth notwithstanding, China (and Vietnam as well) have exchanged the problems of a sclerotic, bureaucratic socialism for those of an exploitive capitalism and unbridled corruption accompanied by extreme inequality – only time will reveal their extent and gravity of the consequences. Roughly 100 million people in China's rural areas were unemployed in 1999 and by then one in four rural workers had moved to the cities – where they receive few social benefits. Far more peasants are moving to urban areas than can be absorbed there; their marginality and poverty are potentially very dangerous to social stability. By 2002 there were anywhere from 15 million to 30 million urban poor, comprising 4–8 percent of the urban population, much higher than in 1999, and their number continues to rise.

The proportion living on the land has declined since 1980 from over four-fifths of the population to 60 percent in 2002, but in the latter year there were still about 800 million people – with an average annual income of $285 – dependent on agriculture and their income has changed very little. Peasant discontent has produced innumerable protests, occasional riots, and general alienation. Until 2000, taxes fell on rural residents far more than on urban dwellers, and while reforms made taxes somewhat more equitable, social benefits per capita in the urban areas are still over three times higher than those for the rural population. Corrupt party cadres still subject many peasants to arbitrary taxes, land requisitions and evictions, and the like, and demonstrations and other forms of protest, including violence in some cases, increased from about 8700 incidents in 1993 in both rural and urban areas to ten times that, involving about 4 million people, in 2005. Too many peasants are being displaced and affected by changes ranging from the consequences of China's adherence in 2001 to the World Trade Organization, which opened it to cheaper foreign foods, to rampant corruption. By 2004, China had an important and increasingly serious food deficit; its food imports are burgeoning and it will soon be heavily dependent on them – thereby abandoning the food self-sufficiency which was one of the tenets of its Maoist heritage. In the urban areas, which accounts for most of China's relative affluence and growth and whose prosperity has greatly increased the disparity between urban and rural residents, the liquidation or reform of state-owned firms has resulted in 40 million workers losing their jobs between 1995 and 2002. There is rampant exploitation and primeval working conditions for many workers in the private sector. Most have lost the elaborate social benefits – housing, health care, and pensions – that for decades were part of their lives.[11]

By 1995, the richest one-fifth in China received 47.5 percent of the personal income, making it more unequal than the United States or Western capitalist nations. It was at least that high in 2004. The richest one-tenth of the population owned 41 percent of the total wealth in 2002 – 59 percent for the wealthiest one-fifth. In 2005 the gap between China's average urban income and the average rural income was one of the most unequal in the world and it has risen constantly since 1990. The regime was forced to attempt to reduce rural taxes, rampant corruption among local cadres, and increase subsidies and infrastructure development – quixotic gestures which have failed in the past. The so-called middle class is still only 5 to 7 percent of the income earners, according to one account, but not more than 15 percent if one uses official figures; it is urban, and mostly connected with joint ventures.

China's transition to capitalism has been characterized by so many forms of corruption that knowledge of its extent is only very approximate. From 3 to 5 percent of the GDP disappears as corruption (it is probably higher in Vietnam), ranging from kickbacks on governmental purchases to publicly funded projects diverted to private gain. Part of this amount ends in capital flight, estimated at an average of $20 billion annually in the late 1990s. China has a huge and growing trade surplus and a large foreign investment inflow, but a good part of these sums fail to show up in China's foreign exchange reserve figures. Much of it is stolen or misused, and in August 2002 the banker in charge of much of it – an ally of Jiang Zemin, China's premier – was expelled from the party and slated to be prosecuted for "absolutely vile" crimes.[12] Rarely do these thieves get indicted, and only then do we obtain glimpses into the crucial relationship of politics to economic success.

Even given highly incomplete data, the richest man in China – ranked by *Forbes* magazine as nearly a billionaire – is the son of a former vice-premier. Six of the ten richest men have made their fortunes wholly or partly in real estate – by definition an activity involving politicians. When at the end of 2002 the Communist Party dropped its self-designation as the "revolutionary" party of workers, peasants, and soldiers and formally opened its ranks to the "vanguard" of the Chinese people, "advanced elements" – business people – it simply formalized a long-standing reality. The children of senior party leaders – the "princelings" – have been prominent among the new rich, and political influence has become an important basis of money-making. One-quarter of the 100 richest people were already party members, and 13 percent belong to the Chinese People's Political Consultative Conference, an important party body. There were in excess of 2 million private businesses in China in 2002 compared to 90,000 in 1989. The party is today formally the organ of the entire ruling class, and the private sector is now larger than the state economy. But the party has a monopoly of political and state power and is the principal conduit for economic accumulation in all its forms. It has perpetuated the myth of itself as the party of the masses.

Unlike China, Vietnam does not allow capitalists to join the party but members are encouraged to become "entrepreneurs" so they will "be in a better position to help the poor."[13] In both nations the party cadres have merged with capitalists and the managers of state enterprises – often tied by kinship and social networks – to create a political and economic hybrid that rules and lives privileged existences in a variety of state capitalism. By 1993, the richest one-fifth in Vietnam received 44 percent of the income.

The transformation of the Communist economies to inegalitarian capitalism was one of the greatest and most rapid shifts of public resources to private hands – largely by outright but sanctioned theft – in all history. It was an inordinately complex process, involving party bureaucracies and dynasties as well as residues of Leninist ideologies, but also much else. There is simply no theory that prepares us for, much less describes, one of the most important economic and political events of the entire modern era.

From the United States' viewpoint, however, China may turn out to be far more dangerous and intrusive in its capitalist incarnation, with its overflow of textiles, garments, and trade in general, than it was when it was Maoist and proclaimed an absurd ideology. It has roughly a trillion dollars in foreign exchange reserves, more than any other nation, and its small currency reforms in the summer of 2005 were negligible responses to European and American pressures to reduce its export flow. China will be dominant and irresistible to its neighbors. It has settled its border disputes with the 14 nations that are contiguous with it, and it has managed its currency and economic strategy to optimize stability in the region. As an economic superpower, pragmatic and non-ideological, it is in a far better position not only to challenge US strategic and economic dominance in the entire Asian region – and there is every indication it intends doing so – but also to become a formidable rival for raw materials, especially oil and gas, on other continents. Its long-term trade strategy and geopolitical ambitions extend from North Asia – Japan and all Korea – to South Asia. It is modernizing its military and will soon be even more of a nuclear superpower with all the hardware required for a stable deterrent relationship with the United States. In this process, Asia will inevitably become its sphere of influence and the United States its rival. Before September 11, 2001 there were officials in Washington who foresaw these dangers and designated China as the greatest long-term adversary of American ambitions to retain world hegemony. After several years of downplaying China as the rival and threat to American power in Asia, by the end of 2004 – with Japanese concurrence – Washington returned to this theme. Objectively, notwithstanding its desire for stability in the region so that it can emphasize economic matters, China is becoming an economic colossus that already outstrips the United States in its production and consumption of many vital commodities. Its role as a player on the world scene is very unpredictable, and that fact alone is a crucial development.

Bureaucratic capitalism

In the other nations, especially the low-income ones, but also in many developed so-called parliamentary states, bureaucratic capitalism in its many forms, from corruption to hijacking welfare to privatization, further confirms politics as crucial to success or failure in the economic process of most (though scarcely all) nations. As a general tendency, the importance of government spending in the electoral and political cycle in Western parliamentary countries makes the marriage of politics and economics the standard virtually everywhere – and it has repeatedly overridden the pledges states in the European Community have made to conform to EU economic criteria, above all balanced budgets. In the United States, successive administrations have routinely manipulated government spending in ways that strengthen the electoral position of the party in power, and such an electoral-economic cycle is an incontrovertible, documented fact of American political life. Many nations, at the same time, declare an unwavering, unconditional faith in laissez-faire principles and deplore the very idea of annual US government deficits – which are now huge, sustained, and threaten the entire world economy. That most politicians, indeed, are quite sincere makes an accurate assessment of American politics' mindset that much more complex. What they all share in common, whether the parties describe themselves as Right or Left, is a desire to retain power, and this obsession causes them to repeatedly abandon nominal principles.[14]

Highjacking welfare, corruption, and favoritism in developing nations is a normal aspect of economic life – in some countries more than others but that it exists widely is a fact. Health and education outlays overwhelmingly benefit higher-income groups and tax systems are generally ineffective in reversing the extremely inequitable income distribution throughout most developing nations – and redistribution is at least as important as growth in ending poverty in a country. IMF conditions intensify inequities, and nations that agree to them reduce social welfare measures and subsidies to lower income groups or cut them altogether in order to balance budgets and produce surpluses – which often go to repay foreign interests. Public and parliamentary opinion must be flouted to meet these draconian conditions and the demands of local and foreign investors for a more congenial environment, reinforcing authoritarian practices. Argentina and the Philippines are but a few of the cases which best illustrate this anti-democratic pattern. Even a growing number of World Bank and IMF experts now admit that economic conditions in low-income countries have scarcely improved after receipt of the IMF's advice and a trillion or more dollars of IMF, international bank, and foreign loans and aid. In fact, by 2003 some of them conceded that there was no proof that the IMF formula for financial and trade integration in the world economy had increased growth beyond what it would have been anyway and that much of the volatility and economic difficulties that these developing nations faced after 1997 reflected the extent to which they followed the IMF's policy advice – and that the negative consequences and instability of their having done so far outweighed any benefits.[15]

An important cause of stasis in developing nations is "the kleptocratic state," which has corruptly enriched members of the mafias of politicians who run various countries, and they often encounter rival groups that have different members but identical goals. How these rivalries are resolved is the stuff from which "politics" is composed in many nations, not just Africa – a favorite topic for the IMF – but elsewhere as well. Throughout much of the world it is usually the control of the political process that determines who wins or loses materially. No conventional theory deals with these realities.[16]

But whatever the myths concerning the origins of modern economic development, even the most passionate defenders of the past acknowledge that the present and future are beset with economic volatility. A growing number of true believers – including key IMF leaders – now reluctantly admit these challenges are increasing both in size and frequency, not only in developing nations but everywhere. Increasing liquidity and capital mobility has become the hallmark of the world financial order, and instead of producing benign results, instability has grown. All foreign direct investment reached a peak in 2000 largely because of mergers and acquisitions, which in many cases were concocted by investment bankers anxious to get fat fees. Many of them proved disastrous. By 2002 and 2003 these private flows for mergers and acquisitions worldwide fell to almost one-quarter of the 2000 peak, and about one-third of the 1998 to 1999 volume. Most of it was direct equity investment – useless gambling.

Increasing liquidity and volatility in the world financial system was in large part due to the fact that President Bill Clinton was beholden after June 1991 to Robert Rubin, the head of Goldman Sachs, and his cronies on Wall Street for decisive backing in gaining the Democratic nomination, and he was highly responsive to the financial services industry. Rubin became Secretary of the Treasury and he successfully had Washington push everywhere for the radical liberalization of capital movements, which American banks and brokerages strongly desired. The bankers were motivated exclusively by their own welfare, which included repayment of monies owed them. Clinton, his coterie, and many of their foreign peers believed that doing what the financial communities demanded was crucial for economic stability and efficiency. Joseph E. Stiglitz, chairman of the President's Council of Economic Advisers from 1993 to 1997, argues that the Clinton Administration intensified the "hegemonic legacy" in the world economy, and Bush just followed it. The 1990s, he writes, was "A decade of unparalleled American influence over the global economy" that Democratic financiers and fiscal conservatives in key posts defined, "in which one economic crisis seemed to follow another." The United States created trade barriers and gave large subsidies to its own agribusiness but countries in financial straits were advised and often compelled to cut spending and "adopt policies that were markedly different from those that we ourselves had adopted."[17]

The developing nations and a good part of Asia, especially South Korea, could not resist incessant American pressures to open their markets. By 1997, growing risks were the hallmark of the world economy. In East Asia, tax policies and the "liberalization" of financial sectors at the behest of the IMF and local and foreign bankers encouraged a fatal dependence on short-term international capital flows and provided incentives to high returns on capital. This was also true throughout the Western industrial economies. Leading financial institutions leveraged their money through derivatives trading and similar techniques and suffered immense losses after the Russian debt default of August 1998. A large part of the private funds that poured into low-income countries until 1997 subsequently left almost as quickly. The net capital flow to "emerging markets" fell three-quarters from 1997 through 2000 despite the fact these nations have borrowed much more heavily. The readiness of Western banks and private investors to loan money before the 1997 Asian crash far exceeded the "fundamentals" in developing nations which would justify their doing so. But considerably lower yields in the United States and Europe in those years caused them to take the risks, and by 2002 to 2003 the developing nations euphoria – and dangers – returned for exactly the same reasons.

The Third World: poverty and instability

Nations that depend on exports of non-fuel commodities have fared the worst economically. There is a direct link between reliance on primary product exports and extreme poverty, defined as the proportion of the population living on less than a dollar per day. Although prices fluctuate, over the long run the market prices for non-fuel primary commodities have fallen dramatically since 1980, as has the terms-of-trade for the less developed countries – compelling them to increase their export volumes to keep their living standards from falling or to pay mounting foreign debts. Even worse, the processing of commodities in low-income countries, which allows a nation to receive more for its goods, has declined dramatically since the mid-1980s. The IMF insisted on this emphasis on commodity exports despite the fact that subsidies and protection in the richer nations have seriously distorted the whole world trading system and poorer nations are not allowed to exploit their potential trade advantages. But only in manufactured goods has the volume of world trade increased substantially since 1980.

In 1997 to 2001 alone the combined prices of all commodities in US dollars, in terms of the purchasing power for manufactured goods, declined 53 percent throughout the world. Africa – with almost 700 million people – was especially hard hit by this deterioration in the terms of trade, and the lost income it suffered from 1970 to 1997 (excluding oil exporters and South Africa) came to over two-thirds of the net resource transfers to it and more than offset, by far, foreign aid. Had the terms of trade remained stable at their 1980 level, Africa would have had double its share of the value of world exports. One cannot reconcile the IMF data with the United Nations' conclusions, but there is agreement that Africa was the hardest hit in every regard and its foreign debts are more onerous than ever. But Africa also suffers from a never-ending cycle of violence – civil wars and wars between nations – and economic factors are only partially the cause of its problems. Small arms, which come from industrialized states, are also crucial, but poverty is also a major source of violence and disease.

Regional averages can be misleading, because globally the ratio of external debt to GDP of 49 of the least developed nations increased from 64 percent in 1985 to 81 percent in 1999. Since then, the external debt of the developing nations increased steadily, over one-quarter between 1999 and 2006 alone, and their debt service payments with them. But the ratio of external debt to GDP has declined in some regions, such as Africa and the Middle East, while it has increased in the Western hemisphere. Low-skill manufacturing nations have been somewhat better off but remain in precarious financial condition and still have high poverty levels. The economies of the poorer countries were "globalized" much more, indeed, than in the high-income OECD economies, with trade as a percentage of the GDP in low-income nations increasing from 31.5 percent in 1987 to 1989 to 50.8 percent in 1997 to 1998. This has not led these countries to experience higher growth; on the contrary, the GDP of Africa and Latin America in 1960 to 1978 increased nearly three times the annual rate as in 1978 to 1998, and in per capita terms they grew far faster. Again, both growth and per capita income in the former European Communist states was negative until about 1996, and the decline was precipitous, especially compared to their 5.3 percent per capita growth rate during 1960 to 1978. But once China is factored into all these numbers, from poverty to investment flows, gains elsewhere are far less impressive – even ignoring the crucial methodological dimensions of assessing and measuring poverty and differences among analysts.[18]

Most developing nations, eager to obtain loans conditonal on accepting them, implemented the IMF's "structural adjustment programs," with its limits on spending (especially for food and fuel subsidies for the masses), its elimination of tariffs on basic staples, and criteria for budgets. Nations that ignored the IMF's strictures generally fared far better. Trade liberalization proved a source of weakness and helped eliminate rice, corn, and other food producers who no longer had protection against subsidized and much cheaper American and European farm surpluses. Thanks to the IMF, it was far easier for the rich nations to export to the poorer ones than vice versa. Meanwhile, the US banks that made loans to these nations were the first repaid when the IMF and other banks bailed out Mexico, Brazil, and others.

The IMF and World Bank are mesmerized by deductive theories that have scant relationship to reality, but their political consequences are often decisive because their philosophies produce recipes for disaster. Moreover, the world economy has become far more complex – and vulnerable – since both institutions were created in 1944. A few of the important IMF personnel are aware that "the complete market model is too far distanced from reality to be useful," for it offers no insight on how social and political institutions that ultimately shape the economy in practice are created. Markets models "assume so much that is unrealistic," making solutions to problems seem far easier – and they fail. But notwithstanding such moments of candor, the "Washington consensus" and IMF orthodoxy entirely determine the basic assumptions that guide the policies these institutions impose.[19] The extent to which these critics remain powerless was reiterated when the United States conquered Iraq. From May 2003 onward, essentially because the Bush Administration also shared its orthodox faith, the IMF's advice and managerial support defined Iraq's economic trajectory. About 200 state firms were privatized and classic IMF conditions and neoconservative tenets of faith were strictly implemented. The immediate result was sharply rising unemployment, which fed the insurgency, and even more chaos and protracted war. But ideology triumphed.

The Latin America experience illustrates how pursuing the "Washington consensus" intensifies a myriad of economic and political problems. And nations that borrowed large sums – in a word, over-borrowed – and then fell into financial difficulty and took the IMF's advice, as in the case of Argentina, then discovered that the IMF only greatly compounds its troubles. Its debts mount, and poverty with it. It was precisely when the Latin American nations abandoned autarchy and linked their trade to each other, so that crisis in one of their larger countries affected all of them, or geared more of their trade to exports to the United States, Europe, and East Asia, that their economies became most unstable.

By 2003 Washington was far less sure that its and the IMF's strict formula on fiscal policy, social legislation, privatization and numerous other issues were producing the right results either politically or economically, not the least because the US government's annual deficit of nearly a half-trillion dollars is the consummate antithesis of the advice it gives to all. Indeed, it was increasingly obvious that the IMF was as much a cause of economic problems as a cure, a reality that was implicitly recognized by the IMF's most ardent supporters. First, there was a growing awareness that monetary policy was not working in the United States or elsewhere. The world economy and development was proving more obdurate and complicated than the IMF's high priests with their inflexible rules admitted, and the major industrial nations were increasingly less enthusiastic about the draconian IMF recommendations – which worsened world as well as the Latin American economies. This has not prevented the IMF from attempting to impose its anti-state subsidies policies in Brazil and elsewhere, but it is less confident about its conventional wisdom than ever. Worse yet for it, fewer nations were going hat in hand to the IMF, and by 2005 its new loans had fallen to the lowest level since the late 1970s – its power was therefore declining. By mid-2003 even the Fund's experts belatedly and reluctantly admitted "there is no quick or easy fix" for the developing world's accumulated economic problems.[20]

Much of the IMF's pessimism was due to the Argentina financial meltdown, which terminated at the end of 2001 as the largest national default in history. About $140 billion in sovereign bonds to private creditors and the IMF were involved. The Argentine case is especially interesting as well as superbly documented. International bankers throughout the 1990s were eager to loan Argentina (among many others) money regardless of its ability to repay it; bankers collect fat fees at the inception of all transactions and so they created a huge bubble long after economic realities ceased to warrant more loans and so-called swap deals. They were fully aware of the dangers their clients were assuming. IMF and all other rules, including elementary prudence, eventually became meaningless because the money was available no matter what a nation did. Wall Street and the Argentine authorities behaved as if the good times would roll on forever. The IMF tried valiantly to rescue Argentina after 1999, in part because the financial crises in East Asia and Russia strengthened their determination to avoid yet another. But the US government, in part because of its fear that an Argentine debacle might drag the region with it, overrode IMF conditions and successfully insisted that huge sums be loaned to the Argentines. More good money was thrown after bad. The crisis dragged on interminably and the Argentines could resist draconian IMF demands and its structural reform program – if not wholly at least to an unprecedented extent – in large part because of the divisions existing among bankers, in the US government, and within the IMF itself.

In the end, the bankers, IMF, US government, and Argentines worked at cross-purposes and the outcome was enormous debts – and economic and political chaos. The currency crashed, the GDP fell precipitously, unemployment soared, and from 1999 to 2002 poverty doubled to almost 60 percent of the population, while indigence about tripled to nearly 30 percent. The result was countless riots and demonstrations – and a succession of five presidents and political upheavals which ended when Néstor Kirchner was elected president in May 2003.

Argentina, indeed, initiated a much stronger national resistance to IMF diktats and this crisis marks the beginning of the end of its role in directing the Latin American economies, a role that had produced worsening conditions for the masses and low growth if not stagnation. Argentina defied its creditors and at the beginning of 2005 finally was able to get about three-quarters of its creditors to accept about one-third of the sums owed them – proving that the conventional rules can be successfully flouted. As for the IMF, Argentina paid off its nearly $10 billion debt to it at the end of 2005, thereby removing it from the scene entirely. One consequence was that Argentina began to recover by whatever criterion one employs, and the growth rate in 2003 was 8.7 percent, the second highest in the world, and it was about as high for the next two years; its inflation rate was under 4 percent compared to as much as 26 percent a few years earlier, although it began to mount thereafter. But in 2004 unemployment was still almost one-fifth of the labor force. Neighboring Brazil, led by a nominal radical, followed IMF advice and did not fare as well.

Part of Argentina's new prosperity, true also of much of South America, is due to the fact that China's demand for its major commodity exports – copper, iron, soybeans, and the like – has burgeoned, a development welcome in the short run but with the same longer-range dangers as overdependence on raw materials exports. Important too was the higher price of petroleum, which gave exporters like Venezuela and Ecuador far greater leverage in dealing with Washington. Indeed, Venezuela bought at least a billion dollars of Argentina's bonds and helped eliminate the IMF's leverage as Kirchner leaned increasing toward the left. But in the short run, in a pragmatic way many of the nations in South America – Brazil, Argentina, Uruguay, Ecuador, Bolivia, and Venezuela are the best known in this growing pattern – began moving away from the United States' traditional hegemony and, at least in part, the "Washington consensus" to reconstruct their relations to each other and the rest of the world. By any criterion, from annual real growth to inflation and current account balances, Latin America has prospered since 2003. While the populist rhetoric its leaders employed meant very diverse things in practice, what they did have in common was a mutual determination to escape Yankee domination.[21]

Poverty, stagnation, and hunger

Data on world poverty and its reduction, its measurement and the criteria for assessing it, or trends in the income gap between the least developed countries and the others, are mired in statistical controversy – although there is agreement that present inequalities are very great and so too is poverty. In 1997 to 1999, 69 percent of the population of primary commodity exporting nations lived below $1 a day as opposed to 63 percent in 1981 to 1983 – $1 being the definition of extreme poverty. But over 80 percent in mineral-exporting nations existed at this extreme level in 1997 to 1999. The number of people living in extreme poverty in the commodity-dependent nations increased 105 million between 1981 to 1983 and 1997 to 1999. Some regions, notably in Asia and especially China, increased exports of low-value manufactured goods and services dramatically. Poverty declined in these nations, but those living in extreme poverty in even such favored regions increased by 10 million. The number of people in developing nations (excluding China) living below the sparse World Bank poverty criterion of $1.79 (in 1993 purchasing power) per day increased 15 percent from 1987 to 1998 – to 1.4 billion people in 1998 – but given population growth fell by four percentage points of the total global population. For all the less developed countries (LDCs) combined, using $1 a day or under as a criterion, the percentage of the population living below it grew from 48 percent of the population in 1965 to 1969 to 50 percent during 1995 to 1999, meaning that the number of people in extreme poverty more than doubled during that period from 138 million to 307 million people. Economic growth in countries with 653 million people – mainly sub-Saharan Africa and former Soviet bloc members – was negative from 1990 to 2003, and poverty increased in these places, especially in the former Communist states, where it – measured as $2 or less daily – increased from 23 million in 1990 to 93 million in 2001. The HIV/AIDS pandemic has been, above all in Africa, a new cause of abject poverty, and a major reason why poverty has been falling since the mid-1990s at one-fifth of the 1980 to 1996 rate. But violence and conflict have been crucial in over half the nations that have done worst economically since 1990, so that poverty and war are intimately linked and must be confronted as a single problem.[22]

The International Labour Organization (ILO), on the other hand, estimates there were 550 million working people in 2002 living on $1 a day or less, and the unemployed would make that figure far higher. The ILO believes 1237 million people lived in absolute poverty in 1990 and 1100 million in 2000, but China and India account for most of whatever progress has occurred. In 1993, 76 percent of the globe's population lived in countries that received only 29 percent of the world's income, and the developed nations – Western Europe/North America/Oceania – accounted for 16 percent of the population and 58 percent of its income. Economic integration via trade and investment since then has benefited only the 12 developing nations that obtained most of the foreign investment going to poorer states. And nations already developed still received about three-fifths of all direct investment.[23]

The IMF, World Bank, and most developed nations for decades urged the poor countries to end their import-substitution and industrialization policies, predicting faster growth rates for the poorer nations and a lessening of the gap between the rich and poor nations or the class structures within each. Loan conditions usually stipulated such changes, and in the 1990s there was a quantum jump in publicly guaranteed international bonds in developing countries – most linked to financial liberalization. There was also a growing intellectual consensus that reinforced the immense number of national regulatory changes which occurred in the 1990s, in part due to the collapse of the Soviet-inspired economic models. Whatever gains that occurred in poorer countries have tended to bypass the rural sectors, and rising rural–urban income differences, especially in China, have caused the inequality of income shares to increase and the quality of social services to decline precipitously.

The rich nations, most of which are in the West, are generally growing faster than the poor ones. The per capita GDP gap between the 20 richest and 20 poorest nations has more than doubled between 1960 and 1962 and 2000 and 2002 – from 54 to 121 times. The rules of the international system, from national protectionism and subsidies to marginal industries and farmers, intellectual property protection and the like, have worked against poorer nations for decades. Inequality among countries was about constant in the 1960 to 1982 period but worsened over the next two decades. In 1998, 93 percent of the poor lived in poor nations, which is no surprise, but there are fabulously rich people in the poorer countries. Depending on the way calculations are made, the richest one-tenth of the world's population received anywhere from two-thirds to 71 percent of the world's income in 1998. The world's 500 richest people listed by *Forbes* magazine have an income which exceeds that of the poorest 416 million people. Increasingly unequal income distribution after taxes in many developing nations – China was among the most unequal, and worse than India, Indonesia, or South Korea – explains part of this persistence, as well as grossly inadequate economic growth and dependence on commodity exports. Global inequality, no matter how it is calculated, is very great and it is increasing. It is increasing between the wealthier and poorer nations but inequality within them is also greater. Of the 73 nations for which it has data, the UN Development Program (UNDP) in 2005 calculated that 53 (with over four-fifths of the world's population) have rising inequality while only nine countries (with 4 percent of the population) have seen it fall.[24]

Education, health, and transfer programs in developing nations did not reverse this growing inequality and in most nations they benefited mainly upper income groups. Political democracy in its many forms, ranging from the nominal to the real thing, has not prevented oligarchies from becoming richer or remaining as powerful as ever. Social objectives are even more crucial. Latin America did especially badly, with utterly inadequate social safety nets and in some nations a reversal during the 1990s of gains made in preceding decades. Basic economic security in all its aspects and protection against unemployment is a condition that exists for a small minority of the world's population – principally in Europe. The United States ranks twenty-fifth in terms of economic security among nations, and the number of its population – in absolute and relative terms – living in poverty (12.7 percent in 2004) and without health insurance has been rising since the late 1990s. In 2004,15.7 percent of the population was not covered by any health insurance. Both US employment and real wages have been declining since 2001.[25]

Global open unemployment, the ILO claims, grew 188 million in the decade ending 2003, in large part due to trends in Latin America, Southeast Asia, and East Asia. This persistence shows up when such measurements as the percentage of underweight children under 5 years are utilized. More than 1 billion people drank unsafe water in 2005 and 2.6 billion (about 40 percent of the world's population) have no access to basic sanitation. Indeed, the gap in health-care standards between the rich and poor nations has widened since the mid-1990s and in some countries, especially in Africa, the medical progress made over past decades has been reversed. In all, the economies of 54 nations with 12 percent of the world's population contracted from 1990 to 2001 – especially sub-Saharan Africa and East Europe – and another 71 nations, with 26 percent of the world's population, had zero to low growth and often failed to keep up with population increases. Per capita income of only 16 developing nations grew at more than 3 percent annually between 1985 and 2000, and mean per capita GDP growth throughout the globe in the decade ending 2003 was about one-third of the 1961 to 1968 increase. China accounts for most of the statistical progress that has occurred in East Asia and the entire world.[26]

The problem of hunger is linked to unemployment and underemployment but also to violence, which has been increasing despite the growth of world GDP. In 1993 there were 141 million unemployed in the world and looking for work but 186 million in 2003. Reliable figures on underemployment do not exist, but it is an immense problem. Unemployment is greatest in the Middle East and North Africa, reaching 26 percent in 2003 among youth in those nations – with predictable political results in the form of extremism. In China unemployment is rising because of the shift from agriculture to more precarious manufacturing and service jobs, but in the other transition economies unemployment lessened in 2003.

Hunger in the world fell to 37 million people during the first half of the 1990s only to increase by 18 million during the second half – AIDS, civil wars, and drought reversed the global decline of undernourishment. There were 852 million undernourished people in 2004 – an increase of about 18 million since 2000. Most of them are subsistence farmers, and at least 5 million children die each year of hunger. Regionally, only Latin America and the Caribbean, as well as China, succeeded in reducing the number of hungry in the late 1990s. Globalization exacted a very high price from all of them.[27]

Economic risks were not merely unanticipated and poorly managed, but after 1997 they migrated from one country and region to others in unprecedented ways, infecting (to varying degrees) the entire international order. Uncertainty became the leitmotif of the world economy, and losses and imbalances – for example, in current account deficits, which went up after 1999 to unprecedented sums – became far more common in many nations, above all the United States, which both in absolute terms and as a ratio of GDP has, by far, the greatest net inflow of capital and the potentially dangerous vulnerability that accompanies this dependence. Indeed, over-leveraged companies deeply in debt, both in the United States and Europe, were prime candidates for bankruptcy in case the liquidity bubble burst; by 2005 financial experts considered this increasingly likely.

The United States and IMF throughout the 1990s pressed the poorer nations to introduce capital account and investment liberalization. But by 2001 the global investment flows had become highly unstable, not only to the developing nations but to other industrialized states as well – partially because corporate mergers and takeovers proved in many cases to be unprofitable chimera as well as credit excesses by individuals and banks. The net result has been increased instability in the relations of the poorer to the rich economies. Most cross-border capital flows occur between developed nations, but as the merger and acquisition flurry between Europe and North America petered out after 2000, and stock prices fell precipitously, a larger share of the considerably smaller investment flows went to developing nations – China above all, which totaled only $25 billion in 1990 but $448 billion by 2002. The post-1997 crisis in East Asian economies made banks and investment funds shy of most of these nations until 2003, but as much higher returns on equities and bonds there returned so too did high capital flows.

As has happened so often in the world economy over the past century, it is as if nothing was learned. China still remains one of the riskiest places for outsiders to put their money, and although it has immense foreign reserves (close to a trillion dollars at the end of 2005) the fact that most of them are held in the form of depreciating US dollars leaves it increasingly intertwined with the United States' growing economic problems. China's willingness to buy US Treasury bonds has allowed the United States to consume well beyond its output for some years, but Washington must eventually confront its sustained record-breaking deficits and debts, and then China's export-led growth is likely to end, perhaps dramatically. China has unrivalled growth rates and a potential for becoming the dominant nation in the dynamic Asian economy; it also has monumental internal social and economic problems symbiotic of its becoming a capitalist economy. It could have a social and political implosion. Whatever the reason, the international economy is just as unstable and dangerous as ever.

All of these seemingly impersonal numbers and trends have dire social and political consequences, and they are potentially the most decisive costs of capitalism and its ethos. The resurrection and continuation of atavistic philosophies and ideas, or tribalism in its many forms, is due in large part to the existence and growth of poverty as well as, of course, to the collapse and failure of secular programmatic reform alternatives because ambitious corrupt opportunists have led them. In the Middle East, large parts of East Asia, and Africa, the failure of export-oriented capitalism and the "Washington consensus" has encouraged separatism, Islamic fundamentalism, and varieties of prejudice and ignorance that have increasingly led to chaos. The absence of an alternative vision of social change, the commitment to justice and equity, has left an enormous intellectual vacuum and aggravated many of the world's problems and resurrected obscuritanism. At the inception of the twenty-first century it is an evil harbinger of things to come.

After 1997 "contagion" entered into the vocabulary of discussions of the world economy – even though remarkably similar analogies can be drawn with the world banking system of the 1920s and the onset of the Great Depression. The major industrial capitalist nations aimed then at not merely increased trade but also greater financial stabilization. It was this very integration that was a major factor in driving many economies into depression at the same time. Until the late 1990s the IMF and many other investment luminaries sought to argue that the basic trends in the world economy reflected economic "fundamentals" and "rationality" rather than fear and dangerous liquidity. But the capital account liberalization that the IMF, World Bank, and American bankers and government advocated was adopted by most important nations, and the outcome is more frequent financial crises. Control over national exchange rates and monetary policy has passed increasingly to foreign economic experts and bureaucrats but also to avaricious speculators.

Every change in such abstract statistics had untold human – and often political – consequences. One example of many: the financial crisis in Asia that began in 1997, which caused the real 1998 GDP to drop from nearly 6 percent in South Korea to 13.7 percent in Indonesia, by late 1999 had pushed at least 15 million to 75 million people – depending on criteria employed – below the poverty line. In the Philippines the GDP fell substantially and in 2002 was only equal to the 1994 level; but in Indonesia the per capita GDP in 2002 was not yet back to the 1993 level. Subcontractors and firms abandoned what were once low-cost operations in various nations because devaluations made it even cheaper to go elsewhere. Malaysia, which ignored the IMF and imposed capital controls, was spared the worst effects of the 1997 crisis. An exhaustive internal evaluation of the IMF's 1997 to 1999 performance in Indonesia, Korea, and Brazil admitted in mid-2003 that the IMF had failed badly and that its advice exacerbated these nations' problems. Its projections and risk assessments were inaccurate, its fiscal remedies were unwarranted, its structural reform measures were often uncalled for, and its advice was not based on knowledge or insight because it employs a purely deductive theory of how nations should run their economies. IMF programs are not identical in every country but it proposes certain minimal and very conservative norms everyplace. Actual investment rates were below its projections in 60 percent of its cases – in one-quarter of the cases it was dramatically wrong. It advocates a value-added tax (a regressive measure which has become almost universal since the mid-1980s) as the principal way to design a modern tax system and austerity, and a balanced budget as the way to solve a nation's economic policies. Experience has repeatedly shown, as in Bolivia in early 2003, that these measures often will trigger mass discontent and political instability, frequently forcing an administration out of power. In the case of Russia in 1998, both ignorance of basic information, overconfidence in their ritual solutions, and political imperatives explain the IMF's actions and policy recommendations. It has only continued to set major obstacles in the way of innumerable countries managing their own economic affairs rationally and equitably.[28]

After a decade of being dormant, nominally leftist political parties revived in much of Latin America, and they are once again in the ascendancy in many nations – Brazil above all, where the Workers Party was elected to power, but also Venezuela, where Hugo Chavez created an eclectic radical and populist ideology. In October 2003, Bolivia, which had loyally followed IMF advice and seen unemployment burgeon and the economy decline, the president resigned after sustained demonstrations and riots. At the end of 2005 a radical was voted Bolivia's president. Washington's futile appeals that the region create more free trade accords, even while its subsidies to American farmers are at their peak, have produced indignation at Yankee hypocrisy.

There are enormous problems in all of the continents. In 1982 to 1990 more money poured out of Latin America in profits and interest than it attracted, and since 1999 this net transfer out has resumed and become increasingly onerous. In places like sub-Saharan Africa the rich routinely hold much of their private wealth abroad – about 40 percent in this region.

Enormous sums flowed into Asian and other areas, but the capital flight out of Thailand, South Korea, Malaysia, and Indonesia after 1997 was estimated at about a quarter-trillion dollars. The capital flow of private bank loans out of emerging markets was $62 billion in 1997 but grew to $172 billion by 2000. But the return on foreign direct investment in emerging markets was still 15 to 20 percent from 1995 onwards, and the only losers were the numerous countries that allowed themselves to be exploited. "Herd" behavior and mentality has become crucial, as investors act together. Macroeconomic indicators proved next to useless in anticipating the problems that were to emerge in the "Asian miracle" nations – the "tigers" in popular parlance – where governments gave huge subsidies and credits to strongly encourage exports and were "well managed" both by IMF standards and especially compared to Latin American and African nations. Basically, most of the East Asian economy, Japan included, was unhealthy – its banking flows, exaggerated stress on exports, the price of real estate, and much more – and waiting to fall precipitously. Indeed, Japanese banks were as aggressive and adventurous in Asia as any, and suffered huge and permanent losses – losses the state had to assume partially when in May 2003 it authorized a special agency to buy $84 billion worth of bad loans from the banks (slightly under a quarter of the total) to "revitalize" an ailing Japanese economy.[29]

But these were only a part of many, often interrelated and reciprocal problems that made the world's economy so vulnerable to crises. The burgeoning US external trade deficit was one major conundrum, inadequate private and public risk management yet another. Indeed, by 2003 the immense US trade deficit was possible only because Asian governments, eager to sustain their exports, accumulated two-thirds of the American deficit in order to prop up the United States' economy. The triumph of the Washington-led system and consensus, with the help of the IMF and World Bank, produced unprecedented and greater profit opportunities – and risks – for the major international banks and corporations, of which the Americans were the most important but certainly not alone. Capital account liberalization plus the doubling of assets managed by "mature market" institutional investors between 1990 and 1998 (reaching an astonishing $30 trillion) also made the swings in capital flows much more volatile. The IMF often discusses how highly leveraged, off-balance-sheet structures and exposures turbulently amplify financial shocks and transmit them across countries and regions in an unpredictable fashion.[30] The Bank for International Settlements has been warning since at least 2000 that the world financial structure is plagued with mounting instability and contradictions. All these developments and the very complexity of the world economy have only made the structural flaws inherent in the existing national economies, ranging from unequal distribution of income and wealth to imbalances in existing policies, corruption, and much else, all the more dangerous – and the people will pay for them. Crises are now intrinsic to the world economy.

The crisis in capitalist practice – and theory

In the long run, since 1881, economic downturns (whether called "depressions" or "recessions" is purely a semantic question) have been endemic in all places at various times, and they affect many nations simultaneously – a decline in fixed investment is one of their more serious features but there are also innumerable human costs, and these often have decisive political consequences. The period 1950 to 1972, which was the height of the Cold War, with rearmament-sustained growth, was relatively the most prosperous, and 1919 to 1939 was the most troubled era economically, ending in fascism and war. The frequency and the duration of financial crises has increased dramatically since 1972 and the intensity of recessions after 1972 as a percentage of lost GDP exceeds those of the prior 22 years. The severity of recessions, indeed, is now greater than the pre-1913 period. Mainly because of the greatly increased complexity of the world financial structure and its systemic instability, IMF analysts counted at least 15 crises and cases of market turbulence in 1992 to 2001 alone that endangered ever-larger parts of the world economy. Until now, good luck rather than market surveillance and policy design, such experts warn, has kept the world economy from entering a profound crisis. The political context of economic cycles is always decisive, and in some nations it has been profound at times. Measurement techniques and the data change, but the IMF has released increasingly dour prognostications. Economics is less politically decisive in Europe than before 1939, but elsewhere it is still often determinant, and very broad historical estimates do not even begin to approximate its political potential. Above all, the vast expansion of unregulated and increasingly volatile cross-border financial instruments have made the world financial structure much more precarious.[31]

Reform of the components which make up the increasingly complex, convoluted world economy has become the order of the day. But pervasive confusion has been the hallmark of all such efforts, not the least because there is no consensus among the people and nations that count if changes are to affect reality significantly. The world economy's much greater size and complexity has made the task of controlling it much more difficult, and its risks now far outweigh the means for reforming it. Supervision, accounting reform, or what is euphemistically called transparency have not solved the problems of the domestic or world economy, which have become far more complicated with computers and legal loopholes. Banks in one nation often belong to foreign interests, and herd behavior in capital movements can – often does – produce nearly instant huge flows that defy the order and rationality that is the necessary, if not sufficient, precondition for greater stability in both regional and world economies. Those in the IMF and World Bank who are supposed to guide economic affairs are now confused – and humbler. They still favor open capital markets but also acknowledge that their very existence can lead to disaster in some countries – which in turn can have dire implications both regionally and internationally. But while many of the nations and experts who favor liberalized investment and capital flows, privatization, and crucial components of the "Washington consensus" now admit all are antithetical to long-term sustainable growth, they still press for it. The IMF still makes certain that there are public guarantees of the safety and return of foreign private investments in most nations, a condition which encourages more foolish investments and the "moral hazards" such assurances create.

The September 11, 2001 crisis in the wake of the terrorist destruction of Wall Street's two biggest buildings produced collective central bank cooperation for a short time only but it did not prevent the loss of well over a trillion dollars in paper values on the American stock exchanges alone – and at least as much in Europe. The events of September 2001 and subsequent American wars in Afghanistan and Iraq further reinforced the intimate yet wholly unpredictable linkages between economic and political-foreign affairs.

But what measures to end the myriad of dangers that beset the world economy can those whose opinions count agree upon? What is feasible as opposed to desirable? Should there be capital controls? On inflows as well as outflows? Floating exchange rates? Intervention to provide liquidity, and by whom? What about hedge funds and similar financial creations? Property prices are too volatile and inflated in the Anglo-Saxon countries, having already wreaked havoc in Japan, the United Kingdom, and Scandinavia in the early 1990s, and by 2005 financial experts thought it was too late for the leading Anglo-Saxon economies to avoid paying dearly for their immense property bubble. There are simply too many problems. Increasing complications have been piled on already complex relations in virtually every area of the economy, whether national or global, and out of this unregulatable, intertwined jumble, the chances of a serious crisis of long duration become more and more likely. The US current account deficit is enormous, and insoluble even if the US government implements protectionist measures and abandons many of the free trade measures that have been laboriously created globally since 1947. The value of its dollar, which is falling rapidly, is now at risk. Banks are imprudently giving the hedge funds enormous credits, exposing themselves to potential immense losses. The "severe risks" of these financial concoctions are now often discussed in the financial press, and the chief risk officer at a leading Wall Street firm admits that banks are forced to "stay in the game": "It's like a game of musical chairs. You just hope it is somebody else that gets hurt when the music stops."[32]

What, in light of trends such as these, does a realistic development strategy entail, especially vis-à-vis the existing world economic structure and the IMF, banks, and others seeking to define the appropriate route for each nation? That is the dilemma that countless countries confront, and it is also the contradiction of those who think that capitalism is a viable system that can be made to work better. It cannot.

Socialism became decisive in the world after 1917 because of capitalism's wars and failures, but today socialism as a real movement of change is dead and capitalism remains as destructive and unstable as ever. Capitalism is not, by any criterion, a sensible basis for our civilization. We should not be optimists but we must be realistic: either there are dramatic, radical changes in the way the world operates, its assumptions and goals, or civilization as we have known it is headed toward far greater crises that risk its destruction. That too is our dilemma, one demanding that we think creatively and comprehensively about the future – while there is still time.

The greatest error one can make is to postulate a coherence and rationality to the existing economy and social system which assumes it is deliberately integrated and viable, so that a functionalist vision of it emerges. According to this view, there are few missed steps, no failures of omission or commission. In this interpretation, planning, order, linkages, and a high degree of class intelligence exist. Many radical critics also assume that positivist powers of understanding and control guide the prevailing systems, and they imply that the system has a higher logic. Everything fits and can be explained, and grand models, each larger and more comprehensive than the last, are often thrown in to account for what is not obvious. Globalization, world systems, trilateral linkages, and the like have become standard concepts in the critics' lexicon. At best they are incomplete and myopic; often they are just plain wrong factually.

The shortcoming of such a vision is that it takes scant account of accidents, stupidity, or failures of intelligence due to bureaucratic or ambitious players. It cannot explain breakdowns and crises, much less predict them. Why things go wrong – as they very often and increasingly do – is incomprehensible. It assumes that there is a higher capitalist intelligence, a "logic" that defines events, and not merely a will to attain rational control but also the ability to do so. But wholly disinterested political intervention in an economy rarely occurs – anywhere. Greed and stupidity, in a word, erode the integrative functions of the ruling system and those who guide it.

But purely domestic factors – economic, political, or social – have not been the decisive elements in the evolution of nations, and here all nineteenth-century thinkers were fatally wrong. The international system, wars of various scales in particular, has been much more determining, and while the world does not fit any neat models – globalization, for example – it remains incredibly precarious. How it evolves precisely is subject to wild guessing save in one regard: it will remain at least as unstable and dangerous as over the past century, and the commercialization and proliferation of increasingly destructive weaponry makes it very likely that the worst is yet to come – unless the premises and goals of powerful states change dramatically and solutions begin to keep pace with problems. We know from tragic experience not only that the worst happens but also that it is often very likely, usually not in the way that its detractors predict but it occurs nonetheless. If there are objective economic and political factors that will create disorder, sooner or later they interact and come into play. And then we have disasters: wars, depressions, and the like. We have only the history of the past two centuries to instruct us, not theories.

7 The future

Where and how

Socialism's political and ideological failure has spared modern capitalism from a credible opposition but it has not remedied its inherent instability and vulnerability to crises. Despite repeated efforts since at least the beginning of the twentieth century, politicians, industrialists, and bankers – both within major nations as well as internationally – have failed in their many attempts to introduce stabilizing rationality into the economy. Resistance to capitalism does not exist now but it will reemerge once the people are called upon to make the sacrifices in blood and well-being for its follies. It has in the past, and it will again in the future.

The economic successes of capitalism have been more than offset by its endemic inability to avoid wars, a process that is stimulated by atavistic ideological and cultural reasons – nationalism being one of them – as much, if not more, than economic factors. Its achievements or failures during peacetime can be debated but a justification cannot be made for the repeated belligerence of many nations that have capitalist economies. Their capacities to resolve their internal problems are limited decisively by the fact that so many capitalist nations have again and again embarked on protracted conflicts and wars. Even ignoring the role the state has played in capital accumulation, capitalism cannot be defined merely as an economic system seeking to apply such principles as the market or other purely economic categories. It has much larger political, cultural, and social consequences which are decisive. Any economy which contributes to such tragic upheavals deserves to be rejected.

The reality is that there has been for over a century a massive waste of human lives and funds in the form of the military establishments of so many nations – resulting, ultimately, in local and world wars. While detailed proposals for reversing this drainage are superfluous here, if the world is to avoid destruction there must be a major reallocation of resources now devoted to arms, beginning with far-reaching arms control of nuclear and chemical-biological weapons and delivery systems as a first step toward even more radical measures leading to total disarmament of strategic weapons and the reduction of conventional armies. Universal disarmament with effective inspection is, by far, the most preferable means of attaining it, but to reach this goal requires the real and potential nuclear powers to make profound concessions. At this time, they will not. The United States is, ultimately, the most crucial nation involved and its continuous, expensive modernization of its arsenal is due at least as much to the companies that produce advanced military technology, much of which is useless, as illusions regarding military power among its leaders. It is to the utmost interest of the people of those nations most likely to go to war that these firms be recycled or abolished altogether. Both from the viewpoint of the misallocation of resources as well as ultimate physical security, getting the demons of military folly and the arms race under control is of highest priority.

In the most general and strategic sense, those who have guided and run the parliamentary nations over the past century have been masters at acquiring and holding power but, with a few exceptions, they have not understood the full ramifications and consequences of their policies and actions. No social theory, whether of the Left or the Right, possesses a serious concept of leaders and their possible role in politics. Successful leaders, for the most part, are cynics who believe principally in their own careers. Facts – and truth – are merely expedients that are treated purely instrumentally; if it suits their purposes they accept them, but if not they employ myths and lies. This is about as true of leaders on the Left as on the Right, especially since 1945 – the age of disenchantment. Innumerable leaders of politics and business, of all ideological colors, are on top because they are simply consummately ambitious and not because they have the impersonal attributes which qualify them to be in authority.

Accommodating to dominant vested interests is the easiest way for parties to engage in successful politics but it only postpones an overdue reckoning if the basic social institutions are incapable of meeting the larger challenges facing a nation – in brief, of doing much more than merely satisfying short-run political needs and interests of those who rule. Leaders have behaved with consummate irresponsibility in making crucial decisions. Integrationist, corporatist, and regulating theories of all kinds, which have been especially popular among leftist intellectuals, overlook the Right's grave foibles and ignorance and the many ways it has traumatized the historical process again and again with fascist and totalitarian movements. Advocates of revolutionary change who have come to power by non-parliamentary means have scarcely been abler, succeeding largely by chance or, as in the case of Leninists, because of traumatic circumstances (linked mainly to wars) not of their own making. That they failed to redeem societies permanently when in a position of power is the logic not only of their authoritarian ideologies but also of the essentially accidental way they attained power and their endemic inability to deal with real conditions after doing so. Overall, of course, those on the Right of the political spectrum have been in charge of many more places, far longer, and their values and social goals – with all of their negative consequences – warrant much more attention. But while there has been a difference between policy errors nominally motivated by very distinct values and assumptions, in the end what emerges as most crucial from the sad history of the past century is the way a basic consensus between Right, Center, and Left has evolved, and how political exigencies have caused each to concede enough to the other to make their common practice and actions far more consequential than their nominal distinctive ideologies. In large part this consensus was the inevitable result of the similar ambition, cynicism, and lust for power on any terms that has driven the leaders of all factions, regardless of their ostensible ideologies.

Issues of transformation

No economic strategy is "logical," much less inevitable, on its own terms – and both classical and Marxian economists have utilized essentially accounting calculations in assessing the durability and prospects of existing economies. In some fashion or another, all economic systems are profoundly "inefficient" to some constituencies, and the fundamental questions are those of goals and priorities – to whom is one responsible. Economics, the naivety of economists notwithstanding, can never be self-sufficient or isolated from a much larger and decisive context. By interacting with political and social factors, economies profoundly affect the total environment which produces economic development – wars included. The only question is who gains or loses from them and what each basic economic form accomplishes. In brief, what total risks are there in each economic system and for whom? It is simply not possible or historically accurate to say that industrialism inevitably imposes major constraints and consequences on society, regardless of the political and social context. All judgments must include every aspect of capitalist society or any other economy, although they may nominally have nothing to do with industrial organization but are crucial to the character of any society: the press, leisure, media, and the mentality and culture it encourages. Even if we cannot transform industrialism in certain technical regards, and must accept some constraints on the parameters of change, most decisive aspects of it are subject to important modifications. These larger dimensions are also vital to assessing whether or not a given organization of society is rational – even if we can do precious little, at least at the moment, about replacing it.

The truly pressing question is defining the minimal political and economic conditions for human survival and their basic institutional prerequisites. Whether or not we have the freedom of real choices, including more moderate ones, is less crucial at this point than our finally attaining realistic clarity about the consequences of different options; that is, where the world is heading with or without our opinions and input. If past responses have usually evolved from crises rather than preconceived plans or desires, the result has been the accumulation of inappropriate solutions. The question confronting the world today is what must be done to reverse various mounting challenges, and the minimum decisions and social forms that are essential for doing so.

We have to appreciate the constraints that conventional wisdom and political practices and institutions impose upon us, but also the grave – and probably fatal – costs of the status quo's continued failures. This means a thoroughgoing realism, regardless of the implications of such candor to our sense of optimism or pessimism.

The dominant capitalist doctrine, as inconsistent as it is, is the ideology of the winners who seek to maintain their mastery in the name of "objective laws" – which are no more objective than those Marx propounded. But has capitalism triumphed by overcoming those problems I outlined in the preceding chapters or has socialism been defeated? To claim that socialism's failures (which in its Leninist and Social Democratic versions is today an indisputable fact) are due to the success and enduring viability of capitalism averts the very real nature and tensions that system confronts, both within the fully industrialized world and in its relations with developing nations. For in certain key regards, capitalism has been weakened: its avarice and very scale and greatly increased complexity are only the most obvious aspects of monumental problems that capitalists must resolve – but cannot. Above all, wars are likely to reoccur and they will be far more destructive than ever.

It is essential to outline some general assumptions both regarding the direction in which we wish to guide social organization but also some of the preconditions for a much more rational society. Priorities vary dramatically in different nations, and what is absolutely essential in some will not be in others. A country with a food or water deficit, or a principally export-based economy or rural population, to name but a few key factors, will have very distinct objectives and problems. This diversity will always remain, and my concern is mainly with the United States and developed industrial societies – though the differences between the industrialized nations are often more important than their similarities. But whatever the nation, there must be a much more realistic definition of "pragmatic politics" and the criterion for determining what is truly pragmatic as well as meaningless existential and symbolic fashions and nonsense. Simply stated, it is not primarily a question of what enables a party or its leaders to come to power but also the extent to which a strategy will actually resolve, rather than merely defer, basic problems that lead to major crises. So far, the politics of "responsibility" has won jobs for those who advocate this brand of change but it has succeeded far less than existential posturing to meet the crucial issues confronting humankind.

The status quo has far more freedom to make errors in most nations than it did when a large, self-confident Left existed. But as the upheavals after 1917 showed, there are indefinable but decisive limits to the blunders existing elites can make. It is this endemic incapacity to get things right that must be addressed, and while the Left's historic failure makes the task much more difficult, those who still wish to save our civilization from committing more follies must embark in new directions if mankind is to escape the destructive fate which awaits it if its rulers continue to base their politics on the primacy of individual profit, war, and the maintenance of those social and economic conditions which make superstition and irrationality flourish. Action cannot wait for ostensible historical laws to unfold because they will not. Marx was completely wrong to allege it, though many of his contemporaries did also, because the end result is conformity and inaction. History's outcome is never certain, much less automatically desirable. It is in the very nature of the human experience that just as descriptions of reality are always contingent, the results of our efforts to alter it can never be guaranteed. In the most general and strategic sense, the only defense – if there be any – against illusions and failure is constant, critical thinking.

Nationalism and secular ideologies have also failed, partially because the United States, above all in the Middle East, for decades nourished religious fundamentalism and obscuritanism as an alternative to both socialism and nationalism. But there is no gainsaying the reality that secular movements in many nations also discredited themselves, largely – but not exclusively – because their leaders were venal and opportunist, and they ceased to be credible to more and more people as true advocates of serious changes in society. Islamic fundamentalism emerged stronger than ever but there are nonetheless nuances in its various forms, depending on the country. What is crucial today is that the vacuum into which irrationality has marched often has as its goal – however vague it may be – the transformation of status quos of every sort, ranging from hedonism and secularism to the unconscionable pursuit of personal interest above all else. These alternatives often posit a return to ancient societies and values that are often described in mythical terms, but they oppose the status quo as socialism once did. Moreover, fundamentalist extremism is symbiotic on unemployment and economic deprivation, above all among the young, and that it has especially flourished in the Middle East and North Africa is in large part due to the failures of capitalism in this region.

Norms

Norms are neither arbitrary nor peripheral, and while success is highly desirable, failure is far preferable than the sheer opportunism and unprincipled lust for power that social democrats and Bolsheviks made the hallmark of their political actions. A renewed Left or emancipatory social movement – what it is called is less important than what it demands and does – must have norms and values as a basis for its actions, and these should provide a direction to theory. At the very least, this requires that analyses of social phenomena and political events must always be undertaken with as much candor and honesty as we can mobilize. People cannot, as did Marxists, cultivate illusions or think along predetermined lines just because they prefer their consequences to those of more nuanced or sophisticated explanations. We scarcely wish for evil or complex situations but very often that is precisely what we confront when dealing with political events and the forces that shape them.

But there are basic criteria or norms that distinguish real movements for genuine change from those that are merely existential and frivolous. Opposition to war is one of them under virtually all circumstances, not because pacifism is a desirable philosophy but because the practical, functional consequences of wars in the past have been destructive and undermined all rational discourse and change. They have caused severe distortions of human and economic priorities; at this stage of weaponry, wars produce calamities. There simply can be no compromise with this principle; a movement is far better served being defeated on this issue. Politics may be the art of the possible in conventional theory but if the minimum essential for the safeguarding of the human condition is not attained then politics in this sense is not at all what is urgently required today. Politics is an excellent channel for ambitious men and women but it must not be confused with the imperatives of confronting reality, and to pretend that the careers of a handful of people are synonymous with preventing more disasters for humanity is a falsehood we should not tolerate. If the world's fate must be written off – because sooner or later there will be a nuclear war in some region unless a great deal of progress is made soon – then we should be honest about the consequences and meaning of our actions and not evoke people's idealism cynically. We have to remember that had the socialists opposed war in 1914 through their actions and votes then Bolshevism would never have emerged as the dominant force on the world Left, fascism would not have followed, and the entire tragic history of the twentieth century would have been far different.

But socialism was not a theory predicated on war, which Marx and his followers scarcely considered, and socialists came to power, to a significant extent, largely as a response to great human cataclysms. After over a century of relying on Marxism, socialists are still unable to cope with wars as a recurrent and predictable problem. Future critical political programs must deal centrally with the issue of wars, not just its institutional causes but how people must relate to tragedy and evil. The goals of socialism itself – its instrumental social, human, and economic objectives and its values – are far less contentious because they are very much in the rationalist, Enlightenment intellectual tradition which has evolved since the eighteenth century. Socialism's goals, which can be defended in economic or ethical terms, are far less controversial than practical questions of how parties, their leaders, and people should respond to reality. As an organized movement, socialism has failed in all its incarnations. Its goals and objectives have been devalued but they can and must be reasserted along with a rigorous commitment to critical intelligence which is both candid and honest about the failures of the Left as well as those it opposes. It does not have to be called socialism but what it is for and against must be crystal clear. But now its credibility must depend on its integrity and actions.

It is at the point when social crises arise that possibilities exist and innovations are also relevant, even if they are not in the precise forms that we desire. But attempting to consciously guide forces – utilizing parties or organizations – is important. This means that counterrevolution and resistance to change is also a distinct possibility and both have often prevailed in past upheavals, for the very circumstances that lead to possible great changes have also led to great failures. Counterrevolution is scarcely an abstract question and any theory of change that does not deal with it and its dangers to attaining one's goals during a struggle for power is exceedingly naive and an invitation to failure. It may range from guns in the hands of a hostile army to IMF attempts to utilize external debts to dictate economic programs – and usually much else. Radicals must prepare for serious opposition if only to prevent their goals being distorted in the process of coming to power. Innumerable times those who seek basic changes frequently have had to respond to internal or international resistance to it, usually because strong nations like the United States have sought wholly opportunistically for local allies to unwanted radical changes. Counterrevolution has usually mediated social transformation in crucial and undesirable fashions. Men such as Lenin had the will to rule but the manner in which it was expressed, even given their elitist preferences, often was dictated by others.

But while we must acknowledge the fact that real options are usually not ideal, many fewer accidents are imperatively required if problems are to be answered more rationally and really solved. We must be candid about the risks of futility in our actions but also take them when the stakes warrant it. But history is a whole cloth and how it is cut depends on many elements, and the Left's commitments and wisdom are crucial. Radicals must relate to real forces of authority and social constituencies but not mindlessly abandon themselves to them, and here the role of open discussion and criticism within parties is vital.

Just as one can never neatly order change as we wish it, it is even more illusory to believe – as conservatives do – that it can be prevented. Great movements of transformation in history in many nations have had a largely, even entirely self-generating and autonomous quality. Sometimes it is possible to bring the will and reality together, and then options are relevant. Prematurely, a revolutionary directive is farcical, but at the appropriate time in some nations it has been highly germane, even decisive. Without wars such periods of great transformation would usually be unthinkable, but to prevent them is today a prime objective. Yet war is the dominant fact of modern history and the proponents of wars take grave risks with remarkable impunity, frequently losing mastery thereby. Warriors are destructive of human lives but ultimately of themselves also. All this, alas, is simply an aspect of the human experience.

Wars and instability in the world

At the present juncture of history, given the formal American commitment to a doctrine of preemptive interventions, wars are at least as probable as at any time over the past century. The increasingly unstable global context has made it ever more likely and dangerous. The ending of Soviet hegemony in East Europe, and Moscow's restraining influence elsewhere, is only one factor – albeit a crucial one – creating new hazards of great importance. The proliferation of nuclear technology and other weapons of mass destruction, the knowledge essential for constructing them along with the diversity of effective means of delivering them, have made large parts of the world much more risky. At least 30 nations, according to the UN, can retool their peaceful nuclear programs and make weapons fairly quickly. If one adds what can be purchased, the present situation is even more frightening. The arms market is thriving and the United States, Russia, and numerous other nations will sell a great deal to most countries, and private arms merchants are utterly unscrupulous. Europe and Japan are far stronger and far more independent than at any time since 1945, and China's military and economic ascendancy in Asia has far-reaching consequences for the region. Despite what is often inappropriately called "globalization," regions and states are becoming far more economically independent and have intensified their national identities, in part because options are emerging in Asia and Europe which make the United States considerably less important than it was in the immediate postwar era. Whether one calls this "multipolarity" or devises another label, the trend is clear: American hegemony has passed and the world is becoming more diffuse. It is more complex and dangerous than ever, and the decentralization of military and political power is occurring simultaneously as the United States perpetuates its traditional ambitions to guide the destinies of virtually every region, as if the balance of power is the same now as in the 1950s. Together, this is a highly inflammable mixture of forces. All elements considered – the breakup of Yugoslavia, events in Africa, South Asia, and the Middle East, the United States' overweening hubris and global vision, and the like – wars, both civil or between states, remain the principal (but scarcely the only) challenge facing much of humanity. Also insidious are the numerous ecological disasters affecting all dimensions of the environment. This relentless development is accelerated by the unwillingness of the crucial nations – above all the United States – to adopt measures essential for reversing or controlling its damage.

The fact that wars occur more frequently and continuously is the major constraint on capitalism enduring as a system. The strongest argument for basic social change remains not the status quo's detractors and critics but the system itself, its consequences, and the world's grave and growing problems it causes. It is this which makes capitalism just as untenable today as it was a century ago, as it will any other social order which also devotes so much of its resources to preparing for and making war. If its economic failures or achievements in peacetime can be debated and arguments made for both sides, there is no case that can justify its belligerence. The absence of organized opposition may be an indicator of the status quo's social health, but so long as there are wars, challenges to existing social systems will reemerge in some form. Wartime conditions are far from ideal to create desirable alternatives, and the Left will behave in the same haphazard, inadequate way it has in the past unless it is much wiser.

Hence war is central to capitalism's viability in much of the world and to any prediction of whether capitalism can survive in the nations that engage in military conflicts. A population is radicalized the longer a war lasts and the greater its loss of lives and property, producing changes in the class structure or inflation – to name but a few potentially traumatizing forces. Their visions alter dramatically with morale, and political options are redefined dramatically. Then the question is not whether people will or should become social actors but merely when and in what forms it takes – but occur it will, for the process of mass consciousness is telescoped and serious opposition then becomes possible, even inevitable. Fascism and Bolshevism both came to power this way and altered profoundly twentieth-century history. Every time rulers embark on wars they create domestic resistance in ways that either would never have occurred or taken far longer. Then capitalists pay most for wars they condone because the struggle for political mastery and the direction of society becomes primordial, and the masses have as much or more to lose from apathy as from action. As for mankind, the stakes involved touch the very existence of rational civilization and human relations, of which economics is a key reflection of the system's failure but scarcely the sole basis for ultimately damning it. With the spread of nuclear or other destructive weapons the issues are much the same but we have yet to experience wars of this scale of destruction, and we have no gauge of possible human responses save that there is no reason to think that many people, as in the past, will regard their stake and role any differently when their losses are even greater – save that they may reach a level where group action is less possible. Alas, it is likely we will find out.

Capitalism's consummate immorality is linked to war, but so too is its structural fragility. The causes of wars include nationalism and atavism as well as economics, but their quite diverse origins in no way mitigate the grave economic consequences that ensue. What is essential now is the definition of the core premises and goals – the priorities – for any political movement of rational social change. Where and when it emerges is speculative, but that it will, at least in some nations, is as close to certain as the phenomenon of change, and at that point the movement must be able to maintain its commitment to its original promises. This requires not just that radicals be willing to act decisively where warranted but to think carefully beforehand about what they want to do with power consistent with their initial principles. Absolutely essential to this extremely formidable task is the definition of a rational political methodology, both analytically and organizationally, one that is flexible when it is warranted and intelligent in its awareness of both the potential and limits of all social theories, and that offers the prerequisite for continuous guidance to coping with inevitable new circumstances. It must not become, as in the case of Marxism, another sclerotic creed, a set of formal and quite academic opaque propositions transformed into an act of faith.

People who seek change must think both much more clearly and candidly, and they must do so much more often. To attain this capacity, which is the precondition of the revival of critical and truly radical politics, is not a vague abstraction but crucial if the Left parties are not again to be unsuccessful. They must offer solutions relevant to the innumerable crises of the modern age, however far-reaching, that really prevent the calamities of wars and revolutions from again preempting and perverting social change. This axiomatically requires us to confront honestly what was wrong with all of the diverse parties of what has been called the Left for well over a century and why they failed to fulfill its original promises on so many crucial issues. But even more important, it demands an articulate definition of what are the absolutely minimum changes that humanity must implement in both foreign and domestic affairs, and not simply what is attainable. If that is utopian and irrelevant, so be it, but we must take great chances because that precisely is what is now required.

Economic premises

The fundamental problems of any economy are not merely its goals and objectives, growth rates, or who wins or loses most from it – although all of these matters are crucial. Much more important is whether the indirect political, ideological, and social consequences of the existing economic system are likely again to create the political and social chaos that capitalist economic systems have generated over the past centuries. Economists are oblivious to wars and their causes entirely, assign little or no role to how the entire political and institutional process determines who wins and loses in economics, and only very recently have some conceded that ecological factors are also significant. But humanity's survival depends largely on factors such as these.

There is no "best" way of arranging an economic organization; immutable economic laws simply do not exist. There are goals and interests only; but if one sees economic forms as a problem of human adaptation to the imperatives of survival there are certain institutional arrangements that are excluded. How we perceive such matters will affect profoundly the way we reason and what we propose. Today the decisive issues are war and peace, environmental survival in every sense, and man-made misery. These are the criteria for the efficacy and efficiency of an economic system. Growth must have a far lower priority than equity and stability – in a word, it can scarcely serve as a rationale for economic policy. The choice of alternatives is far less their practicality than whether the human species will survive in the direction it is going. It will not.

Economic forms can be adjusted as experience or needs dictate but goals can rarely be modified lest the whole purpose of change be subverted. It is not essential to blueprint precise ways of organizing the economy but only to stake out premises and priorities, and above all objectives, and attain them. But there is nothing sacrosanct in a status quo based on chicanery and theft, and dispelling its myths is one major step in choosing organizing principles for another economy. Clarity regarding what one is doing and how the context and society operates is crucial; it also eliminates many alternatives that conventional wisdom advocates. This demands knowledge, independent of alternatives.

Size is a constraint on all forms of economic reorganization, but it is a fiction that business executives are efficient and honest, and there is much room for experimentation and change. Workers' organizations and parties are as prone as any to be taken over by ambitious individuals and every obstacle must be created to keep "workers' control" from becoming a defense of new elites. Marx's and the anarchists' romantic notions regarding a classless society being simply established at the end of history is fanciful nonsense and dangerous for anyone to believe and use as a basis for change. There will always be a need for some sort of hierarchy in a large economic organization, but we can decide how and why it is created and how immune it is to impersonal standards and recall – and alter the economy in the direction of greater responsiveness and democracy to the extent possible and desirable, but also consistent with a minimum of efficiency. Inherited economic units and the way they are run are far less sacrosanct than political systems, which should also be changed if they are abused, and the principle of democracy is just as relevant in the economy as in politics – and while this allows a degree of freedom it also imposes constraints because there is a public whose general interests must also be a crucial factor in how economic units are organized. There are many options to the status quos that are more consistent with efficiency, and workers can make decisions about how the proceeds of sales are distributed that are more rational than those now made by boards of directors and key stockholders. There is so much chicanery and inefficiency built into the present system, from the products that are commercialized to mergers and acquisitions that are motivated by profits and are utterly irrational technically (and often financially), much less how people rise to the top of the corporate world, that it can be replaced with new forms of control that are more humane, democratic, and probably more productive.

The economy must be as responsive to human needs as politics, and the same principles of equity and respect for the environment should guide it. But just because those who now run the corporations are doing the wrong things does not mean that the workers in them will automatically do the right ones. There must be much experimentation because there is no certain and tried way to reform an economy and how to change it will vary by each situation and by country; in some nations there is no economic organization to speak of, or economic activity is concentrated in fields where forms of control – as in agriculture – can be quite different than, say, with advanced industrial facilities. These range from co-ops to more collective forms of ownership – and yet others too numerous to mention. Conventional wisdom in economics has produced a world of instability, injustice, and much more poverty than there should or need be, but there are no magic and timeless universal answers on how we wish the world to be reorganized. The same skeptical realism that causes us to reject the status quo must also be applied to solutions to escape the present economic miasma. If they do not attain our objectives or fail to work we should abandon them and try something else. What is needed is the will to begin and persist in creating new forms of economic control that resolve problems rationally.

But a prerequisite of clarity and changes that are far more rational than those introduced in the past is the recognition that the exigencies of the moment and foreign influences profoundly shaped what was termed "socialism" in all too many places. This was the rule in the nominal Communist economies but in more subtle ways these kinds of pressures have also affected what socialists and reformers have chosen elsewhere. In the Communist nations the institutions, organization, and commandist mentality appropriate for the seizure of power became habits and the norm in the economy. Such thinking must be avoided at all cost. What is best – much less the most durable – is rarely what is inherited or the result of externally imposed compulsions.[1]

It is a reality that nations that have a more equitable distribution of assets and income have higher growth rates and are also more rationally run. They also have much less stress in every form, including violence and homicide, and far better physical and mental health standards than much richer nations with high inequality. The "social determinants" of health have repeatedly been shown empirically to be crucial. While exact economic forms are less important than the social objectives of an economy and, above all, the priorities guiding it, it is also a fact that the nations that have the highest public spending as a share of the GDP also tend to have the highest growth rate. They are far from perfect but the people in them are, on the whole, happier because their basic physical needs are assured and they have many fewer problems than countries whose assets belong to small elites, as is the case in much of the world. Peasants must have more access to credit, and the government has a responsibility to establish superior education and human capital systems; there is overwhelming evidence for the economic as well as human value of equity. Balanced economic development is far more important than growth at any cost, and prosperity based on war and armaments is sooner or later humanly and materially destructive, but experience shows that equity is more compatible with both sustained growth and social stability. It is far more important to avoid value-added taxes on basic necessities or impose the other regressive taxes the IMF advocates. The very notion of balanced budgets as the goal of fiscal policy should be treated with the greatest suspicion. Social needs and priorities have infinitely greater claims upon budgets, and insofar as funds are needed to pay the bills that accrue, raising money is quite simple. The rich should and must pay high taxes, for they squander money on baubles that no one needs to live a healthy, prosperous existence. Taxes, even more than nominal incomes, should be redistributive until all the basic human and public needs are met – which will be a very long time in nations where systematic neglect has been the rule. Capital flight can be prevented easily enough with draconian penalties on those rich who intend avoiding progressive taxes. But the underconsumptionist premise that unequal incomes create less than optimum and stable economic activity, and are a major cause of economic downturns, should be made a keystone of economic policy.[2]

Marxists propounded many of the crucial assumptions of capitalist economic theories. What is "efficient" by conservative economic criteria is inefficient in social terms, yet most socialist parties accept these basically conservative criteria after they are elected. If a nation's welfare calculates everything from the costs of housework to ecological and cultural damage to the house locks essential in most societies and much else, the prevalent methods of assessing economic progress fall by the wayside and very different but much more realistic estimates emerge.[3] A commitment to maximizing the interests and needs of the great majority *must* guide the policy of future movements of change, for it reflects those essential priorities without which they have no raison d'être. Profit as a consideration must be discarded, along with the myths that all economic doctrines manufacture.

Even when externally imposed imperatives circumscribe the Left's ability to shape realities in the manner it prefers, it is essential for it to understand the nature of social history and change – and their responsibilities as well as opportunities to it. It is still vital that institutional criteria for reform be articulated so that the Left will not betray itself or those people whose expectations bring it to power – as it has usually done. It is important to realize that the mere destruction of existing social institutions and forms does not automatically create better ones, and solacing myths do not clear our minds and prepare us for the variety of real options that may present themselves in reality. What is paramount is that the same mistakes not be repeated, and that a movement learns from its errors.

Constraints on social forms are usually a question of financial costs, which are worth paying if the social consequences warrant it. We are not free, as sectarians assume, to do whatever we desire but humanity has been plagued far more with doctrines of inevitability in economics than with notions of freedom, and determinism is the bane of social engineering. Still, the arms race is not inherent in industrialism and technology, but in the social systems that nourish it. For reasons of realistic analyses as well as priorities, we should favor high and equitable taxation, much more equality in society's compensation structure, generous social spending on health, housing, and the like, and a definition of social good in social policy that is implemented in fact and is not merely rhetoric.

The nature and goals of politics

Oppositional politics, whatever its ideological persuasion, encourages the imagination to flourish, but its basic dilemma is what it can and will do if or when it attains power. Power is a great opportunity that usually culminates in disillusion, if not disaster, but there is no way that critical choices, along with their immense responsibilities, can be avoided once in office. Those who seek to replace the established order often lack a program based on careful thought and knowledge, but political failure is also inevitable whenever leaders are egoists who treat politics as an arena for fulfilling their personal ambitions.

But as problematic as it is, politics will never go away and the real issue is what we must and can do, given the profound legacies of past errors, with the precarious tools at hand. This entails priorities as well a far more realistic estimate of the risks and consequences of bureaucracies and their origins, mentalities, and people within them. We have not merely to outline desirable social forms but undo the immense legacies and errors, both structural and intellectual, of the past century of wars. Indeed, these two tasks must be undertaken together.

So-called leftists should particularly be carefully and critically assessed, not so much to devalue their objectives, whose betrayal in no way legitimizes alternatives to them, but to possess an accurate perspective of the nature of the social and political processes that define and compromise modern political life. They cannot rely on or cite axiomatic notions of the mechanistic legacies of nineteenth-century optimism, which merely justify political irresponsibility. There is a need for unsparing candor as well as intelligence when it comes to defining political realities, and this means discarding myths of all varieties – capitalist, socialist, and the like – and a critical analytic method that often appears essentially negative. We require a thorough and realistic appreciation of the social context within which humankind has operated for some centuries past, and is very likely going to continue to function in the future unless we can alter it. By social reality I mean the distribution of economic and social assets, the nature of the education system to the extent it is invidious (as it is at many levels), the character of the media and the ways it aids the process of political and social illiteracy, and much more. And such thought also requires value judgments as to what kind of society we seek to create. We need a minimum understanding of the problems that are to be confronted and resolved, which includes not only war but also the nature and causes of action or inaction by the people, the workings of institutions and power and the personalities who possess it, and much else.

To state that all politics is inherently constrained and foredoomed to compromises and dilution is to miss the crucial point. That innumerable socialist and Social Democratic parties have shown faintheartedness in the face of great challenges, or share a far greater consensus in power than differences with the parties that preceded them, does not require repeating. Socialist parties have failed to transform old orders and challenges and have not been effective vehicles for radically altering the world's course. The only way to do anything radical is to do it, and there is no substitute for actions in the face of deplorable conditions – both domestic and international. The political parties and assumptions that circumstances have bequeathed us over the past century have failed to prevent ever-greater disasters and the attempt to reform basically the world as it is (and is going) is worth the risk of failure, even if it is very large. Otherwise we can await doomsday.

Political movements committed to solutions of the myriad problems confronting us require not only new constitutional forms, which are not easy to attain in parliamentary systems, but also especially innovative party structures that have workable procedures of recall, circumscribed tenure, and discipline that are all wholly autonomous of state constitutions. These must be imposed upon every leader in ways that none can evade. And they must be deliberately encumbering and based on the historically justified assumption that leaders as a class can never be trusted uncritically, and it is far better to eliminate good ones prematurely or unjustly than to have to suffer interminably under the others – which is far more likely. Cliques based on geographic, personal, and religious ties – mafias – exist in all parties and lead to favoritism, corruption, and the like. We must have defenses against personalities and careerists and egoists. It is not only an organizational question but also intellectual, and inviolable received wisdom has been bureaucracies' best defense. Such people cannot flourish in an intellectually open, inherently skeptical environment. If doubt and politics do not mix well, still far worse is dogmatism and sclerosis. Only the critical opposition, which alone has a self-assigned historical obligation to transform societies to the core, imperatively requires such open, frequently cumbersome organizational strictures and methods and must, in effect, creatively reinvent both parties and politics in order to attain their goals. Conservatives can, and do, serve their systems faithfully even if they are personally corrupt.

The public should get used to a party that really believes what it says – and if people refuse to support it, so much the worse for all concerned; then politics is an illusion and a chimera. But political democracy means very little when parties abandon their original pledges and purposes. The programmatic efficacy of a party and its conformity to its basic commitments can never be above discussion, and everything is to be gained from such frequent reviews. The dangers from an excess of democracy have to be weighed against a paucity of it, for it is a historical fact that lack of it has caused most Left parties, from German Social Democrats in 1914 to the Bolsheviks and the British Labour Party today, to fail calamitously at critical junctures. The time-consuming liabilities and imperfections that come from internal democracy are far less onerous than those that accompany efforts to stifle free discussion. They simply must be lived with if there is to be a renewal of radical politics and belief.

We have long since reached a point at which criticism, however uncomfortable it is to the prevailing political process, is not only called for but also essential to reverse existing trends and renew social thought and action. There are costs to both being "relevant" as well as uncompromising, and we can have no illusions about either of these, but there are ample numbers of people willing to be the former and there are far too few with good sense and knowledge in the opposition. Isolation from the mainstream is scarcely desirable per se. Even worse than sectarianism are illusions and a readiness to embark on the chimeras of "responsible" politics that deprive nations of essential analyses and options when they need them most. It is more crucial today to have clear, pertinent, and genuine alternatives based on an intellectual process that is committed to objectivity and candor, and so those who advocate a critical new politics may very well be a small minority for some time. If after articulating relevant solutions they remain isolated, then there is scant hope to reverse the tide that is ruining human civilization and even threatening its very existence. There is absolutely no guarantee that clarity will lead to victory. It may not, but it is a risk we must take.

It is important to articulate a critical and positive theory. Capitalism and the foibles of socialist politicians offer many targets. It must also include the nature of power, history, and the direction of international relations – in brief, the structure and weaknesses of key institutions and the ways existing social systems have distorted technology. But besides defining what it desires to attain, a renewed radical theory should make clear what it doesn't want, a task that also gives required direction to its goals. This is an awesome mission compared to the simplisms which have sufficed in most ideologies until now, and while it calls for great intelligence, intelligence is only a prerequisite and not a guarantee. The best basis for confronting problems such as these is the truth – a commitment inherent in the principles of creating a social philosophy that I outlined in Chapter 4. Commitment to the truth is also a way to avoid the cynicism and depolitization which the denial of reality produces. It rejects the existence of a fantasy opposition – ideas which nourished the Left from its inception – but also the myths of the mainstream ideologues and spokesmen. It requires constant critical thinking.

What is relevant today is the staking out of the core premises and goals – the priorities – for any political movement of rational social change. Absolutely essential to this extremely formidable task is not only a readiness to act decisively where and when warranted but also the definition of a rational political methodology, both analytically and organizationally, one that is flexible and intelligent in its awareness of both the potential and limits of all social theories, and that offers the prerequisite for continuous guidance to coping with inevitably new circumstances. This preliminary effort, which is the precondition of the revival of critical and truly radical politics, is not a vague abstraction but crucial if the diverse parties of the Left are not to once again fail to confront relevantly the innumerable crises of the modern age. This axiomatically requires us to consider what was wrong with all of the diverse currents of what has been called the Left for well over a century and why they failed to fulfill their original promises on so many crucial issues.

Changes and reforms that are relevant in one nation or region often are not appropriate in another, save in one regard: radicals must transform institutions and reject theories of economic growth based on classic, neo-liberal models, in large part because they are false illusions. But even if they were not, the kinds of societies they envision are both inherently undesirable and unstable in the medium and long run. There is nothing intrinsically wrong with growth, but if the costs include social turmoil and its negative consequences, wars, and the kinds of problems most of the world has experienced over the past century then something far better must be articulated than the conventional wisdom which the "Washington consensus" preaches. A renewed Left must think through these complex questions and confront them in some appropriate manner, applying solutions to the specific conditions and demands of their own nations. Their responses have to take realities into account but they must also be principled in intention – and revised accordingly if need be.

At the very least, however, a new radical, democratic ideology must not only spell out its objectives but also indicate how the practice of a movement which evokes idealistic goals can also betray them. There must be a criterion of success but also of failure, and when theory and practice diverge dramatically then a party must have the mechanisms by which to acknowledge it – and avoid repeating errors in the future. If a movement's leaders are fascinated by power then such self-reflection and correction will be very difficult, if not impossible, and this is the history of Communist and most Social Democratic parties. A party cannot be so filled with doubts and contingencies as to be unable to formulate a program or function politically, but the lust of individuals for authority is simply a constant challenge as well as a dilemma for reformers to acknowledge and overcome. A radical party needs values as guideposts, and none is more basic than individual freedom of thought and the ability to express dissent when need be. This requires radical creeds but also radical people who want to achieve them, and whose critical conduct and commitments assure that goals have meaning at all stages. Parties of change must never again become simply vehicles for ambitious people, aspiring leaders and gurus, caudillos and heroes, or the like. If this sounds idealistic it should, but whether it is unrealistic too remains to be seen. What is least acceptable is the continuation of the ideas and patterns of behavior and institutions that now are guiding a hapless humanity to more wars and social ills of every sort and variety. If such change and these criteria are utopian or irrelevant then the world is destined to spin its fate out as it has for over a century, and that is too dangerous to be accepted as inevitable.

The nature of the Left

Socialism as a political movement has disappeared in all but name; parties that use that label are anything but radical. But capitalism, new weaknesses and contradictions added, remains intact. We must revitalize the norms of equity and rationality, not to resurrect socialism as a phrase but to prevent capitalists from pursuing the destructive and antisocial direction the world's economic and political institutions are now following.

The Communist world was based on authoritarian leadership systems both in theory and practice, and tyranny, corruption, and nepotism were their only legacies. But Social Democratic parties have since their inception also been plagued with serious leadership difficulties, from the domination of ambitious opportunists to a lack of internal democracy, especially when parties were the most successful and this very fact strengthened the power of their heads. Intolerance of internal dissent was worst in the Leninist parties but Social Democratic parties have also suffered greatly from it.

The creation of responsiveness – which means welcoming democracy's encumbrances – within a party, which few if any Left parties have attained, means that they must be ready to pay very substantial but necessary costs to achieve it. This includes mandatory retirement from leadership posts after a relatively brief number of years and the loss of seemingly successful and charismatic people in key positions. It means that the party should not permit dynasties based on personal, regional, and other ties. Electoral success should not become an excuse for authoritarianism, as it has in the case of the British Labour Party after 1997 and, to various degrees, in many others. Frequent party meetings that actually have the power of recall are mandatory, and it is far better to have too many safeguards than too few. All this requires party constitutions that are strictly enforced and place a higher priority, if the choice must be made, on the prevention of oligarchies emerging than on taking power. The dangers of the betrayal of principles and potential tyranny are ultimately far more crucial concerns than simply gaining office. Only such rigor can create the precondition for parties that genuinely conform to their principles. And if their principles mean so little then they are much more a liability than anything else, for they mislead those who believe in them. Truly radical parties require continuing social legitimacy, which means they must institutionalize a mass line and guarantee the formal powers and rights of its members – including minorities.

One of the most difficult and crucial issues confronting radical politics is the control of leadership and the political class that all parties create. Authoritarian leaders, alas, have affected all political tendencies – Left, Right, and Center – to some degree, but egomania and social transformation have been and can be a dangerous mixture. Just as good people are not sufficient to make good causes, good causes most assuredly do not guarantee good leaders, and while the numbers of good people in history have far exceeded the bad ones, many appropriate answers to the problems that afflict various nations have been betrayed and distorted by bad leaders. It is by far safer to operate on such a pessimistic basis than to give ambitious personalities the leeway for repeating the compromises and abuses of authority that have blighted socialism and all political systems over the past century. Such a position is not Hobbesian, and no theory justifies fatalism, or optimism, in social and political affairs; it is simply historically based and empirical.

It is always very much easier to describe a set of changes than to make them, not the least because those who advocate change usually find themselves in power in a vacuum – when the old order collapses due to war or other circumstances and they have great responsibility before they are equipped programmatically to do anything with it. Good causes need more than good people to succeed, although they require them also; they need as much clarity as is possible and necessary, or they will fail. The way beliefs interact with the parameters of reality is a dilemma intrinsic in the politics of social change and it will always be present because there is no axiomatic way to resolve it. It is a constant challenge to be confronted over and over again, but it is greatly simplified if people have beliefs as a basis for action and are not merely fascinated, like the vast majority of so-called radicals and dissenters, by acquiring power.

There is, however, a more or less important element of ambiguity in every political act, one that is both inherent in the choice of alternatives as well as the very nature of the political process. History does not deliver neat, simple alternatives or solutions that justify any calculated a priori strategy, and the sources of change – the parties, nature of elites and their antagonists, the degree of spontaneity, and much else – make it very difficult, if not impossible, to predict the precise forms and context in which future changes will happen. There are powerful vested interests in many old systems that often have the capacity to affect events. But basic change *will* occur, with or without guidance. To reject complexities, much less to deny their existence, is to ban oneself to isolation and irrelevance. We can never make a virtue of necessity and accept reality as it comes to us because this means abandoning both reason and imagination. We have fewer choices to make than would be ideal and we should acknowledge the limits of past experiences but we must also transcend them when we have to and can do so – which is far more often than the Left has throughout the past century. Realism plus idealism offers a basis for durable struggle. But this means assessing not merely the internal forces of change but the impact of external interventions – of which those the United States has mounted have been the most crucial since 1945 – on the internal political and economic dynamics of nations. Fortunately, there are important growing economic alternatives to the United States, and although it remains formidable it has far overextended itself and will, despite its illusions, be less of a challenge to radical social change in the future than it has in the past.

There is today precious little of the historic Left's rhetoric that still possesses credibility. Despite the emergence of fairly significant social and political movements, above all the ecological, the Left is still characterized by an inability to define and choose alternatives in the real world. And personal opportunism, to varying degrees, plagues every party. The leaders of the Left remain, as ever, a danger as well as a necessity. And in nations with traditional self-styled socialist parties, many people who consider themselves leftists still insist on supporting such parties even though they do nothing when they come to power to alter the conservative policy thrust. Indeed, they often do what conservatives dare not. Events in the form of wars or social injustices gave a raison d'être to actions and demonstrations, a sense of community, and much else. But in "normal" times, socialist parties that opportunistically pursue conservative strategies continue to get the support of good people who do not want to – or simply cannot – confront the enormous complexities of reality and the difficult, radical choices it requires. These are generally people with noble hearts but their political intelligence has lagged far behind their emotions and many still hold great illusions.

Abandoning oneself to the tides of history leads to condoning the betrayals of Communist or Social Democratic bureaucrats and opportunists. Such parties were facts of life and they have failed, unevenly and often quite catastrophically, but at certain key moments they nonetheless mobilized the time and commitments of millions of good, well-intentioned people as well as those relatively few who saw these causes merely as vehicles for their own ambitions. It is crucial to comprehend the reasons why these nominally ideologically diverse parties were so successful and how they kept many on their side long after they were emptied of the slightest scintilla of radical pretension, how and why their failures occurred and, above all, how to avoid repeating this history of betrayal again. In the case of Communist parties, corrupt elements were protected by the immunity from criticism that Leninism gave them – and still does in China and Vietnam. But Social Democratic parties, as the recent history of the British Labour Party has shown, also insulate their leaders, especially when they bring jobs to the activists. It is also necessary to always recall that mass mobilization over the past century has been far greater during wartime, and that most people who have become political have done so in this context. Normally they much preferred their own private lives and it is a fact that creating a mass political consciousness during peacetime – with all of its assets – is far more difficult.

There is absolutely no comfort or intellectual clarity to be gained from respecting inherited socialist doctrines and icons that have failed to provide an adequate basis for either understanding or changing the world, much less have only deepened the gap between ideology and reality in ways that only intensify the profound demoralization that today permeates the entire Left. Those who seek definite assurance regarding the past and future destiny that dogmatic and comprehensive creeds have offered, the sort of theory which originated in the nineteenth century's sanguine and mechanistic mentality, had best live cloistered existences and leave the problems of social reality to others to confront. But it must be constantly remembered that while Marxism is suffused with this totalistic and dangerous way of thinking, the concept of the inexorable workings of market capitalism, as close to conventional wisdom today as any doctrine, is a similar dogma. This makes the use of the term "socialist" a pragmatic consideration only. What is crucial is the sufficient transformation of those essentially capitalist institutions and precedents – those material or ideological forces that led to atavism, conflict, and war – that traditional socialists failed to alter when in a position to affect history. The term "socialism" itself is scarcely sacrosanct and warrants being replaced wherever a better definition is articulated.

The problem, for now, is strictly semantic. What cannot be dismissed is the larger but admittedly amorphous rationalist, humanitarian, internationalist, and radical tradition from which socialism emerged, which preceded Marxism by at least a century and ultimately was irrevocably committed to the transcendent goals of equality and social cooperation both within and between states. These premises and objectives are more relevant and imperative than ever, to be refurbished and reasserted. Socialism was an effort to counteract the negative consequences of capitalism, and it can still play this role if "socialism" is defined not as a comprehensive analysis – as Marxism is – or as a fairly precise agenda but simply as a broad priority-value system for confronting and making societies and international relations humane and far less belligerent. The social logic and tradition from which socialism evolved remains relevant to the problems of today but its nineteenth-century legacies are vestiges of the analytic moods of that innocent period. Socialism as a political movement emerged largely out of crises, when the overwhelming pressure of events caused people to make choices, but it proved impotent or Leninism grossly distorted it. It is close to certainty that crises will reoccur because capitalism still produces instability and wars.

The vitality of the socialist vision of a equitable distribution of wealth and income is not that it is the perfect way to organize an economic system but that it is, by far, preferable given the alternatives, their impact on human and social forms and, above all else, their consequences for peace or war in the future. It probably does not maximize economic incentives and growth in the strictly short-term manner that conventional economic theory calculates, but it does stabilize economies and societies in ways that are much more likely to prevent the emergence of atavistic, reactionary, and ultimately materially highly destructive as well as dangerous political forces – right-wing populism, authoritarian heroes who suffer from illusions of grandeur, and the like. It is social stability within states that remains the precondition for peace between them, and capitalism has not attained it. For the central issue of economics today is civilization's survival and the preservation of the resources with which the earth has been endowed, and whatever increases the chances for peace as opposed to war and militarism is essential. This was socialism's original impulse and its strongest justification, and although the socialist movement and ideology failed there is more reason than ever to abolish capitalism.

A Left party's actions are generally defined by three factors: first, its ideology and the goals articulated from it; second, a lack of knowledge of options, which the myopia of determinist socialist theory and imagination has reinforced; third, the decisions which historical circumstances impose, and here we must include not only when political events compelled it to act but also when conditions allowed it to procrastinate endlessly and do nothing save administer the status quo more or less effectively. The first is of historic origin, and the reason why most thoughtful people join a party, and the second reflects the profound general analytic shortcomings of the Left. The third is very often the decisive factor, and parties that make a virtue of necessity are far more the rule than the exception. The Bolsheviks were the most ready to do so because they were fascinated principally by the acquisition of power. But social democrats also repeatedly betrayed their ostensible goals because, while parliamentary politics is very often constrained by what is possible, they usually failed to recognize a crucial distinction between making necessity a virtue to be accommodated to as opposed to acknowledging constraints that are a fact of life to be overcome as soon as possible. While there is no predetermined formula, depending on the issue – and war or peace is surely one, basic environmental needs yet another – it is much more important to take the right position and act on it to the optimum extent possible than be a part of a government that pursues calamitous policies. Solutions to crucial problems are ultimately not technocratic but reflect profound policy commitments and a willingness to act that cannot be fatally diluted or forgotten, above all in times of crises. This is not an argument for sectarianism but it is absolutely essential for a radical political party to retain its own identity and actively comprehend its basic obligations and mission, both to its supporters and to well-being in general, and to act to achieve them when it can or must. Being part of a government and sharing power is never an end in itself, and the moment that becomes its overweening goal the so-called Left party will go the way of the major socialist parties – Social Democratic and Communists in West Europe – that have preceded it.

Determining the purely economic aims of a renovated radicalism – again, what it is called is far less crucial than its substance – is the least difficult aspect of the task, for institutions must remain instrumental and sufficiently flexible to create stable nations in a peaceful world. This automatically excludes a wide variety of social forms, now deemed by the United States and many nations, the IMF, and other quasi-official world organizations as desirable. More difficult is the need to create mechanisms and controls that prevent personalities, parties, and institutions – including those that evoke the socialist tradition – from becoming unresponsive and authoritarian. But in the last analysis, how such means and ends are defined must be constrained only by a quite simple dedication to being on the side of the oppressed, the disadvantaged, and – whenever the basic criterion of who should gain or lose in a society is applied – the people who are ready to work to earn what they spend. These priorities are ultimately the only ones that make the entire historic tradition of reform, the improvement of society, and socialism both meaningful and consistent. Such a dedication alone defines the ideological if not actual differences between the Right and Left which have been a central if not exclusive focus of the politics of virtually all nations for well over a century. Integral to this commitment is the prevention of war and the elimination of its causes. We can desire reforms for moralistic, class, and other reasons, but we must also decide what is the minimum essential if the world is to survive in an inhabitable form.

We live in an age of disorder, without the moorings which redemptive ideas

– and myths – that were uncritically accepted provided in earlier centuries. Reality needs far better explanations than have been offered, including comprehension that should ostensibly emerge from the radical tradition. This disorder is scarcely restricted to Leninists and socialists, but it is universal and reflects a much larger crisis that affects all of the social theories produced over the past two centuries. But politics continues because apart from the fact that there will always be those ready and anxious to become leaders, politics is inherent in the nature of things. The world can scarcely afford more false counsel and guidance, or more of the same illusions. This was true a century ago, but far more pressing today.

People should never apologize for attempting to do good, nor making necessary but difficult choices. Nor do they have to apologize for making errors when they occur, although they have a serious intellectual and political responsibility to attempt to avoid committing, much less repeating, them. Everyone must assume the obligation to think as clearly as possible, and to reach their political conclusions after subjecting their own assumptions to an honest, rigorous process of critical examination – in a word, to be intelligent.

But politically active people must still remember that if they make the wrong decisions they very frequently did not create the world's paradoxes and ironies – those who have power and create hapless victims do that – but responded to them. The worst of all possibilities is for a person to be apathetic in the face of evil. It is far better to work oneself into an ambiguous situation than remain silent, but it is even far more preferable to resolve serious problems intelligently – and this the Left has usually failed to do. If evil-doers and immense human tragedies and wars were to disappear then so many intellectual and political enigmas would not exist for others to confront and resolve. Indeed, radical innovations themselves would hardly be necessary. The difficulty is that it is essential to alter many of the important institutions, attributes, and patterns of conduct if the very critical problems confronting the world today are to be solved. Opposition for its own existential sake is a luxury we cannot afford in perpetuity; there must be some important changes quickly if humanity is to survive. A party that says it wishes to solve problems must actually do so when it comes to power. The problem is not to assert that socialism has not been tried but to comprehend – if only to avoid repeating their errors – how those who embarked upon the effort to attain it failed to do so. Leninists and Social Democrats did not capitalize on capitalism's profound failures to create social arrangements and positive precedents for others to follow, thereby gravely tarnishing socialism as an ideal and creating the need for a fundamental intellectual and ideological renovation that does not repeat its failures.

It is true that positions often do not emerge full blown but evolve under the pressure of external and internal forces and reflection. But this way of arriving at choices is often sloppy and incoherent in many contexts, and it should be avoided whenever possible; it frequently is not. Yet if priorities and goals are constant, this is crucial to avoiding the limits of simply reacting to the pressure of events. Still, it is essential that those who express their indignation at the political and economic trends now dominant in much of the world maintain a sufficient degree of clarity to see their own dilemmas and to assert as soon as possible their rationally defined values and objectives. The logic and necessity of responses and actions does not demand mindlessness, and only by guarding the critical, rational process of political thought can a movement react far more ably and intelligently to future challenges than it has in the past. People should avoid passivity and in most cases there is a need to protest even when equivocal situations exist, as they frequently do. There is often permanent tension and dilemma in relating to injustice. We must act, because the world's injustices brook no indifference. Radical politics will continue to require difficult choices, which is the strongest argument possible for rational thinking as a political guide.

No system was ever threatened by an opposition party alone. The context was decisive, and as I have repeated ad infinitum, wars and the threat of them account for most crises that have occurred over the past century and have been the principal catalysts of the radicalization and militancy of the masses. Now that the Left is demoralized, and in many places has ceased to exist for real political purposes, the critical question is whether the structurally hobbled status quo can survive alone, as well as whether new political forms of opposition will emerge to confront it. The virtual demise of an organized Left in many nations has given conservatism an important political respite but its economic and social problems not only still exist but they are increasingly aggravated. Precisely because of such ongoing problems, a genuine opposition – what it is called is not so crucial as the fact itself – may yet emerge to challenge conventional wisdom. The more wisely it does so the more effective and dangerous it will be. The strongest argument for basic change, to repeat a point I have made before, is not the system's detractors – who for the most part have been incapable of resolving the crucial issues facing humanity – but the myriad problems the status quo has created.

People were far less converted to socialism by ethical and rational arguments than outraged by the pressure of events and the destructive consequences, both at home and abroad, of capitalism – expressed principally in wars but also in economic depressions. The irreducible argument for the retention of the older social goals and priorities of which socialism was but a part is its larger sense of human values and needs but, above all, the persistence of urgent economic and political problems to be resolved and the inability of capitalism to create a just, peaceful basis for society. A rational and radical alternative will remain essential so long as these problems exist. The superfluous intellectual trappings that socialists adopted in the nineteenth century must be discarded, and the demise of Leninist parties was a vital precondition in this process. Socialism failed abysmally during its first 150 years of existence but so too did capitalism, which is now far more destructive and irrational. Hence alternatives to capitalism still remain imperative, and that is the reason why a political movement with the same final aims as socialism remains both essential and vital. Today, capitalism's only menace is itself, which will resurrect some form of opposition in the future just as it always has in the past during social emergencies, but now the opposition that emerges cannot simply come to power or retain it by default. It must exploit its transitory success to finally do a great deal more about the failings of the status quo than it did earlier.

People and their roles

Under ordinary circumstances of peacetime, the vast bulk of the population will remain passive. They have been acquiescent in terms of their obligation to become social actors until mainly war-induced upheavals have pushed or compelled them to, and then it has most often been too little and too late.

But people are not free to remain passive without paying a price that is far greater than many have been willing to accept, and it is during such rare occasions that mass action becomes both possible and socially meaningful. Then inhibitions fall aside, conventional wisdom is completely discredited, and social and political radicalization occurs relatively quickly. Economic deprivations and physical risks for the masses transform military conflicts into political struggles. Parties relate to these upheavals and often give them direction but outside this context they and their leaders are of minor importance. The question of the working class's role is when, why, and how it has behaved in historical reality – as it has at rare but crucial junctures. Its importance as a historical agent of paramount importance does not end because Marx and those who followed him were entirely wrong about its roles and motives. During most peacetime periods it has been co-opted and tamed by a variety of forces, ranging from the laws intended to keep them restrained to – more often – trade union and Social Democratic and Communist cooperation with ruling parties. National experiences differ somewhat, but workers' docility for the vast bulk of the time is a historical and sociological fact. Marx's theory of the proletariat was based on the wishes of intellectuals only and no more scientific than alchemy. Again, the factors that interceded to make Marx's prognostications wrong ranged from migration in its many forms to real economic developments. The vision of an inherently radical proletariat is a myth because what people will do varies greatly by the occasion and place. But the identity of workers as a class and their readiness to act under certain circumstances is also a fact and wars telescope the process of their consciousness. Precisely the same can be said regarding the middle classes, bourgeoisie, or however one describes them. The question of the role of the working class is not how its role in the future is projected as being inevitable but rather what it has done – when, why, and how. In this sense, the question of the working class is anything but irrelevant but rather one to be studied in a much more historically realistic context.

Stability requires a just economy, which will be expressed in the forms of full employment and the equitable distribution of income and wealth, both of which still remain valid radical ideals and goals. If states engage in wars then they will confront opposition and challenges to their legitimacy and power. Then the masses sometimes become important actors, but until now it is the ruling classes' follies that have caused the masses to act. The role of the people, therefore, notwithstanding the simplifications of various socialist theorists, remains a very open question.

Solacing myths, whether of electoral politics or "spontaneous" action by the masses have not helped, and candor about conventional radical wisdom is imperative if we are to overcome limits that realities impose. The importance of ideas and ideals as motivation cannot be overstated without falling on idealism but there are sufficient instances – Vietnam is one of them – where their existence was crucial, and even in less cataclysmic contexts they are decisive. Because history is not predestined we must attempt to be constructive as well as accept the formidable risks that events may also impose constraints on us. Hence a radical vision of the future is relevant; it was ignored in the past when power was thrust upon leftists, with dire results. A better and more adequate future is possible, never certain, but we must try where others have failed. Yet just as one can never neatly order change it is even more illusory to believe – as conservatives do – that it can be prevented. Great movements of transformation in the history of many nations have had a largely, even entirely self-generating and autonomous quality. Bringing the will and reality together is the only way of determining if options are relevant when social changes occur, but often this has not been the case and reform movements that have no moorings and scant principles save power have been dissipated and distorted, not just by counterrevolutions from the Right but also by the ambitions and opportunism of leftist leaders. Prematurely, a revolutionary directive is farcical, but at the appropriate time in some nations it has been highly relevant, even decisive. Without wars such periods of great transformation would be unthinkable, and this is a grave risk that militarists take with remarkable impunity, frequently losing power thereby. They are unintentionally the most radical force – malignant and destructive of human lives but ultimately of themselves also.

Human choices everywhere, at all times, are limited by the constraints that historical circumstances impose upon them. If the ever-present risks of surprises and undesirable complications from our idealistic commitments and action were always to inhibit our resistance to social evils and war, people would constantly remain morally passive and tolerate injustice and oppression – with far greater dangers as a result.

So long as the world is so interdependent it is an illusion for anyone to suppose they can avoid the ultimate political and personal consequences of a refusal to oppose injustice, war, and oppression. The question is not whether resistance to these indignities should occur but how best to express it. Throughout this past century, vast numbers of initially apolitical people believed that its terrible convulsions would not also sweep them up, either as victims or resisters, but they ended up as participants in the countless events, ranging from small meetings to revolutions, that sometimes resulted in great social changes.

The personal meaning of passivity in the face of evil must always be weighed against the risks of opposition to it, but there are serious perils either way. We can never avoid such dilemmas because the world inevitably imposes difficult choices upon most of us. For most people, delays are far more common than timely action, and struggles are frequently fought after the possibilities of success have declined significantly. To the extent it preempts and constrains those who may assault civilized society, idealism and action is also the logic of self-interest.

We can never know in advance the ultimate results of our behavior in a world in which political forces and actors are inherently unstable, often in complex ways that they themselves fail to comprehend. If we were to require an absolute guarantee regarding the outcome of our conduct, we would always remain passive, and the negative functional and moral results of our inertia would be far greater. Such assurances are neither desirable nor possible, and no one has immunity from risks. Thinking rationally and often, unencumbered by illusions, is the only safety we have, and there was far less of it over the past centuries than was absolutely essential.

Commitment to a cause or a position can never become an unconditional moral blank check lest we make sustained errors. It must include an acute critical self-consciousness regarding the essential intellectual safeguards that protect political responses from illusions and abuses. Ultimately, regardless of those who cause it, our safest guide in this world of ambiguous choices is to oppose injustice and oppression wherever it exists and whenever we confront it.

In a world full of continuous injustices, we rarely select the time and place we must face them; those who create iniquities force choices upon us. Because we live in human society as it is, whether we wish to or not we function within those constraints inherent in this absence of freedom, and this necessarily constantly imposes difficult options upon us. Profound ambiguities and dilemmas are always predictable, and for those who attempt to challenge a society's evil there will always be enigmatic quandaries. Errors of judgment, either by errors of omission or commission, are also inevitable. Good intentions can never wholly justify such mistakes but they are far less dangerous or morally culpable than apathy and egoism, which surrender by default to those who would perpetuate the world's follies and catastrophes.

If justice and rationality defined the major political experiences of our times then we would not encounter great moral choices. We cannot escape politics and society, and it is an illusion to suppose that we can avoid their dangerous social consequences. Whether we are passive or active regarding them, our lives will be engulfed in major, sometimes critical, ways, and often such choices define the great challenges we confront during our lives and the kinds of human beings we become. But even if we seek to make our world more rational and humane, there is no assurance whatever that we will change it sufficiently to reverse the great challenges we now face.

When people cease to be willing to accept these responsibilities when they should and must, a dark night of despair will overcome humanity. But the very future of our world now depends on banishing dogma and ignorance and acting with far greater wisdom.

Notes

1 The power of reason: a world without limits

1 Barrow 1998: 78–79; Russell 1946: 750–56, 802–08.
2 Spencer 1967: 216. See also ibid: xix, 214–17; Ginsberg 1934: ch. 1; Barnes 1948.
3 Veblen 1948: 241–42, 258, 271; Polanyi 1944: 114–15, 123–27.
4 Hegel's ideas are adequately illustrated by Hegel 1956: 25, 38–39; Hegel 1975: 28–29. See also Popper 1952: 28–37, 46, 66; Russell 1946: ch. 22; Cohen 1947: 13, 88; Schumpeter 1954: 411–14, 437.

2 The legacies of socialism: theory

1 Engels 1959: 37–39, 157, 226.
2 Rosdolsky 1977: 95.
3 Mehring 1935: 155.
4 Marx 1906: 25. See also Marx 1988: 146–60 and passim.
5 Engels 1959: 16.
6 See Rosdolsky 1977: xii–iii and passim; Lukács 1971; Moore 1963; Korsch 1977: 140–44.
7 Schumpeter 1954: 455. See also ibid: 452–58. Karl Korsch, who defended orthodox Marxism most of his life, in 1950 concluded that "Marx is today only one of the many precursors, founders, and developers of the socialist working-class movement. The so-called utopian socialists from Thomas More to the present are equally important." Marxism's assertion of a "monopolistic claim . . . to theoretical and practical leadership" decisively inhibited the definition of a truly "revolutionary theory and practice" (Korsch 1977: 281).
8 Marx 1906: 13–15, 837. See also Rosdolsky 1977: 414 on Marxism as science.
9 Marx 1906: 478n. See also ibid: 17, 566, 673; Veblen 1948: 277–78.
10 Veblen 1948: 283. See also Marx 1906: 334, 532–34, 552 and passim.
11 Marx 1909: 47–48, 209, 794, 798, 806, 856–61. See also Marx 1906: ch. 25, 830–37.
12 Engels 1959: 43.
13 Rosdolsky 1977: 51–52, 118, 192n, 374.
14 Marx 1906: 707, 836–37. See also Rosdolsky 1977: 297–307, esp. 379–81.
15 Marx 1988: 243; Marx 1906: 837.
16 Engels 1959: 385–87.

3 The legacies of socialism: organizational successes, and failures

1 See Lidtke 1985: 192–95; Beilharz 1992: 94–96 and passim; Schumpeter 1954: 453–44, for the hodgepodge of romantic, utopian currents in the socialist movement – among Marxists also.

2 See Michels 1949; Nettl 1965: 78–81; Lidtke 1985: 4–5. For the United States, see Lasswell and Blumenstock 1939.
3 Nettl 1969: 119–20. For this entire affair, see ibid: xxv–xxvii, 94–105, 132ff.; Nettl 1965 : 68–69, 73–81; Gay 1952: 60ff., 106–10, 131ff.
4 Labriola 1908: 29, italics in original.
5 Luxemburg 1937: 32–33.
6 Luxemburg 1974: 304.
7 Lenin 1902: 203, 248. For Lenin in general, see Solzhenitsyn 1976.
8 Lenin 1917: 41, 44.
9 Lenin 1920: 13–14.
10 I have analyzed these larger historic patterns and revolutions in much greater detail in Kolko 1994. Detailed sources will also be found there.
11 Russell 1938: ch. 1.
12 McInnes 1964: 6. See also Levy 1987a; Cammett 1967; Levy 1999.
13 Slezkine 2004: 348–52 treats this well. For the earlier period, see Levy 1987b.
14 Elbaum 2002 for a good account.

4 The role and limits of social theories

1 Cohen 1953: x, xiii, 85–87, 348–50 develops these themes.
2 Dewey 1948: 45, 59.
3 Dewey was ready to grasp any idea that might help attain goals he thought desirable, and so, for example, he exploited the role and meaning of religion functionally in an effort to enlist it in the cause of reason and progress. He was not in the least concerned with religion's validity. See Dewey 1934; Kolko 1957.
4 See Cohen 1953: 108, 362–67; Popper 1952: 262–68; Kolko 1961.
5 There are many treatments of these problems, but Kuhn 1970 is excellent.
6 Useful accounts of these issues are Barrow 1998: viii–ix, 26, 64–67, 248ff.; Kuhn 1970; Cohen 1947: 36–38, 45–46; Cohen 1953: 155; Popper 1952: 220–22; Frank 1961: 21, 34–35, 187, 190–95, 202–03; Moore 1998: ch. 7.
7 The reader can find more justification for my reasoning in Russell 1931: xix, 47, 105; Popper 1952: 262–70, 278–80; Peirce 1940: 56–59.

5 Capitalist realities: economic development, the state, and the myths of the market

1 I deal with the so-called transition economies in Chapter 6. Space prevents discussion of such nations as Turkey, Indonesia, and countless others, where corruption is pervasive and "bureaucratic capitalism" based on political ties determines many, often most of the winners and losers in the process of capital accumulation. See Kolko 1989, 1997a.
2 See Kolko 1967; Slezkine 2004: ch. 1, for examples of family systems; Fligstein 1990: ch. 9.
3 See, for example, Bradley 1996: II, 1815ff.; Perelman 2000.
4 See Kolko 1961; Mathias and Pollard 1989: 44; Ha-Joon Chang 2005, 36ff., 50–51.
5 Bairoch 1993: 34–37, 40, 52–53. Today, with massive and growing trade deficits, important American conservatives are now questioning the relevance of free trade and the Ricardian theory of "comparative advantages," which they regard as utterly outdated in an era when the factors of production are increasingly mobile.
6 Goodrich 1960: ch. 8 and passim; Lively 1955; Broude 1959: 4–14.
7 Gershenkron 1962: 44–47; Kindleberger 1964: 6, 34–43; Lewis 1978: 48–50; Milward and Saul 1973, 335ff., 501; Mathias and Pollard 1989: 714–15, 726–27.
8 Mathias and Pollard 1989: 753. See also Gerschenkron 1962: 15–19, 126; Roehl 1976: 255.

9 Aitken 1959: 36, ch. 6 and passim.
10 Halliday 1975: 57–60; Macpherson 1987: 40; Lockwood 1965: 148, 500–15; Rosovsky 1961: 23ff.; Mathias and Postan 1978: 148, 1107ff.; Norman 1975: 234; Ohkawa and Rosovsky 1973: 16; Beasley 1963: 146–47, 217; Dower 1999: 534–46.
11 MacIntyre 1994: 4–5, 116–36, 160–61; *Financial Times*: Nov. 5, 1999; Sept. 23/24, 2000; July 9, 2003; Sept. 29, 2005; *IMF Survey*: July 16, 2001: 243–44; Kwon 2004: 93 and passim; Fligstein 2001: 188; Ha-Joon Chang 2005: 74–78.
12 MacIntyre 1994: 4–5, 116–36; Lim 1998; Deyo 1987: 87, 94–95.
13 Cardoso and Faletto 1979: 128. See also Kolko 1989: 47.
14 Gerschenkron 1962: 354.
15 Slemrod 1995: 373–80.
16 See Kolko 1994: ch. 4 for more detail on war organizations.
17 Denison 1974: vii, 131–32. See also Cipolla 1969: 14, 24, 72; Munnell 1990: 11–13 for just a few of many examples.
18 Kolko 1963; see Kolko 1965: passim re roots of regulation. Arnold 1937 captures the conflict of ideology with reality.
19 The literature on these issues is very large. See, for example, Schuh 2001; Ferejohn 1974: 233–35; Arnold 1979; Cohen and Noll 1991: 53–57; Derthick and Quirk 1985; Kolko 1968: ch. 2.
20 *Washington Post*: June 5, 2005. See also *Financial Times*: Dec. 8, 2003; Oct. 7, 2004; Dec. 7, 2004; June 1, 2005; *Wall Street Journal*: Oct. 7, 2003.
21 *London Review of Books*: July 7, 2005; *Financial Times*: Dec. 12, 2003. See also *Financial Times*: Jan. 31, 2005; Feb. 8, 2005; June 13, 2005, and the *Los Angeles Times*: Feb. 20, 2004 for lobbyists.
22 *Financial Times*: July 19, 2004; Aug. 2, 2004; Oct. 20, 2004.
23 *Los Angeles Times*: Dec. 15, 2004; Dec. 18, 2004; "Missile defense funding request tops $10 billion," *Arms Control Today*: March 2004; Center for Defense Information (CDI), Space Security update 3, 2004; CDI update 4, March 19, 2004; *San Francisco Gate*: March 15, 2004; April 24, 2004.
24 David Talbot, "How technology failed in Iraq," *Technology Review* (MIT): Nov. 2004: 2 and passim. See also *Financial Times*: Feb. 3, 2004; July 14, 2004; July 20, 2004; Nov. 30, 2004; *Los Angeles Times*: March 11, 2004; March 12, March 15, 2005; *Washington Post*: Oct. 5, 2005.
25 US Congress 1960: ch. 4; Stiglitz 2003: 206–07; *Financial Times*: March 15, 2001; July 23, 2001; May 10, 2002; Sept. 24, 2002; July 31, 2003; Dec. 5, 2003; *New York Times*: Dec. 24, 2000; Sept. 1, 10, 2001; and esp. Environmental Working Group's (EWG) Farm Subsidy Database. US spending on agricultural subsidies in 2005 was $22.7 billion.
26 *Financial Times*: May 31, 2000; Dec. 20, 2001. This issue has been contested for years and is likely to be around a long time. See *Washington Post*: July 23, 2005; *Financial Times*: Dec. 9, 2005.
27 *Financial Times*: Feb. 25, 2004; Oct. 16, 2004; Nov. 11, 2004; *Washington Post*: July 13, 2004; and esp. Paul Krugman in *International Herald Tribune*: April 28, 2004.
28 There is a large literature on these topics. See, for example, *Financial Times*: Aug. 6, 2004; Feb. 24, 2005; March 11, 23, 2005; May 2, 11, 14/15, 18, 23, 25, 30, 2005; June 6, 2005; July 13, 2005; Dec. 29, 2005; Feb. 8, 17, 2006; March 20, 2006; R. Rajan in *Finance and Development*, Sept. 2005, 42: 54–55.
29 *Financial Times*: Sept. 23, 2005. See also ibid: April 13, 2005; June 17, 24, 2005; July 4, 2005; Sept. 29, 30, 2005; Oct. 6, 21, 2005; Nov. 1, 2005; Feb. 6, 2006; March 20, 2006.
30 Chandler 1977; Fligstein 1990; Bradley 1996; Kolko 1963.
31 Browne and Rosengren 1987: 2–6, 11–16, 19, 24–27, 31–32, 44; *Financial Times*: March 31, 2005; Kolko 1963: chs 1 and 2.

32 Fligstein 1990.
33 Augar 2005: 10ff. is one example. See also *Financial Times*: Dec. 12, 2001; May 5, 2003; April 8, 2005; June 28, 2005.
34 *Financial Times*: April 29, 2003; May 8, 2003; Nov. 20, 2003; March 30, 31, 2005; Stiglitz 2003: 140–41, 167; Fuller and Jensen 2002.
35 Central Intelligence Agency 2005: 9–10.
36 Roach 2003: 3.
37 *Financial Times*: June 28, 2005.
38 *Financial Times*: Jeffrey Garten, Oct. 31, 2005, and Stephen Roach, Nov. 1, 2005. See also *Financial Times*, March 15, 2006.

6 Capitalist realities: the way the world lives

1 For Enron and privatization in general, see Beder 2003: 144–45 and passim.
2 Moore 1998: 100. The World Bank publishes a very informative regular publication on the former Communist economies, *Transition Newsletter*, later titled *Beyond Transition,* which I use extensively thoughout this chapter. See *Transition*: May–June 2002: 4 and passim; *Financial Times*: May 5, 6, 9, 11, 12, 2005.
3 Anders Aslund in *Transition*: Dec. 2003–April 2004: 26. For this and following discussions, see also Kolko 1997a: 25 and passim; Goldman 2003: 75 and passim.
4 *Beyond Transition:* Oct.–Dec. 2004, 4–5; Goldman 2003; Reuters: May 12, 2004; *Financial Times*: Aug. 18, 2003.
5 Victor Krassilchthikov, *Transition*: Jan.–March 2003: 23–25; World Bank 2005: 16–17; Goldman 2003: ch. 10; *Financial Times*: July 26/27, 2003; Aug. 21, 2003; July 23, 2004; March 26/27, 2005; July 22, 2005.
6 World Bank 2002: xiv; *IMF Survey*: Aug. 29, 2005: 258, says Czech and Polish output fell 16 percent but declined 60 or more percent in Georgia, Moldavia, and the Ukraine. They all did badly in 1990–2001.
7 World Bank 2002: xiii; World Bank 2005: 3–5 and passim.
8 Gittings 2005 is the best account of the Chinese experience. See also Kolko 1997a: 30–31.
9 *Transition*: May–June 2002: 7; Kolko 2001: 435.
10 Lee and Selden 2005; Gittings 2005: 269–70; *Transition*: May–June 2002: 5–6; UNDP 2005b: 64 and passim.
11 A great deal has been published on these topics. Lee and Selden 2005 is an excellent summation, as is Gittings 2005. See also *Financial Times*: Nov. 7, 2005; UNDP 2005b: 71–73 and passim; Reuters, Feb. 9, 2006.
12 *Financial Times*: Aug. 16, 2002. See also ibid: Dec. 10, 2002; UNDP 2005b: 25–27, 37 and passim; *Washington Post*: Nov. 11, 2002.
13 Prime Minister Pham Van Khai, *Transition*: April–June 2003: 35. For Vietnam see Kolko 1997b, 2001.
14 Alesina and Roubini 1990: 28–30; Tufte 1978: 56–64, ch. 2.
15 UNDP 2005a: 36ff., 71; Kolko 1998; Tanzi 1998: 10–17; Deininger and Squire 1997; Devarajan and Reinikka 2003: 48–49.
16 Charap and Harm 1999: 15–20; Milne 1992: 7–22; Kolko 1989.
17 Stiglitz 2003: 2, 281.
18 IMF 2005: tables 37, 40; UNCTAD 2003: 17–22, 104; UNDP 2005a: 12–13; Ha-Joon Chang 2005: 78–85.
19 Rajan 2004: 56–57.
20 Charles Collyns and Russell Kincaid in *IMF Survey*: May 19, 2003: 144. The IMF Independent Evaluation Office, in its "Report on the Role of Fiscal Adjustment in IMF-Supported Programs," September 9, 2003, says IMF programs are often too optimistic in growth estimates, reluctant to project slow growth and "very rarely" negative growth. Also, social and educational spending does not fall but upper

income groups least in need capture more of it. See also *Financial Times*, Dec. 28, 2005.

21 Blustein 2005; *New York Times*, Jan. 3, 2006.
22 UNDP 2005a: 3–4, 12, 34.
23 ILO 2004a: 1; ILO 2004b: 25–29, 44–46; Milanovic 2002: 7, 13, 20.
24 Milanovic 2005: 44, 78–81, 107–08, 143–44 and passim; UNDP 2005a: 36–38, 54–56; ILO 2004b: 35–37. ILO data support similar conclusions. In 73 countries it surveyed, 48 of them – containing 59 percent of the population of the sample – had rising income inequality between the 1960s and the 1990s, 16 had stable inequality, and in only 9 – with 5 percent of the population – was inequality declining: ILO 2004b: 44–45. But the literature on this topic is very large. See Kiely 2004 for a very useful overview.
25 US Census Bureau: News, Aug. 30, 2005; Economic Policy Institute (EPI), *Job Watch*: April 2, 2005; EPI policy memorandum, Dec. 21, 2005.
26 ILO 2004b: 35–41; Milanovic 2005: 61–81; *Financial Times*: Dec. 19, 2003; *Los Angeles Times*, March 10, 2006.
27 ILO 2004a: 1–5; UNDP 2003: 1–9, 69–71, 77–78, 91 and passim.
28 IMF 2003b: 1–4; IMF 2003a.
29 A great deal on this vital topic has been published, but see especially Lehmann 2002: 5, 24.
30 IMF 2001: chs 2 and 4.
31 IMF 2002: 4–5, 10, ch. 3; Schinasi 2006: 13–14 and passim. See also *IMF Survey:* April 29, 2002: 143–44.
32 *Financial Times*: March 15, 2005. See also the similar observations of Vito Tanzi in *Financial Times*, Feb. 24, 2006.

7 The future: where and how

1 See Kolko 1997b: conclusion.
2 *Financial Times*: March 23, 2005; Deininger and Squire 1997; Deininger and Olinto 2000; Navarro 1999; Wilkinson 2005.
3 Jason Venetouls and Cliff Cobb, "The genuine progress indicator 1950–2004 (2004 update)," Sustainability Indicators Program, March 2004, have produced radically different data showing that there has been much less progress from 1960 until the late 1970s than is usually calculated, and stability or even declines since then. Official American GDP figures show rapid, consistent growth.

References

Adams, C. F., Jr (1871) *Chapters of Erie, and Other Essays*, Boston, MA: J. R. Osgood.

Aitken, H. G. J. (ed.) (1959) *The State and Economic Growth*, New York: Social Science Research Council.

Alesina, A. and Roubini, N. (1990) "Political cycles: evidence from OECD economies," unpublished draft.

Arnold, R. D. (1979) *Congress and the Bureaucracy: a theory of influence*, New Haven, CT: Yale University Press.

Arnold, T. W. (1937) *The Folklore of Capitalism*, New Haven, CT: Yale University Press.

Augar, P. (2005) *The Greed Merchants: how the investment banks played the free market game*, New York: Portfolio.

Bairoch, P. (1993) *Economics and World History: myths and paradoxes*, Hemel Hempstead: Harvester Wheatsheaf.

Barnes, H. E. (ed.) (1948) *An Introduction to the History of Sociology*, Chicago, IL: University of Chicago Press.

Barrow, J. D. (1998) *Impossibility: the limits of science and the science of limits*, Oxford: Oxford University Press.

Beasley, W. G. (1963) *The Modern History of Japan*, London: Weidenfeld & Nicolson.

Beder, S. (2003) *Power Play: the fight to control the world's electricity*, New York: The New Press.

Beilharz, P. (1992) *Labour's Utopias: Bolshevism, Fabianism, Social Democracy*, London: Routledge.

Blustein, P. (2005) *And the Money Kept Rolling In (and Out): Wall Street, the IMF, and the bankrupting of Argentina*, New York: PublicAffairs.

Bradley, R. L., Jr (1996) *Oil, Gas, & Government: the U. S. experience*, 2 vols, Lanham, MD: Rowman & Littlefield.

Broude, H. (1959) "The role of the state in American economic development, 1820–1890," in H. G. J. Aitken (ed.) *The State and Economic Growth*, New York: Social Science Research Council.

Browne, L. E. and Rosengren, E. S. (eds) (1987) *The Merger Boom: proceedings of a conference held in October 1987*, Boston, MA: Federal Reserve Bank of Boston.

Cammett, J. M. (1967) *Antonio Gramsci and the Origins of Italian Communism*, Stanford, CA: Stanford University Press.

Cardoso, F. H. and Faletto, E. (1979) *Dependence and Development in Latin America*, Berkeley, CA: University of California Press.

Central Intelligence Agency (CIA, National Intelligence Council) (2005) *The 2020 Global Landscape: Executive Summary*, Jan. 14, 2005.

Chandler, A. D., Jr (1977) *The Visible Hand: the managerial revolution in American business*, Cambridge, MA: Harvard University Press.

Chang, Ha-Joon (2005) "Why developing countries need tariffs? How WTO NAMA negotiations could deny developing countries' right to a future," November 2005, Geneva: South Centre.

Charap, J. and Harm, C. (1999) "Institutionalized corruption and the kleptocratic state," IMF working paper WP/99/91, Washington, DC: IMF.

Cipolla, C. M. (1969) *Literacy and Development in the West*, Harmondsworth: Penguin.

Cohen, L. R. and Noll, R. G. (1991) *The Technology Pork Barrel*, Washington, DC: The Brookings Institution.

Cohen, M. R. (1947) *The Meaning of Human History*, La Salle, IL: Open Court.

—— (1953) *Reason and Nature: an essay on the meaning of scientific method*, Glencoe, IL: The Free Press.

Deininger, K. and Olinto, P. (2000) "Asset distribution, inequality, and growth," World Bank WPS 2375, Washington, DC: World Bank Development Research group.

Deininger, K. and Squire, L. (1997) "Economic growth and income equality: reexamining the links," *Finance and Development*, 34: 38–41.

Denison, E. F. (1974) *Accounting for United States Economic Growth, 1929–1969*, Washington, DC: The Brookings Institution.

Derthick, M. and Quirk, P. J. (1985) *The Politics of Deregulation*, Washington, DC: The Brookings Institution.

Devarajan, S. and Reinikka, R. (2003) "Making services work for poor people," *Finance and Development*, 40: 48–51.

Dewey, J. (1934) *A Common Faith*, New Haven, CT: Yale University Press.

—— (1948) *Reconstruction in Philosophy* [1920], New York: Mentor.

Deyo, F. C. (ed.) (1987) *The Political Economy of the New Asian Industrialism*, Ithaca, NY: Cornell University Press.

Dower, J. W. (1999) *Embracing Defeat: Japan in the wake of World War II*, New York: W. W. Norton.

Elbaum, M. (2002) *Revolution in the Air: sixties radicals turn to Lenin, Mao and Che*, London: Verso.

Engels, F. (1959) *Anti-Dühring: Herr Eugen Dühring's revolution in science* (3rd edn, 1894), Moscow: Foreign Languages Publishing House.

Environmental Working Group (EWG) Farm Subsidy database, Washington, DC: EWG.

Ferejohn, J. A. (1974) *Pork Barrel Politics: rivers and harbors legislation, 1947–1968*, Stanford, CA: Stanford University Press.

Fligstein, N. (1990) *The Transformation of Corporate Control*, Cambridge, MA: Harvard University Press.

—— (2001) *The Architecture of Markets: an economic sociology of twenty-first-century capitalist societies*, Princeton, NJ: Princeton University Press.

Frank, P. G. (ed.) (1961) *The Validation of Scientific Theories*, New York: Collier.

Fuller, J. and Jensen, M. C. (2002) "Just say no to Wall Street," *Journal of Applied Corporate Finance*, 14: 41–46.

Gay, P. (1952) *The Dilemma of Democratic Socialism: Eduard Bernstein's challenge to Marx*, New York: Columbia University Press.

Gerschenkron, A. (1962) *Economic Backwardness in Historical Perspective: a book of essays*, Cambridge, MA: Harvard University Press.

Ginsberg, M. (1934) *Sociology*, London: Oxford University Press.

Gittings, J. (2005) *The Changing Face of China: from Mao to market*, Oxford: Oxford University Press.

Goldman, M. I. (2003) *The Piratization of Russia: Russian reform goes awry*, London: Routledge.

Goodrich, C. (1960) *Government Promotion of American Canals and Railroads, 1800–1890*, New York: Columbia University Press.

Halliday, J. (1975) *A Political History of Japanese Capitalism*, New York: Pantheon.

Hegel, G. W. F. (1956) *The Philosophy of History*, New York: Dover.

—— (1975) *Lectures on the Philosophy of World History: introduction: reason in history* [1830], Cambridge: Cambridge University Press.

International Labour Organization (ILO) (2004a) *Global Employment Trends*, Jan. 23, 2004, Geneva: ILO.

—— (2004b) World Commission on the Social Dimensions of Globalization, *A Fair Globalization*, Feb. 24, 2004, Geneva, ILO.

International Monetary Fund (IMF) (2001) *International Capital Markets: developments, prospects, and key policy issues*, August 2001, Washington, DC: IMF.

—— (2002) *World Economic Outlook, April 2002: recessions and recoveries*, April 2002, Washington, DC: IMF.

—— (2003a) Independent Evaluation Office, *IMF and Recent Capital Account Crises: Indonesia, Korea, Brazil*, July 28, 2003, Washington, DC: IMF.

—— (2003b) Independent Evaluation Office, *Evaluation Report: The IMF and recent capital account crises: Indonesia, Korea, Brazil*, Sept. 12, 2003, Washington, DC: IMF.

—— (2005) *World Economic Outlook: globalization and external imbalances*, April 2005, Washington, DC: IMF.

Kiely, R. (2004) "The World Bank and 'global poverty reduction': good policies or bad data?" *Journal of Contemporary Asia*, 34: 3–20.

Kindleberger, C. P. (1964) *Economic Growth in France and Britain, 1851–1950*, Cambridge, MA: Harvard University Press.

Kolko, G. (1957) "Morris R. Cohen: the scholar and/or society," *American Quarterly*, 9: 325–36.

—— (1961) "Max Weber on America: theory and evidence," *History and Theory*, 1: 243–60.

—— (1963) *The Triumph of Conservatism: a reinterpretation of American history, 1900–1916*, New York: The Free Press.

—— (1965) *Railroads and Regulation, 1877–1916*, Princeton, NJ: Princeton University Press.

—— (1967) "Brahmins and business: a hypothesis on the social basis of success in American history," in K. H. Wolff and B. Moore, Jr (eds) *The Critical Spirit: Essays in Honor of Herbert Marcuse*, Boston, MA: Beacon Press.

—— (1968) *The Roots of American Foreign Policy: an analysis of power and purpose*, Boston, MA: Beacon Press.

—— (1989) "Varieties of third world elites: a framework for analysis," in P. Limqueco (ed.) *Partisan Scholarship: essays in honour of Renato Constantino*, Manila: Journal of Contemporary Asia Publishers.

—— (1994) *Century of War: politics, conflicts, and society since 1914*, New York: The New Press.

—— (1997a) "Privatizing communism: politics and market economics in Russia and China," *World Policy Journal*, 14: 23–34.

—— (1997b) *Vietnam: anatomy of a peace*, London: Routledge.

—— (1998) "Ravaging the poor: IMF indicted by its own data," *Multinational Monitor*, 19: 20–23.

—— (2001) "China and Vietnam on the road to the market," *Journal of Contemporary Asia*, 31: 431–40.

Kopcke, R. W., Little, J. S. and Tootell, G. M. B. (2004) "How humans behave: implications for economics and economic policy," *New England Economic Review*, First quarter: 3–31.

Korsch, K. (1977) *Revolutionary Theory*, ed. D. Kellner, Austin, Tx: University of Texas Press.

Kuhn, T. S. (1970) *The Structure of Scientific Revolutions* (2nd edn), Chicago, IL: University of Chicago Press.

Kwon, E. (2004) "Financial liberalization in South Korea," *Journal of Contemporary Asia*, 34: 71–101.

Labriola, A. (1908) *Essays on the Materialist Conception of History*, Chicago, IL: Charles H. Kerr.

Lasswell, H. and Blumenstock, D. (1939) *World Revolutionary Propaganda: a Chicago study*, New York: Alfred A. Knopf.

Lee, C. K. and Selden, M. (2005) "Class, inequality, and China's Revolution," unpublished paper, Cambridge University conference, April 1–2, 2005.

Lehmann, A. (2002) "Foreign direct investment in emerging markets: income, repatriations and financial vulnerabilities," IMF WP/02/47, Washington, DC: IMF.

Lenin, V. I. (1902) "What is to be done?" in *Selected Works* [vol. 1, 1960], Moscow: Foreign Languages Publishing House.

—— (1917) *State and Revolution* [1932], New York: International Publishers.

—— (1920) *"Left-wing Communism," an infantile disorder* [1947], Moscow: Foreign Languages Publishing House.

Levy, C. (1987a) "Max Weber and Antonio Gramsci," in W. Mommsen and J. Osterhammel (eds) *Max Weber and his Contemporaries*, London: George Allen & Unwin.

—— (ed.) (1987b) *Socialism and the Intelligentsia, 1880–1914*, London: Routledge & Kegan Paul.

—— (1999) *Gramsci and the Anarchists*, London: Berg.

Lewis, W. A. (1978) *Growth and Fluctuations, 1870–1913*, London: George Allen & Unwin.

Lidtke, V. L. (1985) *The Alternative Culture: socialist labor in imperial Germany*, New York: Oxford University Press.

Lim, T. C. (1998) "Power, capitalism, and the authoritarian state in South Korea," *Journal of Contemporary Asia*, 28: 457–83.

Lively, R. A. (1955) "The American System: a review article," *Business History Review*, 29: 81–96.

Lockwood, W. W. (ed.) (1965) *The State and Economic Enterprise in Japan: essays on the political economy of growth*, Princeton, NJ: Princeton University Press.

Lukács, G. (1971) *History and Class Consciousness*, London: Merlin Press.

Luxemburg, R. (1937) *Reform or Revolution* [1897–99], New York: Three Arrows Press.

—— (1974) *Selected Political Writings*, ed. R. Looker, New York: Grove Press.

McInnes, N. (1964) "Antonio Gramsci," *Survey*, 53: 3–15.

MacIntyre, A. (ed.) (1994) *Business and Government in Industralising Asia*, Sydney: Allen & Unwin.

Macpherson, W. J. (1987) *The Economic Development of Japan, 1868–1941*, London: Macmillan.

Marx, K. (1906) *Capital: a critique of political economy* [1867] (vol. 1), New York: The Modern Library.

—— (1909) *Capital: a critique of political economy* (vol. 3, published 1959), Moscow: Foreign Languages Publishing House.

—— (1988) *Economic and Philosophic Manuscripts of 1844* and [with F. Engels] *the Communist Manifesto*, Amherst, NY: Prometheus.

Mathias, P. and Pollard, S. (eds) (1989) *The Cambridge Economic History of Europe*, vol. VIII, Cambridge: Cambridge University Press.

Mathias, P. and Postan, M. M. (eds) (1978) *The Cambridge Economic History of Europe*, vol. VII, Cambridge: Cambridge University Press.

Mehring, F. (1935) *Karl Marx: the story of his life*, New York: Covici, Friede.

Michels, R. (1949) *Political Parties: a sociological study of the oligarchical tendencies of modern democracy* [1915], Glencoe, NY: The Free Press.

Milanovic, B. (2002) "Can we discern the effect of globalization on income distribution?" World Bank WPS 2876, Washington, DC: World Bank.

—— (2005) *Worlds Apart: measuring international and global inequality*, Princeton, NJ: Princeton University Press.

Milne, R. S. (1992) "Privatization in the ASEAN states: who gets what, why, and with what effect," *Pacific Affairs*, 64: 7–29.

Milward, A. S. and Saul, S. B. (1973) *The Economic Development of Continental Europe 1780–1870*, London: George Allen & Unwin.

Moore, B. (1998) *Moral Aspects of Economic Growth, and other essays*, Ithaca, NY: Cornell University Press.

Moore, S. (1963) "The metaphysical argument in Marx's labour theory of value," *Etudes de Marxologie: Cahiers de l'Institut de Science Economique Appliquée*, 7: 73–98.

Munnell, A. H. (1990) "How does public infrastructure affect regional economic performance," *New England Economic Review*, Sept.–Oct: 11–32.

Navarro, V. (1999) "The political economy of the welfare state in developed capitalist countries," *International Journal of Health Services*, 29: 1–50.

Nettl, J. P. (1965) "The German Social Democratic Party 1890–1914 as a political model," *Past and Present*, 30: 65–95.

—— (1969) *Rosa Luxemburg*, New York: Schocken.

Norman, E. (1975) *Origins of the Modern Japanese State: selected writings*, New York: Pantheon.

Ohkawa, K. and Rosovsky, H. (1973) *Japanese Economic Growth: trend acceleration in the twentieth century*, Stanford, CA: Stanford University Press.

Peirce, C. (1940) *The Philosophy of Peirce: selected writings*, ed. J. Buchler, London: Routledge & Kegan Paul.

Perelman, M. (2000) *The Invention of Capitalism: classical political economy and the secret history of primitive accumulation*, Durham, NC: Duke University Press.

Polanyi, K. (1944) *The Great Transformation: the political and economic origins of our time* (2nd edn 1957), Boston, MA: Beacon Press.

Popper, K. R. (1952) *The Open Society and its Enemies, vol. 2, The high tide of prophecy: Hegel, Marx, and the aftermath*, London: Routledge & Kegan Paul.

Rajan, R. (2004) "Assume anarchy," *Finance and Development*, 41: 56–57.

Roach, S. (2003) *MorganStanley Global Economic Forum*, May 21, 2003, New York: MorganStanley.

Roehl, R. (1976) "French industrialization: a reconsideration," *Explorations in Economic History*, 13: 233–81.

Rosdolsky, R. (1977) *The Making of Marx's "Capital,"* London: Pluto Press.

Rosovsky, H. (1961) *Capital Formation in Japan, 1868–1940*, New York: The Free Press.

Russell, B. (1931) *The Scientific Outlook* (2001 edn), London: Routledge.

—— (1938) *Power: a new social analysis*, London: George Allen & Unwin.

—— (1946) *History of Western Philosophy*, London: George Allen & Unwin.

Schinasi, G. J. (2006) *Safeguarding Financial Stability: theory and practice*, Washington, DC: IMF.

Schuh, S. (2001) "An evaluation of recent macroeconomic forecast errors," *New England Economic Review*, Jan.–Feb: 35–56.

Schumpeter, J. A. (1954) *History of Economic Analysis*, London: Routledge.

Slemrod, J. (1995) "What do cross-country studies teach us about government involvement, prosperity, and economic growth?," *Brookings Papers on Economic Activity*, 2: 373–431.

Slezkine, Y. (2004) *The Jewish Century*, Princeton, NJ: Princeton University Press.

Solzhenitsyn, A. (1976) *Lenin in Zürich: chapters*, London: Book Club Associates.

Spencer, H. (1967) *The Evolution of Society* [selections from *Principles of Sociology*, 1863, ed. R. L. Carneiro], Chicago, IL: University of Chicago Press.

Stiglitz, J. E. (2003) *The Roaring Nineties: a new history of the world's most prosperous decade*, New York: W. W. Norton.

Tanzi, V. (1998) "Fundamental determinants of inequality and the role of government," IMF WP/98/178, Washington, DC: IMF.

Tufte, E. R. (1978) *Political Control of the Economy*, Princeton, NJ: Princeton University Press.

United Nations, UNCTAD (2002) *Overview by the Secretary-General of UNCTAD: The Least Developed Countries Report*, New York: UN.

——, UNCTAD (2003) *Economic Development in Africa: trade performance and commodity dependence*, New York: UN.

——, UNDP (2003) *Promoting the Millennium Development Goals in Asia and the Pacific*, New York: UN.

——, UNDP (2005a) *Human Development Report 2005*, Sept. 7, 2005, New York: UN.

——, UNDP (2005b) *Human Development Report 2005: China*, Dec. 16, 2005, New York: UN.

US Congress (Joint Economic Committee) (1960) *Subsidy and Subsidylike Programs of the United States Government*, Eighty-sixth Congress, 2nd session.

Veblen, T. (1948) *The Portable Veblen*, ed. M. Lerner, New York: Viking Press.

Wilkinson, R. (2005) *The Impact of Inequality: how to make sick societies healthier*, London: Routledge.

World Bank (2002) *Transition: The First Ten Years: analysis and lessons for Eastern Europe and the former Soviet Union*, report 23511, Washington, DC: World Bank.

—— (2005) *Growth, Poverty, and Inequality in Eastern Europe and the Former Soviet Union*, Oct. 12, 2005, Washington, DC: World Bank.

Index